I0889584

Experiences between Philosophy and Communication

SUNY series in the Philosophy of the Social Sciences
Lenore Langsdorf, editor

Experiences between Philosophy and Communication

Engaging the Philosophical Contributions of Calvin O. Schrag

Edited by
Ramsey Eric Ramsey
and
David James Miller

STATE UNIVERSITY OF NEW YORK PRESS

Published by
State University of New York Press, Albany

© 2003 State University of New York

All rights reserved

Printed in the United States of America

No part of this book may be used or reproduced
in any manner whatsoever without written permission.
No part of this book may be stored in a retrieval system
or transmitted in any form or by any means including
electronic, electrostatic, magnetic tape, mechanical,
photocopying, recording, or otherwise without the prior
permission in writing of the publisher.

For information, address State University of New York Press,
90 State Street, Suite 700, Albany, NY 12207

Production by Diane Ganeles
Marketing by Jennifer Giovani

Library of Congress Cataloging in Publication Data

Experiences between philosophy and communication : engaging the philosophical contributions of Calvin O. Schrag / edited by Ramsey Eric Ramsey and David James Miller.
p. cm. — (SUNY series in the philosophy of the social sciences)
Includes bibliographical references and index.
ISBN 0-7914-5875-X (alk. paper) — ISBN 0-7914-5876-8 (pbk. : alk. paper)
1. Schrag, Calvin O. 2. Communication—Philosophy. I. Ramsey, Ramsey Eric, 1960–
II. Miller, David James, 1957– III. Series.

B945.S3264 E96 2003
191—dc21

2002042643

10 9 8 7 6 5 4 3 2 1

Contents

Introduction

In-between Philosophy and Communication Studies

RAMSEY ERIC RAMSEY

If not in *Gorgias*, then at least by *Phaedrus*, Plato understands that he would have to think in-between rhetoric and philosophy if he was going to be able to get at things. As Calvin O. Schrag argued in the article that announced his then-forthcoming book *Communicative Praxis and the Space of Subjectivity,* today rhetoric and communication need to be resituated at the end of philosophy. With that and subsequent work, Schrag has helped make this resituating possible in unique and profound ways.

Those of us who have learned from Professor Schrag—whether as participants in his seminars, readers of his published works, or both—and who teach in departments of communication studies and who work there to philosophize the consequences of this practice, find ourselves having incurred many debts to him. For those as yet unfamiliar with his work, so much remains to be gathered and put to work to assist our thinking about the consequences of communicative praxis across a variety of life-world contexts.

I, along with my co-editor David James Miller, have brought together nine essays by leading scholars whose work has engaged and benefited from Schrag's many contributions and will act in various ways as extensions, explications, and provocations to those studying communicative phenomena. In lieu of a lengthy introduction, we have been given the gift of a full-length interview with Schrag conducted by the editors. The only such interview ever granted, it covers the wide spectrum of issues with which Schrag has dealt in his many scholarly works. Although each contributor to this collection wrote without access to the interview (with the exception of the editors), it is amazing to note the ways in which each produced essays that explore the issues raised in this conversation. The work by the contributors shows how widely and deeply influential Schrag's philosophy is and how much it gives to the future of dialogues concerning theory in the philosophical study of communication.

Recently Schrag's philosophical positions were engaged by Roger Mourad, a philosopher of education, to argue for a postdisciplinary world. Along with my co-editor and all the contributors, I am grateful to be able to make public the following interview and collection of insightful essays of this, if not postdisciplinary, then at least interdisciplinary volume responding to Schrag's philosophical positions from those of us who philosophize elsewhere.

Part I ~ Conversation as Invitation to Dialogue

1 From the Loving Struggle to the Struggle to Love

A Conversation with Calvin O. Schrag

RAMSEY ERIC RAMSEY AND
DAVID JAMES MILLER

INTRODUCTORY REMARKS

RER/DJM: Professor Schrag, we are immensely grateful for the opportunity to reflect here on the richness of the work that marks your distinguished career. We hope that, in some small way, we can offer something here that acknowledges the time, encouragement, and support you so selflessly and graciously give those who are working in philosophy and communication.

It is our intention to conduct this conversation in such a way that it will prove to be useful both to those who are familiar with your work and to those as yet unfamiliar with it. We hope to offer those already familiar with the work, not only further contextualization, but a new perspective on the work as well. We have always believed that the radical implications of your work, implications that have become obvious to us in our many conversations with you, have too often been overlooked, and we hope that in this conversation we can bring some of these implications to the fore. For those unfamiliar with your work, we hope to offer a consolidated, if not a comprehensive, introduction to your thought.

In discussing your work, it will become evident that we have a particular interest in your reflections on the phenomenon of "communicative praxis." We are scholars trained in both the disciplines of philosophy and communication and have been dedicated from the first to an elaboration of the philosophy of communication. It is our hope that in the course of the conversation we can create openings for new generations of scholars concerned with posing philosophical questions about the practice of communication, a practice your work has come to make a central concern.

COS: Thank You. I appreciate your kind words.

ON DOING PHILOSOPHY

RER/DJM: Although you have been labeled a "continental" philosopher, your willingness to move beyond the various demarcations—the boundaries and barriers—that have structured the discipline of philosophy belies the simplicity of this characterization. Before we take this label as a given, we would like to give you the opportunity to situate yourself as a philosopher.

COS: I would situate myself between the either/or that has demarcated the continental and analytic philosophical traditions, as well as within the American tradition of philosophy that this either/or has too often obscured. I would quickly add, though, that this situatedness is neither some species of eclecticism, nor some manner of synthesis. Rather, it is a matter of remaining situated in such a way that forays into, as well as beyond each of these traditions that always remains possible.

With respect to the American legacy, to take the latter first, I have, for example, always been particularly taken by the way Emerson links discourse, thought, and action.[1] In a sense, it complements my own project of communicative praxis. You might be surprised to learn that were I to give an address such as the oration "The American Scholar," which Emerson delivered in 1837 to the Phi Beta Kappa Society in Cambridge, it would deal with many of the same themes he dealt with more than 150 years ago. In that address Emerson spoke of the scholar as one who is educated by nature, books, and action.

Now, admittedly, much of the program at the annual meetings of the Society for Phenomenology and Existential Philosophy (SPEP), which I cofounded with John Wild, James Edie, and George Schrader in 1965, is devoted to discussions of the contributions of philosophers from continental Europe. But one should not forget that there is an indigenous American existentialism and phenomenology, as Bruce Wilshire has so admirably illustrated in his book, *William James and Phenomenology*.[2] My guess would be that an investigation of the nooks and crannies of American intellectual life would also yield resonances of the themes that have come to identify postmodernism, such as multiplicity, heterogeneity, difference, incredulity toward metanarratives, and so on.

It should also be made clear that the purpose of founding SPEP was not as much to confront the dominant Anglo-American analytic tradition as it was to supplement it. We wanted to provide the philosophical community with a more pluralistic agendum. The call for pluralism is a manifestly American request. It is part of our ethos. An ethos that received decisive expression in William James's pioneering work, "A Pluralistic Universe."[3]

Further, I have some deep concerns about the label "continental" philosophy. I am of the mind that the labels "continental" and "analytic" as applied to philosophical discourse have outworn their usefulness. I have yet to meet a responsible "continental" philosopher who is opposed to analysis and I have encountered numerous "analytic" philosophers who are concerned with many of the same issues that elicit my interest. That there are differences of style, attitude, and approach across the spectrum of philosophical movements cannot be denied. But many times these same differences can be found within the movements themselves.

I have always found it amusing that scholars enamored with Edmund Husserl's quest for a universal logical grammar have more in common with the early analytic philosophers than they do with philosophers who have turned from transcendental to existential phenomenology. Or, to use another example, that the representatives of the Ordinary Language School, the second phase of analytic philosophy, have more in common with philosophers involved with hermeneutics than they do with members of the earlier phase of analytic philosophy.

The lesson to be learned from all this is that philosophy of whatever stripe never speaks with a single voice and that if the conversation is to continue it should behoove us to strive to communicate in spite of differences. A multiplicity of voices is needed in the philosophical task, a multiplicity of voices that, in a sense, always remains too narrow.

RER/DJM: In your own work, it is evident you have made an effort to "communicate in spite of differences," engaging the work of many philosophers, philosophers associated with movements such as phenomenology, existentialism, hermeneutics, deconstruction, postmodernism, and so on. Clearly we would be remiss in leaving out pragmatism and other homegrown movements. Yet in these engagements, you have consistently refused to align yourself with any of these philosophical movements. This refusal appears to be indicative of your work.

COS: The philosophical movements that you name are all relevant to an account of my philosophical development. Other philosophical movements or tendencies, of course, would need to be referenced in charting my critical conversations.

However, all along, my response to these movements has been one of critical appropriation. It would be quite misleading to say that I moved from a phenomenological period to an existential period to a hermeneutic period and so on. I have carried on a critical conversation with the representatives of each of these movements as well as others, but never found myself comfortably situated within any one of them.

When I speak of critical appropriations vis-à-vis the individual movements that you have enunciated, I mean that I have taken over the responsibility of addressing the issues, the problems that their thought poses without necessarily taking on their distinctive approaches to the issues. It is important to draw a distinction between a position or a school of thought and the issues that are addressed.

I am reminded here of the response that we received from Martin Heidegger after setting up the Heidegger circle some thirty or thirty-five years ago. We had planned to discuss Heidegger's approach to technology. So we wrote to him, told him about the existence of the circle, and informed him that we were going to be discussing his approach to technology. We received this very interesting letter from him, telling us that he was touched by the fact that we had an annual meeting devoted to a discussion of his philosophical accomplishments. But he urged us not to talk about his approach, but rather talk about the issue of technology.

So that is what I have done in my own work: distinguished position-taking from issues. And my conversation with the different philosophers that I treat in my work has been that of appropriating the issues while remaining critical with respect to their positions. I am hopeful, in this way, what Friedrich Nietzsche always feared can be avoided, namely becoming a disciple or coming to have disciples.[4]

RER/DJM: The suggestion has been made that in appropriating issues rather than position-taking, as you put it, there is a certain refusal of polemics, that time-honored philosophical genre and prominent academic pastime. In other words, a suggestion that you eschew polemics.

COS: It is important that this issue be raised because it gives me an opportunity to address a misunderstanding that appears to be afloat in the neighborhood. I have never taken a stand against polemics or argumentation—which itself would be polemical—nor have I avoided or eschewed polemics.

There are two points at issue here. The first has to do with the placement of strategies and techniques of argumentation within the designs of philosophical discourse. My position here has always been that argumentation clearly has a place in philosophy, but it must remain subordinate to the achievement of understanding and enlightenment. It should not become an end in itself, that is, argumentation for the sake of argumentation, designed simply to chalk up points by obliterating an opponent. The goal of argumentation is not coercion, but rather mutual understanding.

The second point is that although polemic, insofar as it is not abused, comprises a quite legitimate function in the philosophical enterprise, the use of language in its polemical modality is only one function of language. Linguistic usage cannot be restricted to argumentative competence and performance. Language plays within a wider theater of performance and disclosure, exhibiting nonargumentative usages in speaking and writing. Doing philosophy is not bound to the employment of only one language game.

Ludwig Wittgenstein's later work, *Philosophical Investigations*, is a classic illustration of this point.[5] Not a single argument can be found in its 229 pages. What one finds there is the use of language to show that what appears to be the case—to elucidate how something consists in, or counts as something—only within a specified context of circumstances. This is language in its function of showing, of setting forth, of disclosing, rather than language tooled to deliver deductive conclusions or inferential claims. The citadel of philosophy is expansive enough for both of these functions of language as well as others to thrive.

RER/DJM: Taking this into consideration and given that you have characterized your work as a critical appropriation of issues—with an emphasis on the term "critical" here—where do you stand with respect to what has been called the hermeneutics of suspicion?

COS: The triumvirate of Karl Marx, Nietzsche, and Sigmund Freud—the three masters of suspicion, as Paul Ricoeur dubbed them—came to play a role somewhat later in my professional development. I had studied bits and pieces of Marx, Nietzsche, and Freud all along, but what piqued my desire to have another look at them was mainly Ricoeur's pioneering work that teased out a hermeneutics of suspicion from each of these giants.[6] Certainly, there is a hermeneutics at work in the thought of each, and it does not require much investigation of their works to find that they are indeed suspicious about much. Marx works out a strategy of suspicion in his investigation of the ideological underpinnings of false consciousness. Nietzsche directs his attention to the self-deception that feeds the good and bad conscience. Freud uncovers the libidinal energy that motivates behavior from the depths of the unconscious and which the superego is want to cover up.

Now you ask, "How do these strategies of a hermeneutics of suspicion link up with my project of communicative praxis?" Clearly, there is a linkage here. But it is not one of wholesale appropriation. The hermeneutics of suspicion provides us with a necessary deconstructive strategy whereby one dismantles the intrusive ideologies and duplicities of self-deception that obstruct an understanding of self, other, and world. But this is only one half of the loaf—and although one half may be better than nothing, it is desirable to have the other half as well. The other half has to do with a strategy for re-creating a vision of self, of other, and of world that opens up in the wake of the deconstructive dismantling. We must never forget that deconstruction and re-creation always go together.

The hermeneutics of suspicion by itself is too one-sided, too limited, too restricted. It remains largely reactive. It reacts against the techniques by means of which false consciousness, the herd morality of the good and bad conscience, and the repressive facades of the superego cover-up the operations of power. This, of course, is all to the good. But one needs to graft on to this reactive hermeneutics a proactive hermeneutics, that is, an interpretive stance that sorts out the requirements for a more positive and more edifying dynamics of discourse and action. This is precisely the goal of my project of communicative praxis.

PORTRAITS OF THE SELF

RER/DJM: The title of your most recent book *The Self after Postmodernity* hints at what appears to be a life-long project.[7] It is a project already evident in your first book *Existence and Freedom*.[8] From that work onward there seems to be an abiding interest in the notion of the self. Before turning specifically to the project of communicative praxis, we would like to ask about this ongoing interest in the self, assuming, of course, that this is an accurate assessment.

COS: It would be correct to say that the questions of self-understanding and self-constitution are at issue throughout all of my work, from the very earliest to the latest. There are two preliminary points that can be made here that perhaps will help to clarify this interest.

The first point has to do with the accident of one's professional development. Here it was my early interest in Alfred Whitehead, who raised the question about the self in a rather provocative manner. In asking about the self, his position was the self must always be understood as a self in process.[9] Now if the self is always in process, then as Whitehead once put it—and he probably overmade the point, but he did put it this way—Aristotle's doctrine of substance is a complete mistake. I say "probably over-made the point," because Aristotle may have had a more fluid understanding of substance than did René Descartes, for example. But the point, which Whitehead clearly made for emphasis, is that there is no permanent substrate to the self. So, on the one hand, the problem of understanding the self on the basis of an application of the categories of substance and attribute, categories in which the self had traditionally been understood, became a problem for me based on my initial philosophical studies.

The second is the existential and, probably, the more basic point. Namely, to ask any kind of basic philosophical question presupposes some kind of understanding—pretheoretical, to be sure—of what it means to ask a question. The questioner is inescapable here and so the question about the questioner becomes inescapable as well. This amounts to the existential side of the Cartesian problematic: Who is it that doubts before the doubting begins? So, there is, on the other hand, the existential feature of philosophy itself that informs my interest in the self.

Now the pursuit of the question, as you might expect, led me more and more to the disciplines of the social sciences, and probably more specifically to communication. And this was inevitable. As soon as the self is somehow socially or communally contextualized, then there is the requirement to give attention to the social situatedness of the self and the communicative interaction that structures that situatedness.

My most recent book, *The Self after Postmodernity*, provides a kind of consolidation of my life-long interest in the question of the self. Here I attempt to steer a course between the Scylla of selfhood anchored in a stable and self-identical substance, immune to the ravages of time, and the Charybdis of a self dispersed in a random becoming, without any unity or direction. The self, between these unacceptable alternatives, is a self refigured as the "who" of discourse, action, community, and transcendence.

RER/DJM: The interest in the self, as you put it in your second point, is and presumably remains an interest in the existential self. But in speaking of the existential, it is difficult to escape the reverberations of existentialism, which, as you know, has gotten more than its share of bad press. Can we appeal to the existential in spite of these reverberations, and if so, what are we now to understand by the term?

COS: There is the inescapability of self-consciousness, of self-understanding, of self-knowledge in any philosophical inquiry. This mandates, if you will, a return time and again perhaps not to the question "*What* is the self?" but as I suggested in my last book, "*Who* is the self?" or "*Who* is speaking?" or "*Who* is acting?" or "*Who* is in community?" etc. Now this concern with the self is a concern in another guise of the question: "What does it mean to be a human being?" I am reminded here of the statement attributed to Feuerbach: "I do not wish to be a philosopher at the expense of being a human being."

In a sense, this is a kind of recovery of that initial existential question, but now it has matured, gone through a baptism in communicative approaches to selfhood, moved beyond the tendency toward the kind of perfervid individualism in the early existentialists. So, it is not simply a return understood in terms of recovering what somehow was already fixed and finished. Rather, there is a repetition. And here I am thinking of Gilles Deleuze: a repetition with difference.[10]

The inescapable concreteness of the self is, I think, one of the continuing lessons of the existentialist revolt. To be sure, existentialism began by revolting against the abstract philosophy of Georg Hegel, which entailed its own sort of depersonalization. But we find this depersonalization not only in abstract philosophy, we also find it illustrated in the excessive technologization of our current societies. Today, we are required to do battle with dehumanizing strategies of communication and practice, the technologization of communication and practice in which this concreteness is lost.

This is something that has been attended to in much of the postexistentialist literature, in which there is specific attention paid to the relations of power at work enframing self-development and societal development.[11] So that indeed, becoming a self—and it is always a matter of *becoming* a self—is a struggle in achieving selfness, in confronting constraining power relationships in society, and specifically in institutions broadly understood.

RER/DJM: This leads to an interesting aside, the problem of speaking about "the" self in the wake of what you have termed postexistentialist thought. It seems as though no article would be quite right.

COS: This, of course, has to do with the difficulties of speaking about the self in the literature. There is always a problem with articles and connectives in titles—when Martin Heidegger talks about being and time, for example, one slides into the other. It is difficult to know how to handle them.

I had a fight with my publisher about this. *The Self after Postmodernity* was first presented as a series of lectures at Trent University honoring the philosophical contributions of Gilbert Ryle. I entitled the lectures "Portrait of the Self after Postmodernity." Yale University Press agreed to publish the manuscript, but their marketing department, for a number of reasons—none of which I thought were very good—argued that the title *Portrait of the Self* would be a bad title, because the book would be cataloged in libraries under photography rather than philosophy.

Although "Portrait of the Self" doesn't wholly address the concern, it does shift the perspective from a suggestion that what we have here is a kind of complete description of the self—an entity of some sort, to a way of looking at the self, a perspective on the self.

Whatever characterization we ultimately come upon, the issue of the existential remains. Any philosophy that seeks effectuality in our quotidian existence ultimately betrays an existential residue: Someone must act—and, despite appearances, this includes philosophies like deconstruction and postmodernism, which without such effectual effort would be nothing but empty formalism. So, the existential question—the question about the self and its inescapable concreteness—returns not only in experience, but in literature as well.

RER/DJM: Obviously, there are issues concerning the self that you have not yet been able to address in your work. Given this, what do you see as the most pressing concern in articulating an adequate conception of the self today?

COS: I would underscore the requirement for intensive and sustained analyses and interpretations of the role of technology and ecology upon the project of attempting to define who we are within a postmodern ethos. The acceleration of technological innovations during the last half of the century has supplied numerous challenges along the way. Issues having to do with artificial intelligence, which, of course, have been with us for some time, will now become intensified. Developments in biotechnology will have a direct bearing on future definitions of selfhood.

And then directly connected with the development of technology are the ecological issues, which will require our increasing attention. With the unprecedented and almost frightening growth in the world population, and the limitation of both natural and societal resources, we will need to revise some of our jaundiced convictions of what it means to inherit the Earth.

In all this, the need for further study and research in communication becomes quite readily apparent. The world has become a global society as never before. With this comes the requirement to devise means for communication across geographical, ethnological, cultural, and religious divisions. And with this, travels the tough question: What is the *meaning* of communication?

The perfecting of technological devices to send scripted, voice, and visual messages across the land does not provide a sufficient answer to the question of what it means to communicate something to someone else. Wider issues of the meaning of community and communal organization, involving the body politic, also come into play here, and we then quickly see how issues of the self slide into issues of community, politics, and ethics.

RER/DJM: In responding to our questions concerning the self, you have touched, in a number of different ways, on something we take to be central to your interest in the self as well as to your project of communicative praxis. What we find is a concern with alienation or estrangement and the necessity of working to overcome it. It is a theme that first appears in *Freedom and Existence* where, citing Marx, Søren Kierkegaard, and by implication Ludwig Feuerbach, you write of our estrangement or alienation from others, from ourselves, and from nature.[12]

COS: I first studied Marx along with my studies on Kierkegaard and Feuerbach. The three comprised for me the philosophically fresh air of anti-Hegelianism—Marx contesting Hegel's philosophy of identity from the perspective of our socioeconomic existence; Kierkegaard, from the perspective of our ethicoreligious existence; and Feuerbach, from the perspective of our concrete sensory-biological existence.

Hegel's grand hypothesis was that the polarities of essence and existence achieve a synthesis, unity, or coincidence within the dynamics of Absolute Spirit. Marx, Kierkegaard, and Feuerbach were quick to point out that this synthesis appears to occur only in Hegel's head, since all around us we see that the forces of estrangement or alienation are still very much a part of our social, religious, and biological existence. All three were involved, in some manner or another, with what came to be called the "existential revolt" against the Absolute Idealism of the later Hegel.

One of the things I wanted to do in *Existence and Freedom* was to point out the distinction between alienation and estrangement, on the one hand, and finitude on the other, in order to avoid a collapse of the two. It is important to distinguish limitations that arise out of our finitude from alienation and estrangement within that finitude. Alienation or estrangement is, in a sense, finitude gone wrong, which is why we can do something about it—it's not inscribed on our being-in-the-world.

To be finite is not tantamount to being estranged or alienated—a distinction that has, at times, been blurred. Estrangement and alienation amount to a displacement of possibility that is not properly bound to the finitude attached to our being-in-the-world. Although finitude places limits on possibility, the limitations on possibility resulting from estrangement and alienation are not a consequence of this finitude, even though they make use of it and the ambiguous freedom that attends such finitude. Estrangement and alienation are in large measure a result of the misuse of our finite freedom.

It is important, however, in speaking of these matters, to recognize that alienation and estrangement, as distortions of our existence, are not something that can be rectified by linguistic maneuvering. They are material determinants at work in our distorted existence and must be addressed as such.

With respect to my project of communicative praxis, if there were no alienation or estrangement in our communicative activities, I guess there would be no reason to talk about those activities. There is a sense in which my interest in communication is certainly in part, if not to a great extent, motivated by the problems of the distortions of communication. Just as hermeneutics is, in a sense, a project that responds to misunderstanding. So clearly, Kierkegaard, Feuerbach, and Marx—particularly Marx's early work on alienation—are a motivating factor in my project of communicative praxis.

THE TURN TO COMMUNICATION

RER/DJM: As you know, there was an effort to understand philosophy and rhetoric as complementary practices in the work of both Plato and Aristotle. One thinks, for example, of the "philosophical rhetoric" Plato describes in the *Phaedrus*, or again, of rhetoric characterized as the *antistropos* or, as it is usually put, the "counterpart" of dialectic in the opening lines of Aristotle's *Rhetoric*. However, in time, this complementarity, presupposed in one manner or another by Plato and Aristotle, quickly deteriorated into an antagonism in which one was required to make a choice between the two discourses. Subsequently, the task of undertaking something like a philosophy of communication has at least been burdened, if not at times blocked, by this relationship.

COS: That Plato and Aristotle, and the Greeks more generally were interested in the connection between philosophy and rhetoric, and that in later philosophical developments interest in this connection faded, is certainly right on target. Plato wrote two works on rhetoric and Aristotle wrote one of the classic treatises. Moreover, in the medieval trivium, logic, grammar, and rhetoric flourished as overlapping disciplines. But this all changed with the advent of modern philosophy. The rhetorical arts were marginalized at best, disparaged and disdained at worst. Even a philosopher of the stature of Immanuel Kant, who surely should have known better, defined rhetoric as "the art of deluding by means of a fair semblance."[13]

Why did rhetoric receive such ill treatment in modernity? Much, of course, had to do with the "epistemological turn" that began with Descartes' invention of "mind" as a *solus ipse* and the preoccupation with a technical reason that looked to the natural sciences for some sort of unimpeachable criteria for knowledge. The crux of the matter clearly has to do with this imprisonment of the mind as the isolated, zero-point origin of knowledge. The mind in modern epistemology has the responsibility to achieve knowledge. And after it has knowledge, then it may, if it has sufficient time on its hands, decide to communicate what it knows to others.

But does the mind first know and then communicate? Or is communication constitutive of knowledge? Is knowledge a private affair, founded on criteria that are somehow known in advance? Or is knowledge the progeny of what I have called communicative praxis, a quite public affair in which criteria are *post festum* rather than front-loaded, criteria devised and revised in the struggle for an understanding that is the reward and, at times, the disappointment of rhetorical transactions?

One of the important contributions of postmodernism has been to reinstate rhetoric and communication as native voices in philosophical discourse. Nietzsche has played a significant role in this project of restoration. Of particular importance is his explication of truth as "a moveable host of metaphors, metonymies, and anthropomorphisms."[14] And then there is Jacques Derrida, who, in his splendid essay "White Mythology: Metaphor in the Text of Philosophy," has shown, and almost effortlessly, how the grammar of philosophical discourse throughout the history of Western philosophy continued to receive its direction from rhetorical invention.[15]

In spite of this, it is clear that what you call the burden on or blockage to a philosophy of communication attending this historical antagonism remains in force today. And there are two interrelated points I would make with respect to moving beyond this antagonism, one directed to philosophy, the other to communication studies.

On the one hand, there is a responsibility on the part of philosophers to recognize that communication is constitutive of knowledge. This involves a more thorough-going distantiation from the Cartesian legacy in which knowledge is achieved first and then communicated—insofar as it is communicated—as an afterthought. On the other hand, there is a responsibility on the part of communication theorists to recognize that there is a genuine threat of sophistry—of empty formalism—in our communicative engagements. This threat has been pointed out in the tradition going as far back as Plato.

RER/DJM: In the twentieth century, a good deal of philosophical attention has been directed, in one manner or another, toward issues concerning communication. However, it seems that, despite this attention, the phenomenon of communication as such—communication *qua* communication—has, for the most part, gone unphilosophized. What we often find in its place is an appropriation of the phenomenon as a means of solving other philosophical problems. This can be seen, for example, in Husserl's attempt to use communication as a means of resolving the problem of intersubjectivity, or again, in Jürgen Habermas' effort to use communication as a means of establishing a normative ethics.

COS: This is where I differ, not only from Husserl but also from Habermas, each of whom have a kind of instrumental understanding of communication, namely, something that can be used to solve other problems. This is, of course, one possible way to use communication.

Husserl continues the marginalization or subordination of communication in the Cartesian legacy using communication to solve or somehow supplement an epistemological problem. It is a subordination that follows in the wake of the prejudice that knowledge somehow is borne by an isolated act of consciousness. The presupposition is that knowledge is an interior event, an event of a solitary ego-cogito that is somehow able to apprehend its object, either in its givenness as an existential reality or as an object that is meant. After this, communication enters the picture as an instrument used to convey this knowledge to other people.

Now, in Habermas, it's a little more circuitous, and it's not as blandly Cartesian. Communication stands in the service, not of conveying epistemological formulations in terms of assertoric claims, but of opening up a space for ethics. Although I find this to be quite suggestive and to have its own rewards, it seems to me that what Habermas fails to recognize is that in each of the domains of knowledge he maps out—the cognitive, the evaluative, and the aesthetic—communication is always already at work.

Habermas does go beyond the Cartesian legacy in the sense that communication is somehow constitutive of knowledge within each of the cultural domains. But it is constitutive of a rather narrow notion of knowledge. It is knowledge bent upon the discovery of validity claims—that's the whole point of it. Now, to be sure, the validity claims operative in the different culture spheres are operative in different senses, but they are still operative as claims. So, communication is constitutive of each of these domains only insofar as it establishes the claims specific to the domains. These claims, in turn, provide the normative basis for argumentation.

Communication is, for the most part, reduced to the use of language; more specifically language delimited in such a way that it stands in the service of argumentation, which is, in a sense, the long and short of philosophy for Habermas. Communication now provides the resources for argumentation. It substantiates claims—cognitive claims, ethical claims, aesthetic claims, and so forth—in service of the force of the stronger argument.

Reduced to argumentation proceeding from what are taken to be the normative validity claims of each of the cultural domains, communication becomes instrumental, the validity claims themselves standing in service of being correct—a disguised form of epistemology. It is profoundly ironic that Habermas' use of communication is instrumental in spite of itself. Although he has a good sense of the limitations of instrumental reason, moving with great acumen out of the early Frankfurt school and the critique of instrumental rationality, he does so only to turn around and unwittingly make communication itself instrumental.

There is, I think, a significant difference in my understanding of communication. I take communication to be constitutive of philosophical problems rather than something to be used to solve philosophical problems. Communication, by its very performance, poses or sets forth philosophical problems.

And I agree there is a great deal that is left undone in philosophizing communication. You could say Heidegger opened the door—opened the door, but didn't really get much past the threshold. Communication must always be understood as being constitutive of our being-in-the-world. But then I think you have to make a semantic move from communication to community—a move already implicated in the term "communication." Communication clearly has something to do with community. The point is that, in understanding ourselves as being-in-the-world, we are always already communally situated, so that, to move beyond Heidegger, communication/community becomes a structural determinate of our being-in-the-world.

One of the things then that is left undone is fleshing out the significations of communication and community as they play themselves out in the court of sociopolitical concerns. Communication—the meaning of communication—has something to do with the contextualization of the communicator within the polis. Here, communication immediately assumes a kind of responsibility for both a descriptive and prescriptive understanding of politics. And with respect to this, Heidegger clearly came up a little short.

RER/DJM: Communication does not, at least *prima fascia*, always lead to community. Communication can also injure and harm. It can produce separations that destroy community.

COS: Communication and community may be too closely tied together here. In *Experience and Being*, I tried to address this issue by distinguishing community from sociality.[16] Sociality is a rather straightforward and neutral designation of being-with-others that undergoes both positive and negative modifications. There I took community to be a positive modification of sociality, a creative way of being-with-others. And I took what I called conformism to be a negative modification of sociality, a destructive way of being-with-others. Within this set of logical distinctions, there is no deficient form of community because community is, by definition, positive. Strictly speaking, there are only deficient modalities of sociality that entail estrangement, alienation, and the misuse of freedom. Here a kind of communication is at work that articulates stereotypes, that stigmatizes, that refuses difference.

RER/DJM: Would you view this type of communication as somehow being deficient in the same way that Heidegger sometimes talks about deficient forms of care?

COS: I'm a bit reluctant to put Heidegger in this context because of the problem that he has with the unauthentic and the authentic in his ontology of *Dasein*. I think this is principally a consequence of the way he set up the format of *Being and Time*. If you begin with an unauthentic being-in-the-world in which communication is reduced to unauthentic talk—*Gerede*: idle chatter—then you have the problem of distilling out of this unauthentic being-with-others the content and measure of an authentic being-with-others. It is an important distinction, but one that Heidegger made problematic by trying to derive the one from the other. If we are to use the terms, I think we need to take a different approach here. We need to begin with a notion of communication as a kind of neutral space that, like sociality, has different modifications: the authentic and the unauthentic.

At any rate, what I think is significant and helpful in Heidegger's attending to what one might call unauthentic communication, is that there is a kind of ever-present threat to community that is part of the continuing struggle for communication. Interpersonally, the unauthentic would be a failure to respect the other as other, a lack of openness, of receptivity, of responsiveness, a failure to listen and, more importantly, to hear.

This is a threat that is intensified with the advent of technology. Here also, Heidegger pointed the direction, though some of the technological advances that threaten communication didn't really come to the fore until very recently. The threats to authentic communication that travel with advanced technology are threats that require our attention.

There is, for example, an assumption that when we send messages—either scripted, verbal, or visual—across geographical landscapes to disembodied others, then we have communicated. But the virtual recipient is still just a virtual recipient. To be sure, certain dimensions of knowledge can be conveyed in this way, but these are all disembodied dimensions of knowledge. It is important to recognize—and we recognize this less and less—that there is a difference between conveying information and communicating.

As I see it, the threat here is twofold. On the one hand, there is a failure to recognize the abstraction or decontextualization from the communicative context at work here, a failure to recognize that even though something may be gained, something is lost. On the other hand, there is a tendency toward absolutizing certain technological modalities of communication, taking them to be normative of communication itself. This is reductionism in its most violent form.

It is technological enframing as Heidegger spoke of it. And we must see that there is more to communication. More than conveying information in which the decontextualization of communication disguises itself as such. And more than the technological modalities of communication which taken normatively require us to communicate in certain ways at the expense of all others.

Beyond the interpersonal, the unauthentic would also testify to distortions in our sociopolitical existence. For example, in some forms of Marxism, the unauthentic has much to do with the notion of false consciousness or ideology—however you care to put it—that can be generally described as involving unauthentic self-understanding and unauthentic communication. It's interesting how it comes to the fore here. Workers in a state of subjugation are able to communicate. They can talk with each other about all kinds of different things and interests. They can talk about their excitement about a possible raise in their weekly pay. But they are unaware of the underlying conditions of their subjugation. There is communication going on, but communication that belies an authentic understanding of the wider situation.

RER/DJM: In your earlier response, you used the phrase "the struggle to communicate." This seems to us to be a particularly important qualification.

COS: It is Karl Jaspers who uses this rather revealing phrase: communication as *liebender Kampf*—a loving struggle. And it becomes a loving struggle particularly when you are dealing with communicating what he called the truths of *Existenz*—existential truths.

Jaspers lived this philosophy, as I discovered when I had the opportunity to meet with him at the University of Basel. This was in 1955, during the time I was studying at Heidelberg as a Fulbright Fellow. Not only did Jaspers set everything aside to meet with me, but he patiently listened to my hesitant German, rephrasing my questions, answering them, asking if I had understood, rephrasing questions and answers if I hadn't. I still marvel at this great philosopher devoting his entire attention to a young American graduate student—it is one of the most memorable experiences I have had.

It is unfortunate that Jaspers has been so sorely neglected in the recent literature. We forget, for example, that the second volume of the three-volume English translation of his *Philosophie* deals with issues having to do with communication, and that the third lecture in *Reason and Existenz* is on truth as communicability.[17]

When you're dealing with existential truths, the truths of *Existenz*, there is a constant struggle. It is a struggle because there will be inevitable differences both interpersonal and sociopolitical differences, religious differences, cultural differences, and so on. But you have to strive to communicate in spite of these differences. You have to work to keep communication from breaking down, from becoming restricted and distorted. It's a loving struggle because you always have to be willing to recognize that there will be barriers to the communication, and you have to accept the other in spite of an inability to make your point.

AN ILLOCUTIONARY ACT: COMMUNICATIVE PRAXIS

RER/DJM: We would like to turn now to discuss your project of communicative praxis. As a preliminary to this, could you tell us when communication first became an issue for you?

COS: I guess I encountered the issue of communication in my undergraduate studies, but I didn't realize I had encountered it until I was confronted with the need to understand and explain societal structures in my work.[18] The structures of authentic and unauthentic communication are implicated in the very name social science. But it wasn't until I wrote my third book, *Radical Reflection and the Origin of the Human Sciences*, that

I specifically addressed issues in social science.[19] My work *Communicative Praxis and the Space of Subjectivity* followed this.[20]

RER/DJM: In reconsidering the phenomenon—or phenomena—of communication, why did you find it necessary to construct the new locution "communicative praxis"?

COS: A number of factors came into play in my decision to couple communication and praxis. In dealing with the continental tradition, I wanted to avoid what I observed to be the hegemonic and, in a sense, anaptotic—or totalizing—tendencies in the philosophical turn to language, discourse, textuality, and so forth. I also wanted to avoid the tendency in that turn to isolate communication from action. By zeroing in on language, or discourse, or textuality, or whatever, communication was being considered without attending to the actional component of our engagements with others.

In dealing with the analytic tradition, I wanted to avoid the division of communication and action attending the disciplinary separation of the philosophy of language from the philosophy of action. At the same time, I wanted to avoid what I took to be a resurgence of the threat of elementalism within certain quarters of each of these areas of analytic philosophy.[21] In this, an effort was being made to reduce language, on the one hand, and action, on the other, to its fundamental elemental units—its isolated, atomistic, so-called constitutive elements. This, of course, goes back to the beginnings of the British empiricist tradition. The problem here is that in reducing language to its syntactic units or action to units of movement, for example, there is a decontextualization in which meaning is lost.

So, for example, in the philosophy of action, you might be very much preoccupied with the raising of the arm as an instance of action quite independent of the context. Raising an arm is an act independent of the rest of the body—apparently, you can raise your arm without a shoulder, in isolation from one's holistic embodiment. This kind of philosophy doesn't get you anywhere because the actions are isolated, cut off from the social significations in which action occurs.

So I chose the phrase "communicative praxis" in which communication qualifies praxis—is even an intrinsic qualification of praxis, in that it provides the context for the very understanding of the meaning of what goes on in human action. When you link communication and praxis you now have a social form that provides the context for specific acts.

RER/DJM: You make use of the term "praxis" with all of its historical resonances rather than the term "practice" which is more in vogue today. Would you explain your use of the term in relation to its history?

COS: Praxis clearly has been in the vocabulary since the time of Aristotle. And there is a sense in which my effort is, in part, to reclaim the Aristotelian sense of praxis before the separation of theory and practice in the tradition.

Now one might argue that Aristotle was partly responsible for this separation in his division of *theoria*, *poiesis*, and *praxis* with *episteme*, *techne*, and *phronesis* as their attendant forms of knowledge. But with the advent of modernity, the bifurcation of theory and practice widened. When theoreticians tried to be generous about practice and the practical, they said, at best, "Well sure there's practice, but it's always practice as an application of theory, always in the service of theory."

The problem here is twofold. On the one hand, practice, as an application of theory, has to wait upon the determinations of theory for its meaning or intelligibility. On the other hand, while practice without theory is blind, theory without practice is empty.

So, I tried to do a kind of semantic clarification in which praxis—if not on the thither side of this divide—was perhaps somehow between the theoretical and the practical as they are generally understood, and particularly as they are understood in modern philosophy. Praxis as the manner in which we are engaged in the world and with others has its own insight or understanding prior to any explicit formulation of that understanding. Here, of course, I am very much indebted to Heidegger and to Maurice Merleau-Ponty.

Praxis was also used a good deal in the early phase of Critical Theory by members of the Frankfurt School: Walter Benjamin, Herbert Marcuse, Max Horkheimer, and then much later, of course, by Habermas. But there the notion of praxis moves out from a neo-Marxist notion in which praxis is, at least at times, subordinated to *techne*.

Marxism clearly understood the danger of subordinating praxis to *theoria*: "The point is to change the world." But it failed to see the danger of subordinating praxis to *techne*—to forms of socioeconomic organization. The point is to change the world. But how does change take place? Through *techne*: alter the mode of production and everything will follow from that.

So, my effort was, on the one hand, to liberate praxis from its subordination to *theoria* in the modern theory/practice distinction, and on the other to broaden the notion of praxis found in early and later Critical Theory, liberating praxis from its subordination to *techne*. Of course, it must be understood that praxis, as I understand it, is always entwined with communication.

RER/DJM: In a previous response, you described communicative praxis in a way that indicated, if only obliquely, the manner in which we are to understand the relation of these two terms. Communication, you said, is an intrinsic qualification of praxis. By this, we take it that you do not intend the term communicative to designate a particular kind of praxis among others, but rather that all praxis is communicative or, put inversely, that all communication is praxial. Earlier, however, you evinced uneasiness regarding the claims that everything is language, or discourse, or textuality with their hegemonic and totalizing tendencies. Insofar as everything now appears to be communicative praxis, how do you avoid the same dilemma?

COS: As you point out, there has been a recurring problem, a logical problem of sorts, with landing upon one feature, one aspect, one profile, of human existence or being-in-the-world as a means of explication. And then, having settled upon something in this way, having to answer the question: "Well, if everything is discourse or everything is language or everything is interpretation, then isn't it the case that nothing is language, discourse, or interpretation?" But, I think this can be sorted out in such a way that the latter does not necessarily follow from the former.

William James tells a story about an Indian master who explained that the world rests on the back of a huge elephant. Now the master's student wanted to know on what the elephant's legs rested. The master responded that the elephant's legs rested on the back of a huge turtle. The student, James says, still not satisfied wanted to know on what the turtle's legs rested. To which the master answered: turtles all the way down. The answer, of course, is paradoxical because there is no "all the way down," no bottom at which you arrive, no bedrock foundation.

Now I think, in a similar fashion, it can be said that interpretation goes all the way down. Language goes all the way down. Discourse goes all the way down. Action goes all the way down. But that doesn't mean that any one of those items is all there is.

Here the task of philosophy becomes a continuing matter of sorting out, explicating, and clarifying the various expressions entwined in the upsurge of human life in the world: the linguistic expression and the action expression, the interpretive, the descriptive, the evaluative, and all the rest. So I think that's how you surmount the so-called logical problem of appearing to assert that this is all there is.

COMMUNICATIVE PRAXIS: TRANSVERSALITY

RER/DJM: In your project of communicative praxis, there are two notions that have come to play a predominate role: transversality and the fitting response. Transversality serves to delineate the space and movement of communicative praxis, while the fitting response is an effort to delineate communicative praxis in its ethicopolitical dimension. We would like to begin with the notion of transversality and then turn to the fitting response.

COS: Transversality is a very rich concept. It is used in topological mathematics as a generalization of orthoganality, articulating the convergence of lines and surfaces that is not reducible to coincidence. The term is used to describe the overlapping of fibers in physiology. In anatomy, the connection of vertebrae is an example of what is termed transversal unity. In subatomic particle theory, physicists speak of the transverse mass of particles. But you can't reduce its meaning to any one of these areas. It traverses these different contexts as well as others, which is one of the things that intrigued me about it.

I guess I first discovered the notion of transversality in Jean-Paul Sartre, who sort of just throws it out and leaves it dangling. The term comes up in his criticism of Husserl's use of the transcendental ego to ground consciousness.[22] His argument is that before he brought the machinery of the transcendental ego into play, Husserl, in his earlier work on the phenomenology of internal time consciousness, had pointed toward a more promising understanding of consciousness as a kind of unification.[23] There isn't a bedrock unity here. But there is an ongoing unification, a unification in which present consciousness relates itself to the past and future. Sartre calls this "transversal intentionality."[24] I found this very suggestive, but it was undeveloped.

Then, Deleuze came along and provided a more concrete elucidation and illustration of the workings of transversality in Marcel Proust's *Remembrance of Things Past*.[25] This, of course, fell out from Félix Guattari's earlier work in psychoanalysis, from his marvelous description of the possibility of transversal organization in the workings of a psychiatric institution.[26]

In the psychiatric institution, you have different parties each expressing interest in the task of psychiatric healing: the administrators of the hospital, the doctors, the nurses, then of course the patients for whom the hospital exists, as well as the family and friends of the patients. Now all of these individuals should have a say of some kind in helping with the process of psychiatric healing. But what you have to avoid here is a vertical hegemonic structure in which policies are simply dictated from above, without consideration for or consultation with those whom they effect. But you also have to avoid the horizontal converse, a kind of anarchic plurality in which no unity, no agreement, no consensus, can take place.

Guattari uses the notion of transversality to avoid the overdetermination of both the vertical and the horizontal. It is a matter of coming together without the dictates of authority on the one hand, and without the relational indifference of anarchic plurality on the other. Transversality signifies a convergence without coincidence, a coming together in which the integrity of each of the voices—each of these seats of concern—is respected, a coming together constituted in a mutual responsiveness.

RER/DJM: How do you turn the notion of transversality to your own purposes?

COS: In my work, transversality does a kind of double duty in terms of its relevance to communicative praxis, on the one hand, and its ontological significance, on the other. In terms of communicative praxis, it splits the difference between robust consensus and heterogeneous dis-sensus: Habermas versus Jean-François Lyotard. It is a movement of openness refusing the collapse into either. Ontologically, it makes metaphorical use of the diagonal, splitting the difference between vertically anchored universals and horizontally dispersed particulars.[27]

RER/DJM: In terms of its relevance to communicative praxis, transversality obviously cannot be located in one place. Rather it seems to lead us in different ways, by different paths, to something you have called an "in-between."[28] How would you characterize transversality in terms of the "in-between" in which we come to find ourselves?

COS: The first thing that I would say is that the "in-between" is not a "what." It is not a "what" in terms of a specifiable essence, or concept. There is no category of the "in-between." The "in-between" is that which gives rise to categories.

The second thing I would say is that the "in-between" is not a matter of taking the ideas of the addresser and the addressee and then seeing what we can understand in terms of sort of combining the two—trying to get at a meaning through the exchange.

The "in-between" is that which functions or operates in a way that allows for an understanding by the participants in the discourse and in such a way that the ideas are not possessed by any of the interlocutors. This is why when you do a postmortem of a dialogue you find that this bit about "this idea being mine and this idea being yours" is a rather late arrival on the scene.

But there is also a movement here beyond the dialogic. Transversality is not a dialogical understanding, which is why it also needs to be beyond hermeneutics since hermeneutics is fundamentally dialogical. It is instead that which provides the occasion, the opportunity, for the understanding of whatever is at issue.

RER/DJM: Clearly then the "in-between" cannot be understood in the dialogic sense the term might imply. If anything, it would have to be an "in-between-among."

COS: That transversality broadens the "in-between" to "among" is an important point. Clearly, when you move from a face-to-face encounter to the wider sociopolitical fabric, decision making becomes almost infinitely more complicated, as does the need for transversality in communicative praxis. This means that a difficult struggle for openness and humility is required of individuals, a struggle more difficult than is typically the case in dealing with face-to-face relations.

Transversality also broadens the "in-between" to the "beyond." However, I haven't yet developed this to the extent that it might be developed. There is a notion of infinity that attaches to transversality. To use the mathematical concept, a line converges with multiple surfaces and proceeds on to infinity. So, we are not dealing simply with that which is orthogonal to each of the participants. There is something beyond the orthogonal. There is an infinity of meaning. I guess that's something Levinas was chasing down in his distinction between infinity and totality.[29]

RER/DJM: Are we to understand the notion of transversality here as descriptive or prescriptive?

COS: It speaks in a middle voice. The descriptive and the prescriptive fall out from the recognition or acknowledgment of the transversal workings in our discourse and action.[30] In this respect, transversality is older than good and evil. It is older than *différance*. *Différance* is older than Being—Derrida was on to something there. But the structuring movement of *différance* still plays within the economy of identity and difference, of sameness and otherness. Consequently, transversality is older than the *différance* that antedates Being.[31]

RER/DJM: Does this now commit us to a return to origins with all its attendant problems?

COS: The grammar of return and of origins is problematic. And it has to be reexamined repeatedly. But, I still think the grammar is usable, though you have to monitor its signification.

I recall the Marquette conference on the Agenda of Literary Studies in the 1970s—a conference that was supposed to get philosophers, literary theorists, and linguists together. I was paired with Edward Said because I had just written my book *Radical Reflections and the Origin of the Human Sciences* and he had written *Beginnings*.[32] Now Said was very hard on beginnings and origins, so I thought, "We're going to have one hell of a cockfight here between Schrag and Said."

But it's interesting how the rhetorical interaction can work itself out. I thought I was clear in the book—though perhaps not clear enough. But when I explained my position, Said and I ended agreeing with one another. And we ended up better friends than anyone else at that meeting.

I simply pointed out that the origins we are after are neither metaphysical *archai* nor epistemological foundations. Not origins in either of these senses, but rather origins in the sense of a repetition of that which is never completed as an origin. It is only in repetition—the repetition of difference—that you keep open the prospect for invention, intervention, transgression, re-creation, etc.

COMMUNICATIVE PRAXIS: THE FITTING RESPONSE

RER/DJM: As we noted above, the fitting response is an effort to delineate communicative praxis in its ethicopolitical dimension. Could you explain why you turned to the notion?

COS: One of the problems in the development of ethics is that ethical approaches always become essentialized—it becomes a matter of taking up a position. So, we have teleological ethics—an ethics of ends or final goals. Then you have deontological ethics—an ethics of rights and duties. Then you have utilitarian ethics—an ethics of what is the greatest good for the greatest number. And so on. Ethics becomes a matter of choosing between theories.

What I try to do against this historical background, is make a case for the fitting response which I call a protoethic. I call it a protoethic because the question it asks somehow antedates, precedes, is older than the questions: "What is my end?" "What is my duty and what are my rights?" "What is the greatest good?" Now I'm not trying to do away with ethical theory. Although I am apprehensive about the use of theory applied to ethics, the questions that form the basis of these different ethical theories are important questions. But they're latecomers.

RER/DJM: In searching for an alternative to this ethical "theoreticism," what led you to the notion of the fitting response?

COS: It was probably Hans-Georg Gadamer, his tutelage during my time in Heidelberg, who set me on the path of developing the notion of the fitting response.[33] This led me back to Stoicism and the notion of *kathekonta*—that which is fitting, of which Gadamer makes much.[34]

Now, the notion can already be found in Aristotle. But there it supplements teleology, that is, the fitting response proceeds from the question: "What is my proper end?" It is in Stoicism that we find the first ethical view specifically based on the fitting response. In Stoicism, the fitting response proceeds not by first asking the teleological question: "What is my proper end?" but from the existential question: "What is going on in the world to which I must now respond?" Now, the Stoic answer, of course, was quite specific: given that universal reason—the *logos*—is operative, you respond to reason. Of course, the Stoic notion of universal reason had to go, but the notion of *kathekonta* struck me as being very helpful.

You find something like this in Benedict Spinoza's philosophy. Spinoza's ethic is not strictly teleological. It's not deontological. It's not utilitarian. Well, what is it? It is an ethics based on response. Granted you respond to the nature of the infinite substance. Here, response becomes ontological. But the point is, first, you have to ask the question, "What is it that is going on?" and then find out how to respond in the fitting way.

I also found Marx very suggestive. Now sometimes Marx is characterized as having a teleological ethic. But I think you have to be careful there. Maybe later Marxism became teleological when the notion of a classless society was taken to be a kind of proper end. But it seems to me that the main impulse in Marxist ethics has to do with the question: "What is going on in our socioeconomic existence?" The answer is that the workers are being disenfranchised and depersonalized in the conflict between capital and labor. That's what's going on. Now we have to respond and respond in such a way that we redress these issues. So we preenact a state of affairs in which there is no alienation—there is a kind of eschatology here. And we act to bring about change. Now, it might be that Marxism tended to put too much emphasis on the economic determinants of the situation. But even in this, there are glimmerings of the need for a fitting response.

My studies of Emmanuel Levinas' ethics of responsibility further intensified my interest in the notion of the fitting response, particularly vis-à-vis its theological importance. In the ethics of the prophetic tradition, of which Levinas' ethics is a contemporary expression, the basic question is not: "What is our proper end?" or "What is my duty?" and so on. This would lead to a kind of unacceptable moralism. The basic question is: "What is going on and how are we to respond to the situation?"

For example, the question put to Micah: "What does the Lord require of me?" is a *kathekontalogical* question.[35] The eighth-century Old Testament prophets—the so-called minor prophets—weren't interested in abstract questions. Their question was: "What's going on here?" That's why Amos, seeing nothing but religious formalism around him, says: "I hate your sacrifices, I despise your ceremonies, away with all that crap. Let's respond to the injustices that are going on." And then he makes that marvelous statement, "Let justice roll down like waters."[36] That's the fitting response within the area of religious consciousness.

RER/DJM: It is evident from your last example that there are different ways one can ask the question "What is going on here?" It can be a bland, almost tepid question. But it also can be a question coming out of the indignation that arises from the observation or experience of injustice. The latter suggests that the fitting response cannot be reduced to asking the question "What is going on?" and then simply accepting the situation as it is. It implies an active effort to change the situation.

COS: The fitting response is not an accommodation to what is going on. It is not that you simply characterize the situation and then somehow fit in. I think this is a danger in the more tradition-bound analyses of the fitting response. And here Gadamer sometimes comes close to that. For Gadamer, practical wisdom—a reclamation of Aristotle's doctrine of *phronesis*—supplies the criteria for determining that which is fitting and these criteria are always already firmly entrenched and immanent in the tradition. My own development of the notion eventually led me to a friendly *Auseinandersetzung*—a bit of a quarrel—with Gadamer on this particular matter.[37]

Now there is a continuing impact of what we have been upon what we are now—we can't jump over our own shadow. Clearly, we are constantly appropriating the past. But this appropriation is not an uncritical appropriation. We make determinations about what we have done as something either we ought not to have done, or we rejoice in what we have done. It is here that the troublesome notion of the conscience, to which both Heidegger and Levinas have given some attention, comes in.[38] I say "troublesome" only because it's difficult to elicit. At any rate, the point is there is a discernment in which we critically appropriate the past and project the future, a discernment in which we both learn and change.

The fitting response is a questioning. It is always a questioning of what is going on and then making hard decisions regarding the extent to which we can appropriate the tradition and the extent to which we have to intervene in it. There is a creative moment in the fitting response, a moment in which we have to invent something new, project something new, begin to enact something new. And it may call for a radical revision or indeed the overturning of traditional as well as current forms of thought and action.

RER/DJM: Would you respond in a similar fashion to the call for a "return to virtue"?

COS: I have problems with the very grammar of virtue. What happened in the history of ethics is that virtue immediately became subject to an essentialization in which a table of virtues is established having a locus somewhere, we know not where. The locus lies in some kind of transcendent ideal—ontology, or in what Nietzsche described as "herd morality"—the normative. So, we end up with definitions of virtue that have either an ontological or a normative underpinning, or both.

This is why the appeal to return to virtue is problematic, and not only the appeal from the conservative right—William Bennett's *Book of Virtues*, for example.[39] But also when it comes from ethicists like Alasdair MacIntyre.[40] The appeal leaves a lot of problems unresolved.

MacIntyre, for example, lands upon the Thomistic line of Aristotelian philosophy as somehow being the trustworthy norm in the return to virtue. But why conserve the values of this tradition over any other in the evident plurality of traditions? I have been unable to find a satisfactory answer to this question in his writings.

My project is an effort to establish an ethics and a politics that is neither normative nor ontological. The fitting response is on the thither side of the ontological, at least its measure and content is beyond the ontological—Levinas was right, ethics antedates ontology.[41] It's also otherwise than the normative, otherwise than the normative understood as norms or rules—the nomos within the economy of virtue.

RER/DJM: What if this return was a return to virtue in the Greek sense of virtue?

COS: Perhaps I wouldn't have as much of a problem if the return to virtue meant virtue in its original Greek sense: virtue—or rather a doing that is understood to be virtuous—taken in the sense of a performative guided by *phronesis*. Aristotle had a lot of things going for him in this respect. In the *Nicomachean Ethics*, *phronesis* is that which provides the measure of virtuous activity.

But in the end, there is the teleology that underwrites the work. First, you have to decide what the proper end is, the essential determinant of being human. For Aristotle, the human being is a rational animal so the proper end is actualizing reason. This is why the intellectual virtues crown the moral virtues for Aristotle. And the metaphysical justification for all this is the doctrine of teleology. You don't deliberate about ends. You deliberate about means. Ends are given—you discover them. This is how the schematization of virtue gets started and how it starts to get in our way.

RER/DJM: But a very different reading of the *Nicomachean Ethics* would be liberated if this justification were displaced.

COS: That is a good way of putting it. It's not that the *Nicomachean Ethics* itself is now displaced—it's a classic work and it will stand as a classic work. But different readings are always possible. One aspect of a work can be emphasized rather than another.

Now the *Nicomachean Ethics* has a strange combination of teleological and *kathekontalogical* ethics, ethics based upon movement toward the proper end and a more contextualized ethics that may in fact be more Platonic than Aristotelian. De-emphasizing the teleological would provide us with the opportunity to acknowledge and emphasize the role of the *kathekontalogical*—an ethics that requires response based on determining what is going on in the *polis* and what is to be done. Aristotle wrote his handbook the *Rhetoric* for the latter purpose. So, you would have to read the *Ethics* and the *Rhetoric* together.

RER/DJM: This seems to suggest that the fitting response is not something to be determined by what is somehow fitting in itself but rather something circumscribed by what is unfitting—that we learn about the fitting response by suffering the unfit. In this, the delineation of the fitting response would proceed not so much by way of example, but by way of counterexample.

COS: This is certainly analogous to the dialectical relationship between being and nonbeing, though here we've moved beyond the formal question of being and nonbeing. Plato clearly had something going when, in the *Sophist*, he said that being is always somehow determined by what it is not. We know what something is in terms of the finite determinations of what it is and the infinite determinations of what it is not. Being is within the sea of nonbeing. And we sort out that which is by this contradistinction with what it is not.

The fitting response has intelligibility only against the backdrop of a discernment and determination of what is not fitting. And it is out of this that action comes.

There is, of course, a need to acknowledge that what has been determined to be unfitting in the past can, upon future enlightened reconsideration, be revalued. So that the kind of finality the unfit has is determined from our perspective. The unfit is unfit until further notice.

On the other hand, the unfit is certainly more encompassing than the fit. And I suspect there are certain cases in which the finality of the unfit is more final than in others. It is inconceivable to me that at some future time something like the Holocaust or the slave trade could somehow be revalued in such a way that they were no longer gross injustices, were no longer all that evil. In other cases, this finality is more attenuated.

But clearly, the point is that determining what is fitting is much more difficult. It always remains open. Our determinations of the unfit consequently retain a kind of flexibility as well. This, of course, is a constitutive feature of what it means to be human, an implication of human finitude. But this openness is also the possibility of response and its undoing, an undoing that prevents the idolatry of response: "Here now is the response for all time and eternity."

THE GIFT: THE MEASURE AND CONTENT OF THE FITTING RESPONSE

RER/DJM: Understanding the fit in terms of the unfit suggests that the critical questions often leveled against the notion of the fitting response—"How does one determine what is fitting, by what criteria or through what appeal?"—are, in a sense, questions posed backwards. But beyond this, it seems to us that the request for criteria is an effort to determine in advance: to whom, under what conditions, and in what way, one should respond. It is a question motivated, perhaps understandably, by a desire to respond correctly. But this desire to respond correctly—to know the correct response in advance—betrays an epistemological impulse that undermines the fitting response that requires an openness and open responsiveness to what is going on. On the other hand, a request for further clarification would seem appropriate. The notion of the fitting response engendered a great deal of excitement among many scholars insofar as it offered an alternative approach to ethics. But when they tried to use the notion in their work, elucidating the fittingness of response became more than a bit perplexing.

COS: Admittedly, reviewers of *Communicative Praxis and the Space of Subjectivity*—the work in which the notion of the fitting response is first developed—invariably asked about the role and dynamics of the fitting response. The question that came to the fore was: "What is it that makes a response fitting?" The answer to this question is complicated, complicated because, for me, it spills over into the arena of theological inquiry—in particular, into what Kierkegaard called the "religious existence-sphere."

Now in speaking of "religious existence" you have to be careful not to confuse "the religious" with a religion. I learned this from my mentor, Paul Tillich.[42] But Kierkegaard drove the point home for me in his *Concluding Unscientific Postscript*.[43] Recently, Derrida has been speaking of the possibility of "religion without religion."[44] Although the point is left open, I take it that what is at issue is, at least in part, the point Tillich and Kierkegaard had already made clear. A religious manner or mode of being-in-the-world must not be reduced to, or conflated with the belief system of any particular historical religion. So when I speak of the religious, I am speaking of a way of being-in-the-world, not of a religion.

So then, what is it that makes a response fitting? In the end, the answer turns on what I call the semantics of the gift, more specifically on the gift understood in terms of a giving that expects nothing in return. This carries with it—implicitly, if not explicitly—a religious modality of being-in-the-world, of being-with-others. It is a way of being that Kierkegaard articulates—in a way that is unsurpassed—in his *Works of Love*.[45]

The answer to the question "What is it that makes a response fitting?" is, for me, the gift. The relation of the fitting response and the gift is such that the gift provides the ultimate measure and content of the fitting response.

RER/DJM: This is a bit of a departure from your previous works. At the risk of being presumptuous, are you alluding to a work in progress?

COS: I should preface my answer by saying that up to this point, I have written no work in the general area of the philosophy of religion. And this should be somewhat puzzling given my professional development, which clearly began in such a way that both interests, philosophical and theological, were quite intact.

I am currently working on a manuscript that specifically addresses the relationship of ethics and theology. The title, I hope, is descriptive enough to point in the direction that I think one needs to go, *God as Otherwise than Being: Toward a Semantics of the Gift*. In this work, I do approach the question of theology—a *logos* of *theos*—as a discourse about God quite directly, but still from a philosophical/quasi-philosophical perspective. My prospectus is that of investigating what a philosophical grammar permits us to say about the deity and the divine, which in my scheme falls out as an analysis of God-talk in terms of gift-talk.

RER/DJM: Before turning to the notion of the gift and its relation to the fitting response, what is it that motivated you to write a work in philosophy and theology?

COS: A number of things come into play here, some implicit, some explicit. In the background, of course, is the fact that my early influences are as much theological as they are philosophical. Surely, in part, this had to do with the fact that my father was a Mennonite pastor, and there is a sense in which the radical reformers of the Anabaptist tradition have left a significant deposit in my stance on matters religious and theological. Then there is the fact that I attended a Mennonite college as an undergraduate and then went on to the Yale Divinity School before attending Harvard.

Further, it may be that one of the earliest formative influences on my philosophical development was the thought of Alfred North Whitehead. During the time that I was an undergraduate in the latter 1940s, Whitehead was very much in the philosophical news. And there was, of course, the religious dimension in Whitehead's thought itself, which provided the inspiration for the development of the Chicago School of Process Theology.

In any event, it was the philosophy of Whitehead that piqued my interest in those early days and it was the main reason for selecting Harvard for my graduate studies. Whitehead had recently finished his illustrious career at Harvard and had entrusted the continuation of his legacy to one of his brilliant students, Raphael Demos.[46]

However, the predominant influence on my philosophical development during the formative years of my graduate study was John Wild.[47] And then later, Paul Tillich for whom I served as graduate assistant.[48] It was principally Wild and Tillich who were instrumental in shaping my professional career. And here again, we can see how philosophical and theological orientations were entwined. Wild was a professional philosopher with strong theological interests and Tillich was a professional theologian with strong philosophical interests.

Also in the background is my first book, *Existence and Freedom*, a revision of my doctoral dissertation "A Comparison of Kierkegaard's Dialectical Analysis of the Self and Heidegger's Ontology of Dasein," which I worked closely with Wild in shaping up. In that work, I argued that in ontologizing Kierkegaard's work, Heidegger made an important advance over Kierkegaard.

Although I still think it is correct to read *Being and Time* as an ontologization and secularization of Kierkegaard's ethicoreligious categories, I began to wonder whether there might not be some expense associated with what I took to be an advance. It occurred to me—and here things become more explicit—that long before Levinas came to speak of ethics as otherwise than being, and Jean-Luc Marion, following Levinas, spoke of God as God without being, Kierkegaard had, in a sense, already done so.[49]

I began to reconsider my assessment of Heidegger's accomplishments in ontologizing Kierkegaard. Heidegger's negative characterizations of Kierkegaard came to weigh more heavily upon my mind: In *Being and Time*, Heidegger portrays Kierkegaard as having gotten hold of the concept of anxiety but only in an ontic analysis, the ontological understanding remains at a distance.[50] And then in *Holtzwege*, a more derogatory comment: Kierkegaard is a mere religious writer.[52] I recalled that Jaspers had had a falling out with Heidegger over whether concrete existence could be ontologized at all and if it could be wasn't there a need to recognize that something might be lost. In the end, I changed my mind about Heidegger's alleged accomplishment. It was, to put it mildly, a bit of a change in my thinking.

And then I was asked to write a piece on Kierkegaard by Martin Matustik and Merold Westfal for a book they were editing. The impetus for the book was Habermas' Copenhagen lectures on Kierkegaard. Habermas began, as all students in Germany did at that time, by studying Kierkegaard—you had to study Kierkegaard. But then he moved away from Kierkegaard and now seemed to be returning to Kierkegaard. Matustik, whose interest is in Critical Theory, and Westfal, whose area is the philosophy of religion, picked up on this and were putting the book *Kierkegaard and Post/modernity* together.

Now, it had always occurred to me that there was something amiss in the contemporary interest in Nietzsche. It wasn't the recovery of Nietzsche, but the neglect of Kierkegaard that troubled me. In writing the piece for the book, I returned to Kierkegaard and realized that there was a lot that needed to be recovered.[53]

Up to this point, I had never taught a course on Kierkegaard—never in forty-three years of teaching. I thought it would be too difficult since his writing style is so nonacademic. But I decided to go ahead and try. And in doing so, I realized that in teaching the philosophy of religion what I had been doing was representing the discipline and that there was nothing religious about it. Finally, I decided it was time to take a hard look at what was going on.

RER/DJM: What did you discover?

COS: First I should say that because of my interest in the relationship between philosophy and theology, many of my colleagues have been surprised that I have never used philosophy and religion as providing themes for the subject matter of a major work. And I guess it puzzled me as well. But it was simply that I couldn't do it.

In my early work, I wrote some articles dealing specifically with philosophy and religion. And I have been teaching the philosophy of religion all of my professional life—in fact, the job description for my appointment at Purdue specifically listed teaching the philosophy of religion as one of the requirements. But what I was teaching my students in philosophy of religion—and I've been doing this for the past forty-three years—left me uninspired.

I attribute this to the general format of the philosophy of religion itself. The philosophy of religion is grounded in the metaphysics of theism. It is organized around very specific theistic/atheistic questions: questions concerning the existence of God, the nature of God, and God's relationship to the world. And then of course if God is a moral God, there is the problem of Evil and so on. But the metaphysics of theism itself was never questioned. Even those who reacted against it rarely questioned the theistic concept of God.

The notion of God as it came to be developed in the history of the metaphysics of theism is one in which God is somehow pictured as the highest being. You have this in Anselm: God is a being greater than which none can be conceived. You have it in Saint Thomas Aquinas's definitions of God as prime mover, necessary being, first cause, supreme instance of perfection, final cause, etc. If you canvas the history of theology in Western thought what you have is a portrayal of the deity as a kind of supernatural being that crowns the scale of existence from the lowest to the highest. That is the metaphysical picture of God as a being that somehow has control over all the other beings.

Now, such a being remains philosophically problematic—the classical arguments for the existence of such a being fall short of being convincing proofs. And even if the existence of such a being were to be demonstrated in a compelling manner, its religious significance would remain problematic. Such a being, particularly one described in terms of personlike attributes, would resemble a cosmic tyrant whose relationship to the world would be such that it would obliterate all vestiges of freedom—both the freedom that might attach to God and the freedom that might attach to finite beings.

This is the God Nietzsche proclaimed to be dead. Theism was an edifice ready for and requiring deconstruction. Tillich, of course, had already urged us to reconsider theism. One of the more provocative sections in *The Courage to Be* is entitled "Transcending Theism."[53] There, playing with the metaphor of the "God above God," he indicates the need to move beyond the limitations and distortions of the metaphysical concept of God as a supreme or supernatural being. But Tillich remained too enamored with Heidegger's ontological schematization. Rather than a being, Tillich spoke of God as Being itself.[54] In doing so, he remained bound to the grammar of theism, bound to it in spite of himself. So even here the deconstructive task remained.

RER/DJM: Responding to our earlier question concerning the hermeneutics of suspicion, you spoke of the necessity of deconstructive strategies in dismantling obstructions that insinuate themselves in our understanding. But you also spoke of the limitations of such strategies and of the corresponding need for a proactive hermeneutics. How does this work itself out here?

COS: I should begin by saying that, in a certain sense, the deconstruction of theism is nothing new. Nietzsche, Marx, and Freud, who you invoke here in reference to the hermeneutics of suspicion, each accomplished it in their own way, as have others. But they deconstructed theism only to end up in atheism. Now insofar as the Christian theologians and metaphysicians simply took over the metaphysics of Greek thought—if that is what is involved—then it is a justifiable atheism. In this respect, Nietzsche, Marx, and Freud are each involved in a project of justifiable atheism.

The problem is that this atheism remains for the most part purely reactive. As such, atheism remains within the economy of theism—is simply its converse. Viewed from this perspective, the history of atheism is only the flip side of the history of theism. As such, a dismantling of theism necessarily involves a dismantling of atheism. In the process of deconstructing theism, atheism is and must be deconstructed as well. So, in the end, we are left with the pronouncement that the God of theism and atheism is dead—dead as metaphysical cause, dead as a being greater than which none can be conceived, and so forth.

But the demise of the theistic concept of God—of theism and atheism alike—does not necessarily foreclose all inquires into the possibility of a religious dimension of human existence. And I kept wondering what might be on the thither side of this demise, if anything at all? How can we talk about God after the death of the God of theism and atheism? What should God-talk be like? This question motivated me to undertake the present work—a work that is turning out to be more extensive than I had planned.

RER/DJM: How did you attempt to formulate the question—were you able to find philosophical precursors?

COS: Nietzsche has something to say about this. He cannot be considered purely reactive—he still leaves the door open for some viable notion of the divine. For example, the door remains ajar in the *Antichrist* where he tells us that it is the Christian theologians and metaphysicians against whom the war is being waged.[55] And similarly in *Beyond Good and Evil*, it becomes clear as early as the preface that the object of his ire is the concept of God invented by a Platonized Christianity rather than with the notion of divinity per se.[56] It is in the *Will to Power* that he offers us a glimpse through that door. There one can find passages that suggest a retrieval of an authentic sense of the divine.[57] Not surprisingly, this retrieval is often couched in the language of the will to power.[58] And unfortunately, it all remains undeveloped.

Heidegger also pointed out the limitations of Western metaphysics, the essence of which he considered a theologized ontology.[59] But he didn't do much with what might be on the thither side of the onto-theological.

And then there is Levinas, who makes much of the motif of that which is "otherwise than being"—referring specifically to Plato's notion of the Good.[60] In this, he makes use of what is implicit in Plato's notion of the Good in order to give ethics a priority over ontology. The Good is otherwise than being for Plato. But God beyond theism should also be otherwise than being. And I'm not sure that God for Plato was otherwise than being. The Demiurge was a strange kind of a first cause. In any case, the Demiurge—*demiourgos* as the Maker of the world—usurped or not was the beginning of the metaphysics of theism.

The question, then, as I formulated it is how are we to speak of God as otherwise than being? This accounts for the main title of my work: *God as Otherwise than Being*. And to answer the question, I turned to the notion of the gift. This is the move from the traditional questions about God to what I have called the semantics of the gift, hence the subtitle of the work: *Toward a Semantic of the Gift*. The deity understood in terms of the gift, in terms of giving, is otherwise than being.

RER/DJM: Can we understand this in terms of a turn from the traditional distinction of the transcendent over against the immanent to a notion of the transcendent within immanence?

COS: As opposed to the transcendent as a metaphysical category that separates the transcendent from the immanent. And we need to be concerned about this separation. The metaphysical bifurcations at work in theism are evident even from a cursory reading of the history of Western religion: the transcendent versus the immanent, the eternal versus the temporal, the immutable versus the mutable, the incorporeal versus the corporeal, and so on. And when this metaphysical machinery is used to explicate the meaning of God as transcendent, then Heidegger is right: You get to a *causa sui*—God as Being, as first cause—but you don't get to somebody before whom you'll bend your knees.[61]

Now, in making this point, Heidegger still uses very anthropomorphic categories.[62] And we have to be concerned about this as well. Here, I think Freud is very significant. Freud is a much-needed sheet-anchor—a final resort—against any anthropomorphic tendencies in describing the divine.[63]

But in any case you're right. The transcendent here is no longer the transcendent in terms of a supernatural being of some sort, but the transcendent as event. The problem is you get stymied grammatically using these terms because you have to make all kinds of semantic maneuvers to explicate them.

RER/DJM: So, what led you to the language of the gift and where does it now lead us?

COS: Yes, how do we begin by talking of the deity and end by talking of the gift? It reminds me of Nietzsche writing of Thales. "What? The poor guy's been maligned? Just because he asked a basic question and ended up talking about water?"[64]

Nietzsche was the one who opened up the language of the gift for me, particularly in the section on the gift giving virtue in *Thus Spoke Zarathustra*.[65] Here the gift quickly becomes the gift of love. But it is a restricted love. Restricted because of its involvement in the master/servant dialectic, a dialectic in which it suffers the fate of degenerating into pity. In order to move beyond this restriction, we have to turn to a more authentic notion of love.

Tillich, for example, speaks of a love that expects nothing in return, a love that is not conditional.[66] Now in speaking of a love that is not conditional, we need to avoid the metaphysical bifurcation of the unconditional and the conditional. Obviously, everything we do is conditioned in many different ways. It is an unconditional love in the existential sense, no more but also no less than a love that is given freely, given without the condition that it be returned.

Now it should be evident that we are talking about a notion of love that is similar to the one we find in the eighth-century prophets and to the notion of *agape* we find later in the New Testament. But, of course, the Judeo-Christian tradition has no franchise on this notion of love. There is the concept of compassion in Buddhism, for example. What is compassion? It is self-sacrificing love. But even here we need to be careful not to fall into exclusivity, moving from a notion of love articulated in the Judeo-Christian tradition in order to embrace similar articulations found in eastern religion—from one manner of exclusion to another, broader now but nonetheless exclusive.

As a way of being-with-others, it is a notion of love that transcends the particularity of any given religion or nonreligion. The important point is that the notion of love at issue here is such that it is not understood against the backdrop of an economy of exchange: a love given without the expectation of return.

The question is can there be a love that is outside economy? Derrida says this is impossible. We are always in an economy of one sort or another in which there are different laws operating.[67] Well, in one sense it probably is impossible. But there is something other than economy and its laws. In theological terms, it is grace. The gift that expects nothing in return is grace. And grace somehow suspends the law. So, in another sense it does remain possible.

Here we get into the eschatological dimension. The gift that expects nothing in return has this quality of being impossible within the context of finitude, but it is a strange kind of impossibility: an impossibility that enters finitude as eschatological possibility. The gift remains possible as an impossible eschatological event that can somehow be understood as informing or leavening our "economic" interactions with others in our sociopolitical life and in our discourse. It remains possible in terms of what I call preenacted eschatology.

But clearly, the articulation of this requires at least some recourse to paradox. And I think Kierkegaard was right about this move. When you get involved in a discussion of these issues, you have to move from a semantics of dialectic—which he used to analyze human existence, to a semantics of paradox. The eternal isn't in the temporal, at least in the Hegelian sense. Kierkegaard spent his whole life harpooning Hegel because of his mediation of the eternal and temporal. The eternal is in time, as he puts it in *Works of Love*, but always in the future.[68] Again, you get back to the eschatological. So, nothing is unconditional in the conditional, in this instant of time. But it is otherwise in the moment. The moment is never an instant of time because it reaches out to the future.

You need a new semantic to articulate this, one that breaks with the traditional epistemology of representation and with traditional doctrines of recollection as well. The notion of knowledge as representation and recollection, which began with Plato, has in large measure determined the history of Western epistemology and metaphysics. Knowledge is returning to that which has been. But when we move to a semantics of the gift, one that is future oriented, then we have something else again. Something like Kierkegaard's notion of repetition: recollection forward.[69]

That's why I lit upon this notion of preenacted eschatology. It isn't eschatology already realized, somehow actualized—that's Hegel and that's liberal theology coming out of the belief that "the kingdom of God is here." Nor is it eschatology always awaiting its future enactment. It is eschatology preenacted in the moment, in the concrete situation. There is a sense, to quote someone who is clearly one of my favorite philosophers, in which you can live in eternity and hear the hall clock strike.[70] The fullness of time has not yet fully come, but we still can experience the fullness of time. What you have to do here is split the difference between Judaism and Christianity in such a way that the kingdom of God has not yet come, Judaism is correct; but the kingdom of God has already begun to come, that's the point made in Christianity. Here we have the eschatological dimension of love.

RER/DJM: You quote Kierkegaard in relation to this preenacted eschatology: "living in eternity yet hearing the hall clock strike." How are we to understand the notion of eternity?

COS: In the history of philosophy, which is basically the history of metaphysics, time and eternity serve as correlative descriptions of the finite and the infinite, the immaterial and the material, and all the other oppositions that travel within the economy of metaphysics. So, time and eternity are understood as oppositions. The eternal stands outside of time: Plato's forms are eternal, Kant's noumenal world is eternal, Spinoza's infinite substance is eternal, and so on.

What I'm trying to do, is reformulate this metaphysical distinction in ethical-existential terms. So, the eternal has to do with the gift that expects nothing in return. The gift is eternal in that it is not subject to the temporal succession of expectation and return. As such, it is outside the economy of exchange and its laws but also effectual within it.

In giving without the expectation of return, the gift is complete, without remainder. Not complete in terms of some sort of metaphysical presence but as the existential embodiment, the sublime experience of the fullness of time. Eternity, as Kierkegaard so marvelously puts it, is the fullness of time. Time stands still. But within temporality, the fullness of time is never fulfilled—time continues. So, we have to move to the semantics of paradox, or, in my grammar, to the moment of giving as eschatological preenactment.

RER/DJM: And how are we to understand the gift?

COS: The gift is an event. Although in one sense, the gift is incarnate in both the one who receives as well as the one who gives, in a stricter sense it lies somewhere in between, somewhere in the mutuality of call and response.

There is the call that calls for response, the call of the visage and voice, as Levinas puts it. For Levinas, who I follow here, this is the call that issues from the face of the stranger, the widow, and the orphan—the disenfranchised.[71] In these faces, alterity transcends mere otherness. For Levinas, God is present in the face of the disenfranchised as a call to responsibility, a call for response.[72] This call is itself a gift. It is a gift because, in offering itself up—laid bare without the expectation of return—it also lays bare the space for response. The gift of the call makes giving possible.

But there is also the gift of the response, which in giving responds to this call, responds without expectation. And here I depart, in a sense, from Levinas. Response as giving is not a return. It responds freely to the call, without command, without obligation. It is the impossible possibility of a giving not derived from the economy of exchange but nonetheless effectual within it.

In the stricter sense, the gift lies in the meeting of the call and response since it is only in the meeting that giving can take place at all. This is reason the gift is an event rather than the act of the one who gives.

RER/DJM: Have we now abdicated responsibility and obligation?

COS: Not abdicated but refigured. In *Works of Love*, Kierkegaard struggled with a similar issue: the commandment to love. Now a commandment is a law. So how can you command love? You have to ask, what's going on here? You can't command love. If you command love, loving becomes an obligation derived from the law. And what you end up with is obedience rather than love. So, the puzzle, in this instance, is how can you have a commandment that doesn't reduce love to an obligation derived from the law. I think it was one of the most perplexing problems Kierkegaard dealt with in his whole literary production.

Now more directly to the point, I think you can work out a notion of responsibility and of obligation in such a way that while impinging on the economy of exchange, they are not derived from the laws of that economy.

The responsibility that comes from the call does not come in terms of an obligation derived from a law in the economy of exchange. In order for this to be the case, responsibility must be a responsibility one imposes upon oneself in relation to the call. This, of course, does not resolve the problem of obligation. But I think the two are related. Here the question is, when you give a gift to someone in the sense in which we are speaking of the gift, is there, in turn, an obligation to give that travels with this responsibility, or are we dealing with contradictory terms? Well, there is a kind of obligation. But it is an obligation derived from gratitude. And gratitude, which is related etymologically to both gratuity and grace, is something that is freely given. Further, we mustn't forget that the verb "to oblige" has two senses. One can be obliged in the sense of being forced or compelled to do something, or one can oblige in the sense of doing a favor, that is, doing something one need not do. It is interesting to note, if only as a curiosity, that the term "favor" was at one time used to refer to the countenance—the face.

At any rate, an obligation derived from gratitude is an obligation one imposes upon oneself. But one need not return a gift to the giver in taking this obligation upon oneself. This is not to say that there is something wrong with returning a gift to the giver. But insofar as the gift returned is a gift understood within the context delineated here, return is transfigured. The one who gave has become the other who now calls. So, the obligation to give is an obligation taken upon oneself as a self-imposed obligation, a responsibility to give to others.[73] In other words, the obligation and responsibility that attaches to the gift is such that the gift perpetuates itself. Refigured in this way, the responsibility or obligation to give becomes centrifugal rather than centripetal. It goes outward and it does so freely.

Consequently, we can now also say that the event of the gift is its eventuality. This is to say that in the mutuality of call and response, a further gift ensues, one that lies in accepting the gift as such, as a gift given freely without expectation of return, given purely and simply in response to the call. And this gift is the perpetuation of the gift itself. It is a giving on the part of the one who now receives, a giving that lies in the future. It is giving, in turn, to the other who will call.

RER/DJM: With this understanding of the gift, how is it that the gift serves as the content and measure of the fitting response?

COS: The content of the fitting response is the gift, a giving that responds to the call and it is the call that answers the question "What is going on?" The content of the fitting response is a giving that responds to the call by giving what is called for so far as one is able and giving so far as one is able without the expectation of return. And the measure of the fitting response is the gift. The fitting response is measured by the extent to which this giving gives what is called for, by the extent to which the giving gives what one is able, and by the extent to which the giving gives without expectation of return.

The content of the fitting response is the gift as pre-enacted eschatology measured by the eschatology of the gift. But the *eschatos* of this eschatology—the future toward which it reaches—is without specificity outside the concrete event of the gift and, in the end, it remains indeterminate with respect to its eventuality. It is, if I can quote someone who has recently published an essay, all a matter of working and waiting.[74]

RER/DJM: So in our efforts to respond to the call, we move now from the loving struggle to the struggle to love.

COS: Precisely.

RER/DJM: As you know, there will inevitably be requests for instances or cases of the gift.

COS: Asking for instances or cases is, of course, a legitimate request. But you have to be careful with the strategy of using cases. Instantiation can be problematic when you're dealing with matters such as this. Representation, which is always a return, always an analysis *post festum*—literally analysis "after the festival"—runs the risk of displacing the experiential feature of the concrete situation it describes and with it the very thing it is attempting to describe. An analogous problem, though perhaps not completely analogous, can be found in the literature on the sublime and the beautiful, something that is currently receiving a great deal of attention.

Kant already pointed this problem out in the *Critique of Judgement*. Can one provide instances of the sublime? Can one provide cases of the sublime? Cases and instances of the beautiful can be provided. The imagination can always use a concept of beauty, the understanding and will working in tandem to circumscribe cases or instances. However, it is otherwise with the sublime. The sublime cannot be encompassed by a concept. Thrust upon us, it exceeds conceptualization and so circumscription. But there are cases and instances of the sublime. The sublime can be experienced. But it cannot be not represented, or at least represented in such a way that it retains its sublimity.[75]

So the question becomes, can one provide cases or instances of the gift, which in a certain sense is in the region of sublimity? The gift can be said to be sublime. It can be experienced, but can it be represented? On the other hand, if the gift does make a difference, that is, if it has an impact upon the lifeworld as we live through it, then shouldn't we be able to say something about it?

Well, you can offer illustrations, provided the experiential element is retained. Certainly, in the theological literature and even in nontheological literature, there are all kinds of illustrations. Here and elsewhere, I think you have to look for personal encounters where goodness happened. And probably more importantly, you have to look for goodness happening in the area of sociopolitical relations, engagements, and performances.

With respect to the latter, one of my favorite examples is the subject of Philip Hallie's book on the story of La Chambon, a small town in the mountains of southern France.[76] In its nonviolent opposition to the Vichy regime and the Nazis at a stone's throw, this little-known Huguenot community led by Pastor André Trocmé and others saved thousands of Jewish children and adults from Hitler's extermination camps. A kitchen-struggle, he calls it, since the women were the ones largely involved in hiding and sheltering the refugees.

Hallie traveled to southern France to research this. Using first-hand accounts and the unpublished autobiography of the late Trocmé, Hallie came up with this marvelous account of the story of La Chambon where, as he puts it, goodness happened. Trocmé and his parishioners, at the risk of their own lives, did what they did without expecting anything in return. Goodness happened there—against all odds, goodness happened.

It did not end there. Bitter, cynical, and at times indifferent, having for years researched the cruelty and brutality of humanity's inhumanity, the discovery of this unknown town where goodness happened, his work there, changed Hallie himself. And, no doubt, his work will change others.

Here we have a case or an instance of the event of the gift in a concrete sociopolitical situation. So you can come upon cases where there is an expression of a gift given that expects nothing in return responding to a call that in offering itself up imposes no obligation.

RER/DJM: We take it that the fitting response understood in terms of the gift then is not a matter of responding to anyone and everyone. Clearly, in your illustration the response of this community, though it was pacifistic, was a response against what was going on.

COS: The occasion for the fitting response is not the occasion of response in general. It is not a matter of returning what is due within an economy of exchange, be it the exchange of discourse, action, or material goods. The fitting response, as the ethicopolitical moment of communicative praxis, does not function in terms of a kind of distributive justice. Response in general is the work of transversality, and while transversality is operative in the fitting response, the latter is not reducible to the former. The fitting response is occasioned specifically by the call as I have delineated it and occasioned in such a way that—insofar as it responds to the call and in the extent to which it responds to the call—it is constitutive of the event the gift.

Now in the illustration I have offered, the response was pacifistic. But we must make no mistake here, the fitting response, in order to be fitting, will be, at times, no less than militant.

RER/DJM: Can we say that in the end the task of communicative praxis in its ethicopolitical moment is to confront injustice in its concrete manifestations?

COS: To act in order to deal with injustice as it occurs in our quotidian existence, as it occurs in the streets. Yes, that is the permanent existential deposit in my thinking.

NOTES

1. Ralph Waldo Emerson, "The American Scholar" in Ralph Waldo Emerson, *The American Scholar, Self-Reliance, Compensation* (New York: The American Book Company, 1893), 21–46.

2. Bruce Wilshire, *William James and Phenomenology* (Bloomington: Indiana University Press, 1968).

3. William James, *Essays in Radical Empiricism and a Pluralistic Universe* (New York: Longmans, Green, 1942).

4. "One repays a teacher badly if one remains only a pupil." Friedrich Nietzsche, *Thus Spoke Zarathustra*, trans. R.J. Hollingdale (New York: Penguin, 1985), 103.

5. Ludwig Wittgenstein, *Philosophical Investigations*, trans. G.E.M. Anscombe, 2nd ed. (New York: Macmillan Company, 1958).

6. Cf. Paul Ricoeur, *Freud and Philosophy: An Essay on Interpretation*, trans. Denis Savage (New Haven: Yale University Press, 1970).

7. Calvin O. Schrag, *The Self after Postmodernity* (New Haven: Yale University Press, 1997).

8. Calvin O. Schrag, *Existence and Freedom: Toward an Ontology of Human Finitude* (Evanston: Northwestern University Press, 1961).

9. Alfred N. Whitehead, *Process and Reality* (New York: Humanities Press, 1929).

10. Gilles Deleuze, *Repetition and Difference*, trans. Paul Patton (New York: Columbia University Press, 1994). Cf. "The Dicethrow" and "Consequences for

the Eternal Return" in Gilles Deleuze, *Nietzsche and Philosophy*, trans. Hugh Tomlinson (New York: Columbia University Press, 1983), 25–29.

11. The term "enframing" is an allusion to Martin Heidegger, "The Question Concerning Technology," in Martin Heidegger, *The Question Concerning Technology and Other Essays*, trans. William Lovitt (New York: Harper and Row, 1977), 3–35.

12. Schrag, *Freedom and Existence*, 31–32, 144.

13. "Rhetoric, so far as this is taken to mean the art of persuasion, i.e., the art of deluding by means of fair semblance (as *ars oratoria*), and not merely excellence of speech (eloquence and style), is a dialectic, which borrows from poetry only so much as is necessary to win over men's minds to the side of the speaker before they have weighed the matter, and to rob their verdict of its freedom. Hence it can be recommended neither for the pulpit nor the bar." Immanuel Kant, *Critique of Judgement*, trans. James Creed Meredith (Oxford: Oxford University Press, 1988), 192.

14. Truth is "a moveable host of metaphors, metonymies, and anthropomorphisms . . . which have been poetically and rhetorically intensified, transferred and embellished and which, after long usage, seem to a people to be fixed canonical, and binding." Friedrich Nietzsche, *Philosophy and Truth: Selections from Nietzsche's Notebooks of the Early 1870's*, trans. Daniel Breazale (Atlantic Highlands, NJ: Humanities Press, 1979), 84.

15. Jacques Derrida, "White Mythology: Metaphor in the Text of Philosophy," in Jacques Derrida, *Margins of Philosophy*, trans. Alan Bass (Chicago: University of Chicago Press, 1982), 207–271.

16. Calvin O. Schrag, *Experience and Being: Prolegomena to a Future Ontology* (Evanston: Northwestern University Press, 1969), 185–215.

17. Karl Jaspers, *Reason and Existenz: Five Lectures*, trans. William Earle (New York: Noonday Press, 1957), 77–106. Karl Jaspers, *Philosophy*, Vol. 2, trans. E.B. Ashton (Chicago: University of Chicago Press, 1970), 47–103.

18. *COS*: Although I took every course in philosophy that my undergraduate institution offered, my major was not in philosophy but in what is generally called the social sciences. At Bethel College, the Mennonite school I attended as an undergraduate, there was an interdisciplinary program in the social sciences: psychology, sociology, economics, and political science.

19. Calvin O. Schrag, *Radical Reflection and the Origin of the Human Sciences* (West Lafayette, IN: Purdue University Press, 1980).

20. Calvin O. Schrag, *Communicative Praxis and the Space of Subjectivity* (Bloomington: Indiana University Press, 1986).

21. *COS*: I first encountered this kind of reductionism in the philosophy of language when I was a graduate student at Harvard during the postwar years of the fifties. This was very much the age of neopositivism. The protocol statements of the Vienna Circle and Russell's Logical Atomism were standard fare in those days. On the heels of this, of course, came the Ordinary Language School, informed by the thought of the later Wittgenstein, Ryle, and Austin, for which I developed some continuing sympathies.

22. Jean-Paul Sartre, *The Transcendence of the Ego: An Existentialist Theory of Consciousness*, trans. Forrest Williams and Robert Kirkpatrick (New York: Noonday Press, 1957).

23. Edmund Husserl, *Phenomenology of Internal Time Consciousness*, trans. James S. Churchill (Bloomington: Indiana University Press, 1964).

24. Sartre, 39.

25. Gilles Deleuze, "Anti-logos, or the Literary Machine," in *Proust and Signs*, trans. Richard Howard (New York: G. Braziller, 1972), 93–157.

26. Félix Guattari, "Transversality" in Félix Guattari, *The Molecular Revolution: Psychiatry and Politics*, trans. Rosemary Sheed (New York: Penguin Books, 1984), 11–23.

27. *COS*: It occurred to me that the notion of transversality could be used to deal with the longstanding problem of the universal and the particular, specifically as it applies to the resources of rationality. Moving toward a notion of a "transversal logos" opens up the possibility of a principle of a unifying or togetherness, which avoids the unacceptable alternatives of universalism on the one hand, and a complete particularism on the other. My book *The Resources of Rationality* developed out of this. (Calvin O. Schrag, *The Resources of Rationality: A Response to the Postmodern Challenge* [Bloomington: Indiana University Press, 1992].)

28. Cf. Calvin O. Schrag and David James Miller, "Communication Studies and Philosophy: Convergence without Coincidence" in *The Critical Turn: Rhetoric and Philosophy in Postmodern Discourse*, ed. Ian Angus and Lenore Langsdorf (Carbondale: Southern Illinois University Press, 1993), 126–139.

29. Cf. Emmanuel Levinas, *Totality and Infinity: An Essay on Exteriority*, trans. Alphonso Lingis (Pittsburgh: Duquesne University Press, 1969).

30. The movement of transversality is the possibility or condition of the horizontal and the vertical as well as their demise. Cf. Schrag, *The Resources of Rationality*, 148–179 and Schrag and Miller, "Communication Studies and Philosophy: Convergence without Coincidence."

31. "Older" is used here in the sense of a priori—logically rather than chronologically priori. The first allusion is to Nietzsche's *Beyond Good and Evil*, specifically to the transvaluation of values and—following from his earlier work (cf. footnote. 15, *above*)—to untruth as the condition for truth. "To recognize untruth as a condition of life—that certainly means resisting accustomed value feelings in a dangerous way; and a philosophy that risks this would by that token alone place itself beyond good and evil." Friedrich Nietzsche, *Beyond Good and Evil: Prelude to a Philosophy of the Future*, trans. Walter Kaufmann (New York: Vintage Books, 1966), 12. Cf. also Friedrich Nietzsche, "On the Three Metamorphoses," Part One, Section One, *Thus Spoke Zarathustra* in Friedrich Nietzsche, *The Portable Nietzsche*, trans. Walter Kaufmann (New York: Viking Press, 1968), 137–139. The second allusion is to Derrida's notion of *différance* and his critique of Heidegger's ontology in "Différance." "Older" here plays off of Derrida's characterization of *différance*: "'Older' than Being itself, such a *différance* has no name in our language." He goes on to write: "There will be no unique name, even if it were the name of Being. . . . [And] we must *affirm* this, in the sense in which

Nietzsche puts affirmation into play, in a certain laughter and a certain step of the dance." Derrida, "*Différance*," in *Margins of Philosophy*, 26, 27.

32. Edward W. Said, *Beginnings*: *Intention and Method* (New York: Columbia University Press, 1987).

33. *COS*: I had the opportunity to work with Gadamer as well as with his assistant as the result of receiving a Fulbright Fellowship to study at Heidelberg University in Germany.

34. Schrag, *Communicative Praxis and the Space of Subjectivity*, 202 ff.

35. *Micah* 6:6-8. "'With what shall I come before the Lord, and bow myself before God on high? Shall I come before him with burnt offerings, with calves a year old? Will the Lord be pleased with thousands of rams, with ten thousands of rivers of oil? Shall I give my first-born for the sin of my soul?' He has showed you, O man, what is good; and what does the Lord require of you but to do justice, and to love kindness [or mercy], and to walk humbly with your God?" *The New Oxford Annotated Bible* (New York: Oxford University Press, 1973).

36. *Amos* 5:21–24. "I hate and despise your feasts, I take no pleasure in your solemn festivals. When you offer me holocausts, [a line is missing in the mss.]. I reject your oblations, and refuse to look at your sacrifices of fattened cattle. Let me have no more of the din of your chanting, no more of your strumming on harps. But let justice flow like water, and integrity like an unfailing stream." *The Jerusalem Bible*, (Garden City, NY: Doubleday and Company, 1966).

37. *COS*: I would never have thought that the day would come when I would have even a friendly quarrel with Gadamer over a Greek term. I recall doing Plato's *Theatetus* in a course with Gadamer while I was a student in Heidelberg. We had come to one of the decisive passages in the text and Gadamer asked the young woman sitting next to me, "What does the Greek say here?" And the poor woman said, "But Herr Professor, I don't read Greek." To which Gadamer responded, "My dear young woman, if we don't read Greek, we don't study Plato." And there I was trying to slide under the table, waiting for Gadamer to say, "Why don't we have the guy from U.S.A. tell us."

38. Martin Heidegger, *Being and Time*, trans. John Macquarrie and Edward Robinson (New York: Harper and Row, 1962), 312–348. The call is implicit in Levinas' notion of the face. Cf., e.g., Levinas, *Totality and Infinity*.

39. *The Book of Virtues*: *A Treasury of Great Moral Stories*, ed. William J. Bennett (New York: Simon and Schuster, 1993).

40. Alasdair MacIntyre, *After Virtue*: *A Study in Moral Theory* (Notre Dame: University of Notre Dame Press, 1981).

41. Emmanuel Levinas, *Otherwise than Being or Beyond Essence*, trans. Alphonso Lingis (Boston: Martinus Nijhoff Publishers, 1981).

42. Cf., for example, "The God above God and the Courage to Be" in Paul Tillich, *The Courage to Be* (New Haven: Yale University Press, 1952), 186–190.

43. Kierkegaard vividly portrays the distinction while discussing the "Outing to Deer Park." Cf. "The Religious Task: An Edifying Divertissment" in Søren Kierkegaard, *Concluding Unscientific Postscript to Philosophical Fragments*, trans. Howard V. Hong and Edna H. Hong (Princeton: Princeton University Press, 1992).

44. Jacques Derrida, *The Gift of Death*, trans. David Wills (Chicago: University of Chicago Press, 1995), 49. Cf. Jacques Derrida, "Faith and Knowledge: the Two Sources of 'Religion' at the limits of Reason Alone," trans. Samuel Weber, in *Religion*, ed. Jacques Derrida and Gianni Vattimo (Stanford: Stanford University Press, 1998), 1-78.

45. Søren Kierkegaard, *Works of Love*, trans. Howard V. Hong and Edna H. Hong (Princeton: Princeton University Press, 1995).

46. *COS*: Now Demos, who was himself retained on the Harvard faculty until his retirement, agreed with Whitehead that the history of Western philosophy should be read as a series of footnotes to Plato. But instead of continuing to interpret and develop Whitehead's speculative metaphysical system, he defined his professional vocation as that of returning to the source. This meant that I learned a lot about Plato from Demos but very little about Whitehead—with the exception of numerous anecdotes about the personalities of Mr. and Mrs. Whitehead.

47. *COS*: Wild was one of the more contentious critics of neopositivism and suggested that I have a go at Heidegger's *Being and Time*, or *Sein und Zeit* as I knew it, since, of course, it was not yet translated at that time. Needless to say, the going was somewhat arduous, but I persevered. After the task was completed, Wild encouraged me to apply for a Fulbright Fellowship to study in Germany. I did so, received the fellowship, and spent the following year at Heidelberg University studying with the likes of Karl Lowith and Hans-Georg Gadamer. As a kind of bonus, I had the opportunity to do a tutorial with Gadamer's assistant, Dieter Heinrich, who helped me walk through *Sein und Zeit*. Heinrich, himself, quickly ascended through the ranks to become Germany's leading authority of Classical German Idealism, spending the later part of his preretirement years as a professor at Harvard

48. *COS*: It was during the year of my return from Heidelberg that Paul Tillich had been appointed to the prestigious post of University Professor—patterned after the Regis Professorship at Oxford. Upon learning of my philosophical interests and my having studied abroad, he asked if I would be willing serve as his assistant—"Teaching Fellows" is what we were called. I was of course pleased to accept the assignment.

49. Levinas, *Otherwise than Being*. Jean-Luc Marion, *God without Being: Hors-Texte*, trans. Thomas A. Carlson (Chicago: University of Chicago Press, 1995).

50. Heidegger, *Being and Time*, 494, footnote vi. (H. 235).

51. Martin Heidegger, *Holtzwege* (Frankfurt: V. Klostermann, 1957).

52. Calvin O. Schrag, "The Kierkegaard-Effect in the Shaping of the Contours of Modernity" in *Kierkegaard in Post/Modernity*, eds. Martin J. Matustik and Merold Westphal (Bloomington: Indiana University Press, 1995), 1–17.

53. Tillich, 186–190.

54. *COS*: Tillich was quite taken with Heidegger's contributions—they had taught together at Marburg. He once told me that after one of Heidegger's first lectures on the distinction between Being and beings, during the walk in the woods that they always take after lecture, he said to Heidegger, in all earnestness, "That was a great sermon you gave." In my naïveté, I asked Tillich, "What did

Heidegger say?" Tillich was a bit surprised. Heidegger, of course, didn't say anything. What would you say after a pronouncement like that?

55. "It is necessary to say whom we consider our antithesis: it is the theologians and whatever has theologians' blood in its veins—and that includes our whole philosophy." Friedrich Nietzsche, *The Antichrist*, trans. Walter Kaufmann, 574 in *The Portable Nietzsche*, trans. and ed. Walter Kaufmann (New York: Viking Press, 1968).

56. "But the fight against Plato or, to speak more clearly and for 'the people,' the fight against the Christian-ecclesiastical pressure of millennia—for Christianity is Platonism for 'the people'—has created in Europe a magnificent tension of the spirit the like of which had never yet existed on earth: with so tense a bow we can now shoot for the most distant goals." Friedrich Nietzsche, *Beyond Good and Evil*, 3.

57. "—And how many new gods are still possible! As for myself, in whom the religious, that is to say god-forming, instinct occasionally becomes active at impossible times — how differently, how variously the divine has revealed itself to me each time!" Friedrich Nietzsche, *The Will to Power*, trans. Walter Kaufmann and R.J. Hollingdale, ed. Walter Kaufmann (New York: Vintage Books, 1968), 534.

58. "Let us remove supreme goodness from the concept of God: it is unworthy of a god. . . . God the *supreme power* —that suffices! Everything follows from it, 'the world' follows from it!" Friedrich Nietzsche, *The Will to Power*, 534.

59. Martin Heidegger, *Identity and Difference*, trans. Joan Stambaugh (New York: Harper and Row, 1969).

60. Levinas, *Otherwise than Being or Beyond Essence*.

61. "Being as the generative ground [of beings] . . . itself needs to be properly accounted for by that for which it accounts, that is, by the causation through the supreme original matter—and that is the cause as *causa sui*. This is the right name for the god of philosophy. Man can neither pray nor sacrifice to this god. Before the *causa sui*, man can neither fall to his knees in awe nor can he play music and dance before this god." Heidegger, *Identity and Difference*, 72.

62. "The god-less thinking which must abandon the god of philosophy, god as *causa sui*, is thus perhaps closer to the divine God. Here this means only: godless thinking is more open to Him than onto-theo-logic would like to admit." Heidegger, *Identity and Difference*, 72.

63. Sigmund Freud, *Future of an Illusion*, ed. James Strachey (New York: W.W. Norton and Company, 1989).

64. "Thus Thales had seen the unity of that all that is, but when he went to communicate it, he found himself talking about water!" Friedrich Nietzsche, *Philosophy in the Tragic Age of the Greeks*, trans. Marianne Cowan (Chicago: Henry Regnery Company, 1962), 45.

65. "On the Gift-Giving Virtue," Part One, Section 22, Nietzsche, *Thus Spoke Zarathustra*, 186–191.

66. Paul Tillich, *Love, Power, and Justice: Ontological Analyses and Ethical Applications* (New York: Oxford University Press, 1960).

67. *COS*: Derrida is good in pointing this out—how it effects our whole existence. But the mistake he makes, I think, is in assuming that the gift as a love that is not conditional can only be understood in a metaphysical sense—without any condition whatsoever. The possibility that this might be understood existentially as a love given without the condition that it be returned escapes him. Rather than beginning with the experience of the gift, he begins with a definition of the gift that presupposes the metaphysical distinction he then uses to demonstrate its impossibility. The gift is defined as an infinite love which in order to be an infinite love must be a goodness that infinitely effaces itself in forgetfulness. This is then juxtaposed with the responsibility imposed upon finite individuals to love infinitely who in order to be responsible for this love must be capable of answering for what they give. This in turn requires an awareness of the giving which contradicts the requisite forgetfulness. Thus the gift as infinite love can have no effectuality in finite existence. Here the gift is defined before it happens. But taken existentially, it is the awareness—not the effacement—of the possibility of a giving that expects nothing in return that permits rather than prevents its effectuality, even if the possibility itself cannot be fully realized in finite existence. (Cf. Derrida, *The Gift of Death*, 49–51.)

68. Søren Kierkegaard, *Works of Love*.

69. Søren Kierkegaard, *Repetition: An Essay in Experimental Psychology*, trans. Walter Lowrie (New York: Harper and Row, 1964).

70. Søren Kierkegaard, *Either/Or*, Vol. II (New York: Anchor Books), 116.

71. "The Other does not only appear in his face, as a phenomenon subject to the action and domination of a freedom. . . . The face with which the Other turns to me is not reabsorbed in a representation of the face. To hear his destitution which cries out for justice is not to represent an image to oneself, but is to posit oneself as responsible. . . . The Other who dominates me in his transcendence is thus the stranger, the widow, and the orphan, to whom I am obligated." Emmanuel Levinas, *Totality and Infinity*, 215.

72. "In the idea of the Infinite, thought thinks more than it can contain and, according to Descartes' Third Meditation, God is thought in humankind. Is it not like a noesis without a noema? And the concreteness of responsibility, in its extraordinary and nonencompassable future, is it not ordained through its Word in the face of the Other?" Emmanuel Levinas, *Time and the Other*, trans. Richard A. Cohen (Pittsburgh: Duquesne University Press, 1987), 117.

73. *COS*: Of course, someone will come back and say: "Well, aren't you going to feel really gratified that those you gave gifts to now give gifts to others?" Well, of course, you might feel gratified, but that's not the essence of the giving. It's a psychological accompaniment and you can't simply define or characterize the gift in terms of psychological attitudes.

74. *See,* Ramsey Eric Ramsey "Communication and Eschatology: The Ethics of Relief, the Work of Waiting, and areligious Religiosity," *Communication Theory*, vol. 7, no. 4 (November 1997): 343-361.

75. Cf. Calvin O. Schrag, "Ultimacy and the Alterity of the Sublime," in *Being Human and the Ultimate*, eds. Nenos Georgopolous and Michael Hein

(Atlanta: Rodopi Press, 1995), 51–65. The collection is a *Festschrift* in honor of John Anderson.

76. Philip Hallie, *Lest Innocent Blood Be Shed: The Story of the Village of Le Chambon and How Goodness Happened There* (New York: Harper and Row, 1979). Other European communities also came to the aid of Jewish refugees, among others communities in northeast Holland, as well as in Denmark, Bulgaria, and Slovakia.

Part II Publics and Their Problems

2 Communicative Praxis and Collective Decision Making

From Phenomenology to the Politics of Experience to Dialogic Constitutive Practices

STANLEY DEETZ, AMY GRIM, AND ALEXANDER LYON

Everyday conceptions and scholarly conceptions of communication are of fundamental importance. They reflect and influence the ways people work to shape social institutions and participate in sociality and decision making with each other. Specific communicative practices arise as practical attempts to deal with historically situated problems. They are shaped by political configurations and institutional forms, as well as other resources, of the time, and are sustained by sedimentation, institutionalization, and specific reproductive micropractices. As social problems change, older concepts and practices of communication become less useful in enabling productive joint engagement in serious issues of our time.

Calvin Schrag's work has been significant among those working to rewrite the theory and conception of communication within the Western tradition. As such, he has helped to engage contemporary problems by teaching us how to live together in a world where personal identities, social order, knowledge, and visions of a future are a perpetual joint accomplishment in concrete life situations. Schrag's work, from his earliest studies to his most recent, elucidates the positions taken here. No doubt, those who follow projects set by the trajectory of this essay will find Schrag an invaluable ally.

We believe that dominant contemporary communication conceptions and practices loosely organized as "traditional" and "liberal democratic" are fundamentally weak as guidance for engagement in public and private issues of our time. In a world of increasing interdependence and weakening systems of collective choice, insight from social phenomenology can provide better guidance.

After a brief review of the dominant "traditional" and "liberal democratic" conceptions and practices of communication, we will argue that the contemporary problem of making collective decisions is fundamentally different from the conditions under which these conceptions arose. Nonetheless, "traditional" conceptions and practices continue to dominate the less democratized private spaces of the family and the workplace. "Liberal democracy" has been institutionalized in the public arena, especially in the political and judiciary processes. Further, with the relative demise of the public/private distinction, the dominant practices of communication have invaded alternative spaces, leading to some hybrids, much oscillation between liberal democratic and traditional approaches, but few creative advances. The development of workplace participation programs, for example, largely remain under authoritative control while using liberal democratic forms of talk—both of which greatly limit the possibility of creative joint decisions. The complexity of contemporary problems and oscillation between approaches make examination and critique difficult.

A democracy in our contemporary situation either becomes naive or oppressive if framed within either the traditional or the dominant liberal democratic conception of communication. Our focus here will be on the difficulties of liberal democracy, since it offers the more viable alternative and the more traditional model suffers from many of the same limitations.

Both of these approaches have worked with various successes and costs. Both require a fairly high degree of social consensus and widespread legitimacy in order to function. Consensus and legitimacy, however, to the extent they exist, cannot be assumed as an external background for communication; rather, they are an accomplishment of communication. Neither approach accounts well for this more fundamental communicative accomplishment.

Fundamental negotiations are central to contemporary society, but understanding these negotiations requires a different set of communication conceptions and practices. This essay will show how a theoretically and practically driven conception of "open communicative micropractices" grounded in a critical phenomenology offers both the possibility of a situated normative critique and a guided practice focusing on the restriction of moves of disqualification and discursive closure. This way of thinking will then be applied to mediation and restorative justice, both of which are designed to overcome the limitations of liberal democratic judiciary processes.

THE LIMITATIONS OF LIBERAL DEMOCRACY

Communicative praxis in a liberal democratic form rests on three essential conceptions. First, the autonomous individual is seen as the origin of perceptions, thoughts, and feelings. Second, available forums exist where people may freely express these perceptions, thoughts, and feelings to others. Third, persuasion and advocacy are the preferred modes of communication leading to decision. Such conceptions enable the narrow U.S. version of democracy, where democracy itself becomes reduced to the freedom of expression and "free" markets rather than a form of deliberation and decision making where people collectively can make decisions for the good of all. But even outside of the narrow U.S. version, all three limit the capacity of liberal democracy to provide an effective method of discussion and decision making. Let us consider these three conceptions in reverse order, since our greatest concern will be with the first.

PERSUASION AND ADVOCACY OR COLLABORATION

Although traditional conceptions of communication accepted persuasion and advocacy as means of disseminating the truth and inculcating social values, liberal democracy essentially accepted a debater's version of the Greek dialectic. As it has developed, if all engage in self-interested expression, good collective decisions arise through the guidance of some invisible hand. Such a faith fails to consider that while, individually, all may seem to benefit from decisions, they may have negative systemic consequences for everyone in the long term. It also fails to recognize that very different forms of communication can enable creative solutions that were not possessed by any participant, solutions that seldom arise in adversarial situations. Part of the problem of endless meetings in the United States rests on conceptions and practices which assure that "all have made their case" rather than focusing on processes of reaching agreement.

In the United States the preferred political forum is the debate. The one who can best advocate and persuade is declared the winner. Would we select the same person or think the same way about issues if we required the candidates to sit down and solve a problem together? Surely, watching two intelligent people figure out ways to meet the different needs and values of society would be instructive. The candidate most creative in finding mutually satisfying systemic solutions might well be the better leader. But all of this requires a different model of communication.

The judiciary system most fully institutes this model to its credit and demise. Even in cases where mediation processes have shown considerable advantage over litigation, in divorce court and environmental disputes for example, they are conducted in the shadow of the unquestioned adversarial system. As we will argue, in such contexts mediation becomes bargaining over known positions rather than the collaborative accomplishment of diverse interests. Alternative communication models are at best partially developed, and experience, rather than theoretically guided understanding, directs most of these alternative activities. The analysis of mediation and restorative justice below shows some of the difficulties of a practice without a praxis. Our current conditions provide complex negotiation needs, but the model of communication built for rather simple issues with constrained contestations proves to be less than useful.

Places of Speaking or Places of Understanding

Liberal democracy greatly depends on both the freedom of speech and having places to speak. Clearly, more attention has been given to the defense of the freedom of speech than to the preservation of meaningful places to speak. Free speech advocates have not adequately considered unequal access to speaking forums or the difference in "megaphone" size. Freedom of expression is essential because good decision making requires that all relevant perspectives are known by all. Unfortunately, contemporary communication environments do not assure this condition. Freedom of expression is meaningless if there is no one to represent relevant positions, if the one with the biggest megaphone can drown out the chorus of free voices, or if, as in the case of the Internet, the proliferation of opinions inhibits meaningful discussion.

The problem is even deeper. Present interaction processes do not foster the development of all relevant positions. Freedom of expression neither specifies the right of being heard nor does it guarantee that all opinions are expressed. The desire for representation requires building processes that develop alternative perspectives, fosters their expression, and gives them an equal opportunity to influence decisions. The critical function of communication studies is to promote better decisions. Too often in our attention to information and influence have we forgotten that the primary function of expression is to make sure the community does not overlook a position that is valuable for decisions. Rather than attend to the enhancement of participation in decision making, we have treated informing and persuading as an ends in themselves. In media studies, for example, we attend to mass media's role in informing but usually remain silent regarding its influence on deliberation. The restrictions placed on representation may be direct through freedom limitation or coercion, but are often unobtrusive and subtle through unwarranted consent.

THE PRIMACY OF PERSONAL EXPERIENCE OR SOCIAL CONSTRUCTIONS

Both the traditional and liberal democratic models of communication treat meanings as already existing. Either meaning is held by authority, as in the traditional model, or meaning is worked out in the private life of the individual, as in the liberal democratic model. Neither consider the possibility of the social formation of experience. For that we must turn to twentieth-century phenomenology, which has developed a richer understanding of how experience forms. The phenomenological focus on the social formation of experience has brought to light distinct communication issues and enabled the development of conceptions of communication better able to help people deal with contemporary problems.

Around the turn of the twentieth century, Edmund Husserl developed the most original and complete critique of the psychological subject as the center of experience and the equally problematic conceptions of an objective world and proper methods of discovering it. The fundamental argument, now seeming so far ahead of its time, was clear: although sedimentation and reproduction made it difficult to understand, particular worlds and persons are constructions; to the extent that they are treated as primitives in the mind or in the material, we are unable to describe what is necessary for them to appear as they appear; hence, subjective domination in the form of proclaiming the real or natural or in producing a particular world in methods continues. As Husserl increasingly came to understand these constructionist activities as cultural and historical, the conceptual field was sown for an open, reflexive, and liberating social science. Schrag, of course, greatly built upon and resolved difficulties in Husserl's works.

The phenomenological legacy has developed much over time. Phenomenological rethinking has moved from an understanding of the constitution of experience, to an understanding of the social-linguistic structuring of experience, to an understanding of the politics of representation and experience, to an affirmation of the dialogic quality of existence.

The presence of social diversity (even if weakly formed) has helped to situate an awareness of the inadequacy of previously assumed foundations and an understanding of the constructed and negotiated (though heretofore invisible) character of personal identity, social order, knowledge, and social vision of the future. The largely "informational" conception of human interaction that arose out of traditional and liberal views presumes the presence of psychological, sociological, economic, and objective facts, and as such it fails to account for these crucial negotiative accomplishments. A society marked by diversity must be complemented by a conception of social interaction based in phenomenology. In this antifoundational move, the process of communication is seen as the way temporary structures and orders are produced and overcome in interaction.

Even where diversity and the contested nature of experience have been understood and where forums have been developed to enhance participation and democracy, the processes usually share the problems of self-interested expression and collective failure more generally seen in liberal democratic models.[1] The move to dialogic communication is central to the development of a vital new democracy in contemporary society.[2]

A COMMUNICATION-BASED CONCEPTION OF EXPERIENCE

A more useful understanding of communication begins with a phenomenological reconsideration of experience. The phenomenological insights informing communication studies are fairly straightforward. Human beings always find themselves embodied in a worldly configuration and act within this world in ways that reproduce particular selves and realities and produce new possibilities. Human beings, like all living things, are interpretive creatures. We live and work in a world that is formed in particular manners given our specific sense equipment, manners of comportment, and routinized practices. In this sense we respond to a world external to us, but one that is only known relative to the specific characteristics and activities of the subject.

Unlike most living things, however, much of this interpretive mode of being for humans is provided socially rather than genetically. Social routines, linguistic distinctions, and institutional structures operate for humans much like instincts do for other creatures. The body is extended through space and time as the position, point of view, or subjectivity within various technological extensions of the senses and limbs, and as concretized in buildings, landscapes, and patterned practices. Prior social interactions and social decisions thus constitute the conditions of every "personal" perception, feeling, or need. Language, as the primary mode of interaction, is a particular form of institutionalized sensing that directs the attention of other senses, strikes and recalls differences in the inner and outer world that make a difference, and provides system reflexivity. Issues related to language, institutions, and routine practices thus have both political and moral dimensions since they ultimately determine the character and survival of the species (and perhaps all others).[3]

Each psychological state and conception of personal identity arises out of a background of social practices in which such things are constructed as possible, feelable, and imaginable. Every social structure can be seen as an arbitrary, routine, habitual way that social interactions have come to be played out. As such they have no stature except as reproduced and legitimized in ongoing social interaction. In this sense, psychological and sociological theories are attempts at reifying ongoing productive and reproductive interactions, usually for the sake of advantaging certain historical practices over others. Their attempts at explanation merely freeze a process in time, establishing arbitrary independent and dependent variables that are often mistaken as real things. Alternatively, communication analysis properly attempts to describe and explain productive and reproductive processes through accounts of specific ongoing representational practices.

A conceptualized personal identity or a psychological self as origin of experience is thus always a reification of this constituting/constituted self instituted in the world. Reification is made possible by the linguistic possibility of referencing one's lived self, a reference situated by another living relation held as available by the discursive "I" in linguistic constructions. While this relation allows for reification, dualism, and a misrecognized freedom, it also allows for critique and a productive or opening turn on self-referentiality in systems. The same process that makes possible the preservation and naturalization of sameness makes the experience of difference and change possible. It does, however, show how human beings can be creatures with multiple literal and metaphorical genetic programs, and who are active in literal and metaphorical genetic programming through the production and transformation of social institutions. Hence, while the subject is invisible as the constitutive process by which the world appears as object and identities are produced in particular relations to the world, the construction of particular identities and realities is not neutral, for it becomes part of the produced institutional configuration in which the subject is embodied, retained, or transformed.

The concern here is with how meanings, psychological states, social structures, and personal identities are produced and reproduced through specific social processes. Further, since all institutional structures concretize power advantages, institutionally embodied subjects perceive, feel, and need along lines that give preference to certain groups and their produced interests. Experience is thus always political and the reproduction of institutional arrangements and conceptions of identity cannot be separate from systems of power and control.

In the view we are suggesting, communication refers to the social processes by which meanings, identities, psychological states, social structures, and the various means of contact with the environment are both produced, reproduced, or changed.[4] In both its constitutive and reproductive modes, communication is central to how perceptions, meanings, and routines are held in common. In human interactions, perception, meaning and data transmission are all complex, multileveled phenomena produced from and productive of conflicting motives and structures. The complexity of the communication process can be initially seen in the way it both produces and reproduces objects and persons.

Communicative relations can be either open and productive or closed and reproductive in relation to both others and the world. In productive relations, the unity of the "I" is risked as alternative structural relations interrogate the fixed position of the "I" as the very objects of the world are transformed. Productive relations happen as the fixed self/other/world configuration gives over to the conflictual, tension-filled antagonisms out of which objects are differentiated and redifferentiated and preconceptions yield to new conceptions.[5] In such relations, both the power in the weblike configuration and the presumed self-directive power of the individual are challenged. At this constitutive level, a communication perspective draws attention to a politics of perception and person formation.

Productive interactions are responses that range from a relatively stable set of practices and linguistic forms that constrain variety to an actual set of events that could have been described and responded to in a number of fashions (i.e., that potentially demand variety). In productive interactions, identities are utilized improvisationally to provide a moment of articulation which is transformed freely into another, constantly moved by the excess of meaning and possible experience over that which is momentarily present.[6] But when identities are protected from examination in interactional systems, often through either invisibility or processes of discursive closure, they not only distort the development of each participant, they also distort the consensus reached on the subject matter at hand. Domination occurs when a particular moment of articulation of self-other-world relation is frozen or fixed, so that the singular holds sway over the plurality. Much of life and interaction with others, then, gives evidence for reproductive communicative processes with types of closure and distortion.[7] Both traditional and liberal democratic conceptions reduce all communication to reproductive communication; thus they both miss and undermine creative potential and make the examination of forms of consent and domination in reproductive processes difficult.

Both traditional and liberal democratic conceptions draw our attention to contestations among known positions but lead us away from examining contestations in the social formation of positions. Human interaction is filled with practices leading to discursive closure whereby important contestations never occur. Without a richer conception of communication, these are not likely to be examined. In certain historical periods these may have been less clear or important than today.

Eroding Consensus and New Arenas for Negotiation

In certain eras, the difficulties of traditional and liberal democratic models of communication remain invisible. In periods of relatively closed cultures, one grows up in and unwittingly consents to a culture and its political arrangements and does not recognize its forms of domination. The citizen of a homogeneous culture operates with a false sense of freedom; the constraints are barely felt. S/he does not understand that in consenting to that culture, a form of violence is reproduced, violence against aspects of the self (or potentially conflicting selves) and violence against all marginalized groups.[8] Such citizens express "freely" in a liberal democratic sense, but have no "voice."

The presence of unexpected and often undesired diversity creates a problem for that world, but also tremendous opportunity. In a diverse social context these assumptions are seen as only one type of social arrangement—an arrangement that either can be maintained through control or open to constant negotiation. Actualizing the negotiative opportunities requires a new conception of communication appropriate for the new situation and new practices, a new praxis.

Arising from its relatively homogeneous context, Western society traditionally has been based on four foundational faiths or centers that have been assumed as unproblematic in most modern conceptions of people and organizations. In a sense, they have served as a kind of consensual background in which many things did not need to be negotiated. Communication could assume these things rather than be about them. Although they were based in values and support power arrangements, they were rarely questioned. Since everyone accepted the foundational faiths, they appeared as part of the natural order. In this way, potential conflicts over them were deeply suppressed.

These foundations are a belief in the existence of

1. unitary-autonomous psychological persons who know their interests and are capable of freely subordinating themselves in contractual relations,
2. a legitimate consensual-integrative social order,
3. an objective external world and proper methods of discovering it,
4. a grand narrative of a material progress-driven cybernetic.

It is precisely these foundations that can no longer be taken for granted in contemporary society but are nonetheless assumed in institutional arrangements like the judiciary system.

Contestation of the taken-for-granted requires the presence of concrete others. Only in the development of the "other" can the self and experience collaboratively develop.[9] Neither traditional nor liberal democratic conceptions have a strong sense of the other or the community. Ultimately, dialogic communication is not for self-expression but self-destruction. The point of communication as a social act is to overcome one's fixed subjectivity, conceptions, and strategies, and to open to the indeterminacy of people and the external environment. Communication in its dialogic form is productive rather than reproductive. It produces what self and other can experience, rather than reproducing what either has. Self-expression is misleading not because people do not or should not try to express their experiences, but because such expressions in a dialogic view are the raw material for the production of something new rather than the product of self interests. The responsible self cannot simply choose to be open, for that would presume that it has already determined that outside itself. Rather, process subjectivity happens in response to the pull from the outside.

The recognition of "the otherness of the other" disrupts a discursive stoppage by posing questions to any fixed conception or meaning. The "other" exceeds every possible conception of it. In modern terminology, otherness deconstructs. Otherness is property of people, but also of things and events. The fundamental otherness suggests that any possible label or conception of self, other, and world is capable of being questioned. Perception, as well as conception, is the end product of a conflict, a conflict that can be recovered. The conflict represents a struggle between one's fixed identity and conceptual schemes and the excess of the "other" over that. The remembrance of this struggle leaves each and every attempt to form an object potentially open to question. Otherness in this sense is critical to the formation of self and other. Every interaction thus holds both the possibility of closure or new meaning, either a reproduction of the dominant socially produced subjectivity or responsiveness to the excess of external events over these conceptions. Developing an appreciation of "otherness" as a part of dialogic interaction is central to developing a responsibility appropriate to the modern age.

While social diversity provides alternative forms of responsibility and competing forms of procedure and knowledge, neither traditional nor liberal democratic conceptions and practices enable meaningful contestation. Within institutional sites like the judiciary, fundamental conflicts are avoided, key participants are disqualified, and processes and positions are neutralized and naturalized. To the extent that contestation does occur through actions and noncommunicative processes, contestation is often fueled by frustrations. The processes of expression and uptake are often distorted. Open productive discourse is nearly impossible to achieve.

Within the judiciary system, the weaknesses of existing models are at least partially understood. The gradual removal of judicial discretion has reduced some biases but also makes it more difficult to consider local and individual circumstances. Litigation often leaves both parties unhappy, produces large legal costs, and provides few creative alternatives. Justice is laden with values that lead to white collar and corporate crimes being treated far differently than others. The structure fixing individual responsibility fails to account for or hold responsible complex conditions leading to problems. Both mediation and restorative justice have been suggested as meaningful communication-based collaborative alternatives to some of these difficulties.

The Mediation Alternative

Over the last three decades, mediation has become an increasingly popular alternative to adversarial forms of conflict resolution as exemplified in the U.S. justice system. In mediation, decision-making authority is retained by the participants rather than a judge or jury. With the help of an impartial third party, participants are encouraged to collectively negotiate a mutually satisfactory solution. Because participants voluntarily come to the bargaining table with the goal of making a joint decision, the process of mediation holds the promise that individuals are empowered to voice their own perspectives and concerns, that they come to better understand the perspectives and interests of others involved in the dispute, and that they are invested more thoroughly in the final outcome of the process because they have been active participants in it.

Despite the many successes of mediation, particularly in the arenas of divorce, child custody and environmental disputes, it fails to enact an authentic alternative to a liberal democratic model of communication. In theory, mediation is seen as a collaborative process of decision making, but in practice, the process is more often one of compromise, resulting in a decision that the disputing parties can mutually accept rather than one that genuinely transcends participants' socially produced interests. Pervaded by a metaphor of commodity exchange, models of negotiation used in mediation rest upon a set of taken-for-granted oppositions that reinforce adversarial (and patriarchal) communication practices rather than overcome them.[10]

Participants come to mediation with a set of individual interests and objectives that are viewed as incompatible with the interests and objectives of the other parties. Participants express their interests as the mediator listens for areas in which the parties might exchange lesser goals in the service of meeting their overall objective. The mediator then guides the communication to focus on issues that can be exchanged or traded in a reciprocal manner. If party A concedes one of its demands, then party B follows suit by conceding one of its demands. In order to be effective, this trade must be seen as equitable, i.e., the value of A's concession is approximately equal to B's concession. Such bargaining is meant to ensure that no single party dominates the process and that the compromises reached are seen as a fair and balanced. This process underscores the notion that information is a valuable commodity and that communication is a rather simple process of exchanging information. Parties can and do engage in strategic communication by placing some issues on the table while shielding others from potential compromise. Thus, the individual parties are still seen as unitary autonomous persons who know their own interests, are capable of expressing and controlling them, and can freely enter a contractual relation with another.

Another way in which mediation underscores rather than overcomes the liberal democratic model of communication is in the nature of the relationships among the disputants. In traditional negotiation, as in adversarial judicial proceedings, identities and relationships are pregiven. Each participant enters the process with her own set of needs, interests, and goals that are seen as discrete and often incompatible with the needs, interests, and goals of the other participants.[11] The relationships among the participants are taken at face value (e.g., victim and offender or manager and employee) and are seen as instrumental rather than interconnected and interdependent. Thus, the subject positions of the individuals are rarely questioned or open to examination and have little potential of being transformed by the process. Even when a mutually acceptable decision is reached, the participants leave the negotiation with the adversarial identities and relationships they brought to the process intact.

Finally, because mediation is specific to the dispute at hand, few opportunities exist to examine the social order and systemic conditions that enabled the conflict to surface. The typical process of mediation focuses upon reconciling individual interests rather than the interests of the larger community. Indeed, individuals cannot bargain issues such as community standards, norms, and values; they must assume these things for the sake of a productive interaction and instead must focus on the issue and offer proposals and counterproposals over which they, as individuals, have some control. Thus, in traditional approaches to mediation the joint accomplishment of social order is backgrounded as the joint accomplishment of an acceptable solution to the present problem is foregrounded.

This brief sketch highlights the fact that although mediation is seen by many as a viable alternative to adversarial conflict resolution, it rests upon some assumptions and processes that reinforce a liberal democratic model of communication. This is particularly troublesome because the adversarial nature of the process is hidden. Participants and practitioners may believe that mediation moves beyond adversarial means of resolving conflicts, and indeed mediation does mark some progress from traditional forms of dispute resolution, but ultimately mediation enacts a liberal democratic conception of communication that, as argued earlier, is insufficient for generating truly collaborative collective decisions in a complex, heterogeneous society.

THE RESTORATIVE JUSTICE ALTERNATIVE

Restorative justice is a more recent attempt to overcome the limitations of the justice system and to generate truly collaborative decisions. Like mediation, it is designed to avoid the tendency of the criminal justice system to displace communicative and decision-making responsibility on lawyers, judges, and juries. It provides a forum that allows each person impacted by a crime to explain the event and its consequences from his or her perspective with the goal of collaboratively developing creative solutions. Significantly, restorative justice rests upon the assumption that a criminal offense is primarily a transgression of community bonds and human relationships and is secondarily a violation of a law or policy. In this regard, an offender is held responsible for the harm done to individual members of the community as well as the community at large. Instead of imposing sentences or fines, restorative justice seeks to repair the harm and restore the community by attending to the needs of victims, offenders, and the community.

All of this calls for an alternative to the adversarial system institutionalized in court proceedings. In lieu of trials, the restorative justice system holds conferences in which victims, offenders, and members of the community voluntarily come together with a facilitator to discuss the nature of the offense, to explore ways in which the harm might be repaired, and to develop specific solutions that attempt to reintegrate the community. Participants are each given the opportunity to voice their perspective in a dialogical context rather than an adversarial proceeding. Restorative justice is designed to promote new ways of thinking about justice as well as innovative, flexible means of collectively addressing community problems. It fosters collective decision making by empowering community members to have a say in how specific offenses against the community can be remedied.

The restorative justice model overcomes certain obstacles that litigation and sometimes mediation do not. First, the people involved all speak for themselves instead of through a representative so that participants will gain a greater understanding of, and perhaps empathy for, each other. Sharing numerous perspectives may also create a shared experience among group members and lay the foundation for a common sense the group may use to reach a decision. A second salient feature of restorative justice is that decisions are made through consensus. After participants express their viewpoints, the facilitator moves the group toward a decision. Even the person identified as the offender contributes equally to the discussion about the outcomes of the conference. Similarly, the victim participates in the decision and will sometimes work side-by-side with the offender to implement the solution.

Thus, restorative justice attempts to overcome the problems of liberal democratic adversarial communication by creating a dialogue and by opting for collaboration instead of winning a decision. Restorative justice also attempts to overcome the inherent limitations of freedom of expression by insuring that all relevant positions are voiced. However, it would be improper to assume that just because each person is allowed to speak that they are doing so freely. For instance, both the victim and the offender have the right to end the conference and pursue litigation. This may motivate participants to be cooperative, but it also may provide a recipe for consent. The desire to avoid incarceration or fines and the pressures of social desirability may create a situation in which offenders may consent to just about anything the group suggests.

Further, like litigation, the process assumes fixed roles for each participant (e.g. victim and offender) before the conference ever begins. These roles are not negotiated, but rather are pregiven as the subject positions from which each person can speak. These pregiven roles potentially limit the scope of discussion and hinder the advancement of innovative solutions. Moreover, like litigation and mediation, the process of restorative justice is limited to the conflict at hand and is not designed to explore broader systemic questions. By focusing solely on personal responsibility, which is certainly important, the process brackets equally important questions of social and institutional responsibility for reproducing the conditions in which the conflict could occur.

Pulling Together

The contemporary everyday conceptions of interacting with others through traditional or liberal democratic models are conceptually flawed as a basis for responsibility and responsiveness required by a judiciary system. Both mediation and restorative justice offer greater potential for opening deeper contestation if developed from a phenomenologically-based model of communication. Each provides an adequate "forum," but "voice" in the sense of contestation and the presence of genuine otherness is greatly limited. The self is held as fixed and knowable, and language and the social formation of experience are rendered invisible. The constitutive conditions of self and experience production cannot be seen as politically charged. In practice, this gives a false sense of the individual as the originator of meaning and leads to self-expressionism and strategic control of others through expressive acts. The stage is set for control of self and control of others, but strategically positioned outside the illusionary self. Rethinking both alternatives in light of phenomenologically-based conceptions and practices of communication offers a productive avenue of reconsideration and development.

The core concerns are the centrality of contestations that cannot happen and the way communication and conceptions of communication support the suppression of conflicts. The democratization of everyday life is the key critical need of our day. The recovery of basic contestation is central to it. Conflict is suppressed at both the "subjective" and "objective" poles of experience. The former through the maintenance of the unity of the psychological speaking subject and the latter from the failure to understand the constructed nature of objects. Both are aided by practices and philosophies of interaction that see language as primarily representational and communication as largely expressive. Negotiative interaction cannot operate without reclaiming the conflictual nature of self, experience, and world, to open each to redetermination in relation to concrete others.

Few conceptions of communication deal with interaction in conditions of fundamental indeterminacy, where each interactant holds conflicting subject positions regarding a world that can be constructed in many different ways and where the outcome hopes to be a temporary responsive move intending only to open a future with greater options. Interaction studies have focused so much on resolution and clarity that they have made it hard to think of interaction as primarily for the purpose of overcoming deadening certainty. For many different reasons we have accepted the Enlightenment view that the world is filled with darkness and disorder and that we must struggle to produce clarity and order. Our worlds are filled with order, even organized deviance—the struggle is to reclaim some of the disorder out of which responsive and responsible choices arise. The judiciary system becomes an interesting site where new conceptions and practices could grow.

A growing number of scholars have taken seriously the issues of constructionism, showing the ways open interaction is foreclosed and developing ways of thinking about interaction under conditions of indeterminacy. Few of these studies, however, have worked out pedagogical and practical implications and none have considered the judiciary process. Let us suggest a few core practices that could be incorporated into mediation and restorative justice programs.

1. The principal goal of interaction is the discovery/invention of selves and worlds rather than the expression of existing ones.
2. Difference in positionality, rather than positions, is to be prized since it allows for fundamentally different world constructions.
3. Discursive closures in the form of naturalization, neutralization, or disqualification are to be avoided.
4. Forms of self-protection in claims such as grounded certainty or subjective relativism are to be avoided.
5. Interests should be considered fluid and historically derived with the focus on ends to be achieved together rather than preferred means of attainment.
6. Determination of the world should be considered temporary and follow, rather than precede, the question of what we wish to become together.

As shared perspectives and values erode in a diverse society, communication scholars are charged with rethinking the communicative conceptions and practices we use to make collective decisions. The problems of access and "megaphone size" continue to challenge the extent to which we can make truly collective and collaborative decisions about what is valued, what is just, and what courses of action we should take as a society. The problem of voice continues to pose questions that communication theorists and practitioners need to address, questions such as: How does one share her perspective without positioning the 'other' as an adversary? How can we ensure that all relevant perspectives are heard? How do we determine which perspectives are relevant? How do we develop the skills to engage in a type of dialogue so radically different from what we have done in the past?

All of these questions require further attention at both the theoretical and practical levels. Instead of retrofitting old models of communication for the problems of our time, we need a new model of communication that embraces the challenges of an increasingly diverse society, one that foregrounds the creative potential of dialogue, one that sees diversity as an opportunity to forge a new way of being together in the world.

NOTES

1. Benjamin R. Barber, *Strong Democracy: Participatory Politics for a New Age* (Berkeley: University of California Press, 1984).
2. Stanley A. Deetz, *Democracy in an Age of Corporate Colonization: Developments in Communication and the Politics of Everyday Life* (Albany: State University of New York Press, 1992).
3. Karl-Otto Apel, *Towards a Transformation of Philosophy*, trans. Glyn Adey and David Frisby (London: Routeledge & Kegan Paul, 1979).
4. Deetz, chapters 3–5.
5. Ernesto Laclau and Chantal Mouffe, *Hegemony and Socialist Strategy: Towards a Radical Democratic Politics*, trans. Winston Moore and Paul Cammack (London: Verso, 1985).
6. Ibid.
7. See Deetz, *Democracy*, chapter 6 and Stanley A. Deetz, "Reclaiming the Subject Matter as a Guide to Mutual Understanding: Effectiveness and Ethics in Interpersonal Interaction," *Communication Quarterly* 38 (1990): 226–243.
8. Pierre Bourdieu and Jean-Claude Passeron, *Reproduction in Education, Society, and Culture*, trans. Richard Nice (London: Sage, 1990).
9. Tanni Haas and Stanley Deetz, "Between the Generalized and the Concrete Other: Approaching Organizational Ethics from Feminist Perspectives," in *Rethinking Organizational and Managerial Communication from Feminist Perspectives*, ed. Patrice M. Buzzanell (Thousand Oaks, CA: Sage, 2000), 24–46.
10. Ibid.
11. Ibid.

3 Limitations of the Public Sphere

The Repressive Voice of Modernity

RAYMIE McKERROW

Within the modern worldview, rational deliberation conducted by an educated public seems the most logical, if not the only, means to employ in seeking solutions to the problems of a people. Arguments that would retain the space for public deliberation, then, would seem appropriate, even if not cogently presented. But retaining space, in and of itself, or even ensuring through the operation of some set of universal validity conditions (were such ever actualized) that all persons in the sphere had the chance to speak their respective minds, is far more problematic that at first appears. The commonsense orientation—that we simply need to respect others in the space set aside for deliberation, and grant good intentions to our foes (as we would have to if we were to consider the possibility of changing our own minds)—seems sensible on its face. Unfortunately, such is not the world in which we live. The instantiation of the public sphere, in any world other than the utopian dream world of a committed Habermasian, may well possess critical limits, such that the expression of modernity's voice leaves more by the wayside than it includes.

In examining the potential for a revitalized public sphere, this essay calls into question the assumptions of some modernist critics through an examination of five critical elements affecting the construction of a public space for rhetorical deliberation. The role of reason in postmodernity is the overarching frame within which the discussion of these elements will be placed: rational decision making, time, space, composition, and status.

REASON, CRITICAL RHETORIC, AND THE PUBLIC SPHERE

What is the fate of reason in a postmodern rhetoric? Is it to be forever at a remove from discourse, thereby consigning rhetoric to the world of the irrational? If the standards of judgment themselves are exterior to the domain in which reason finds expression, how are we to know if postmodern reason is rational? These are the critical questions raised by those who see in postmodernism the celebration of the indeterminate, the contingent, and hence the irrational.

This is presumed in Dilip Gaonkar's argument that there is a disjunction between critical rhetoric and reason. He argues that the conception of critical rhetoric, to the extent that it ignores "friendlier versions of reason," suffers a fatal flaw:

> Unless McKerrow can show in a convincing fashion that practical reasoning and everyday reasoning are also somehow implicated in erasing situated differences and in universalizing standards of judgment characteristic of formal apodeictic reasoning, he cannot continue to ignore the simple fact that there are different types of reasoning that are active in different spheres of life.[1]

At issue, however, is not simply reason as universalized (as in the sense of Habermasian argumentative discourse), but reason that, while "active in different spheres of life," is precluded from the realm of public influence. The "simple fact" remains that the form of reason in the public sphere is "implicated in erasing situated differences." It matters little that other forms of reason exist if they lack influence when people who, on giving expression to reason, are not given space or time within the public sphere, simply because their "different type" is not recognized as influential in that sphere.

In his keynote address to the 1993 Summer Conference on Argumentation, Joe Wenzel presented a more optimistic picture of reasoned argument's potential in postmodernity:

> A modernist theory of argumentation in the postmodern world would look very much like it always has in its goals and in its substance. It would be informed by a commitment to emancipation. It would understand emancipation as linked to a theory of rational conduct and decision-making. It would remain committed to the cultivation of practical reason in theory, practice and critique. But it would proceed with a sensitivity to the con-

> ditions of power, oppression, and difference revealed in the critical discourses of postmodernity. Hence, it would entail a commitment to the ongoing critique, reconstruction, and refinement of reason, understood as a practical human accomplishment.[2]

Although there is much to value in this picture of practical reason, and much to hope for in its commitments, its realization is not so clearly inscribed in the culture of the present as to ensure its promised outcomes. To the contrary, privileging reason precludes access by those whose voice is not expressed in the forms accepted within the dominant culture. Where the convention of rational debate and decision making governs who will speak with what authority, modernity's voice will dominate rhetorical address, thereby repressing those on the margins whose voice is "other" than that of reason.

There is yet another side to reason as the agent of exclusion. Reasoned argument, sans the emotions, or with *pathos* carefully limited to the service of reason, has been the central feature of Western rationality. This sense of reasoned discourse is continued by those who, in Gaonkar's words, propose "friendlier versions of reason" that attempt to go beyond the strictures of Kantian logic. Taken as a whole, these contemporary conceptions privilege a form of rationality that remains exclusively logos oriented; the practical reason of the community is marked by the exclusion of emotion. Habermasian reason, in particular, rejects rhetoric as an inferior discourse that goes beyond the boundaries of argument in admitting other proofs.

A different sense of reason follows from its habitation within "emancipated" space. Emancipation, the hallmark of the Enlightenment, is positioned within Western culture to preclude diversity: What gets emancipated is determined by those in control of the discourse. As Joan Landes and others have demonstrated, the sphere of activity is gendered.[3] That the sense of reason inhabiting this sphere is also gendered should be obvious. The image of males articulating reasoned discourse—shorn of its emotive grounding—in the public sphere is so well inscribed in our culture that we scarcely notice its presence. In contrast, women remain ensconced in the private sphere, ever the emotive beings. The triadic formula, though challenged, remains dominant yet today: male-public-reason; female-private-emotion.[4]

Constrained as this sense of practical reason is by form, content, and gender, rhetoric can ill afford to allow it centrality in a critique of freedom. Gaonkar's commentary on rhetoric's relation to reason is absolutely on target: "Rhetoric has to find its own emancipatory site not already colonized by reason."[5] The nature of that site can best be dealt with through an examination of the "public sphere." Hence, this essay will focus on the following claim: *Valorizing the public sphere as the site of rational decision making perpetuates the repression of marginalized voices.* In substantiating this claim, I will argue that characteristics of modernity inhibit the kind of discourse that might well save the public from itself.

Rational Decision Making

The preeminent perspective that recurs in describing the public sphere is its commitment to rational decision making. The Habermasian conception, even in its latest formulation, clearly privileges reasoned argument as it "anchors the validity of norms in the possibility of a rationally founded agreement on the part of all those who might be affected, insofar as they take on the *role of participants in a rational debate*."[6] The normative standards are those of "prudent discussion," "prudent choice," and "prudent action" with respect to the issues facing the social world.[7] If there "is no such thing as a referendum on reason" it is precisely because reason is not in question: as "nonspecialized interlocutors" our task is to project reasons (prudently) within the normative constructs of the public.[8] Reason comes from the outside of rhetoric, informing it as to the prerequisites for action, and expects rhetoric to then expedite through expression those dictates.

As intimated above, the sense of reason embraced within this conception of the public sphere is highly problematic. As Rodolphe Gasche notes, "postmodernity and rationality are simply incommensurable" in Habermasian terms.[9] If rationality is to be solely configured in Aristotelian terms, Habermas is correct. If, on the other hand, rationality is reconfigured as "the reason of the plural, the indeterminate, the random, the irregular, the formless, the paralogistic," it finds itself compatible with the terms of postmodernity.[10] The kind of rationality presupposed within this realm is not that of formulaic response to validity claims. Rather, it is dependent on cultural perceptions of what constitutes appropriate standards within given communities of discourse. The sense of reasoned discourse implied is not restricted to "argumentative reason" per se; rather, it is broadened to encompass the full flavor of rhetorical expression whether verbal, visual, or both. Where the emphasis in a Habermasian model is on formal validity claims, the emphasis within a postmodern conception of rationality is on justified discourse which "encompasses both beliefs and values, is truth-seeking rather than truth-certifying, is nonfoundationalist . . . is contextually based, [and] is assessed by recourse to the coherency of belief sets"[11] As Calvin O. Schrag has observed," rationality need not be imported from the outside," thereby leaving the field open for the articulation of a rhetorical rationality that comes from within the field of expression itself.[12]

This pragmatically grounded sense of justification operates across domains in what Schrag terms "transversal rationality":

> Reason remains transversal to the various forms of our personal and social forms of life. It lies across them diagonally; it is neither vertically transcendent to them nor horizontally immanent within them. It operates "between" them in such a manner that it is able to critique, articulate, and disclose them without achieving a coincidence with any particular form of discourse, thought or action. The integrity of otherness—other forms of thought and other social practices—is maintained, accomplishing at once a better understanding of that which is one's own and a recognition of the need to make accommodations and adjustments in the response to the presence of that which is other. Within such a scheme of things, the dynamics of transversal rationality falls out as a convergence without coincidence, an interplay without synthesis, an appropriation without totalization, and a unification that allows for difference.[13]

Seen in terms of transversality, what I have termed "pragmatic justification" is compatible with the task of reasoned rhetoric in postmodernity: Transversal rationality is to postmodern discourse what logocentric rationality is to modern discourse. It allows for the abandonment of the universality of pure logos in favor of refiguring "the logos as a praxial performance of critique, articulation, and disclosure."[14] It allows, further, for the recognition of alternative voices without privileging any one voice as particularly "rational." Hence, within the public sphere, as it is reconstituted in the discussion that follows, reason is no longer bound to argument; the "full play of signification," in Derrida's sense, is allowed to work its will.[15]

Temporality

Although the modernist perspective accords "time" a relatively simple formulation, as in the "right time" for discourse, temporality is a complex, multifaceted concept in relation to the structure of discourse. Time can be discussed in terms of its linear or cyclical directionality, its relatively shallow or deep dependence on a sense of history or the past, as well as its ephemeral or eternal nature. For the purposes of this discussion, the central issue is the conception of time that is salient for the public sphere. Applying Schrag's use of transversal reason to time is not without merit—as one can conceive of time not as outside discourse, but as an inseparable component of discourse. In this latter context, time is constructed through discourse, rather than being conceived as independent of it. The kind of time, whether linear, cyclical, shallow or deep, ephemeral or eternal is likewise not seen as one or the other, but as a "both/and" as one moves across the dimensions to construct that use of time most appropriate for the situation at hand.

Another way to conceive of time, especially in the context of "the right time" is to think of it as fitting into a rhythm. [16] Events are not simply born in the moment, but have a prehistory, a context which assists in bringing them to fruition. They also are implicated in the power relations that are a part of that prehistory. Understanding time in a rhythmical sense is to understand the flow of events—to be "in sync" with the context. This is not to imply that one must only say that which is already complicit with the context, but that one must recognize the rhythm if one is to counter its force, or alter the beat. As I've suggested elsewhere, a rhythmic sense of time also implies a "willingness to experiment, to improvise on the moment in fashioning one's discourse."[17] A transversal conception of time's varying senses permits one to challenge the sense of time salient in any given moment, especially the hegemony of a privileged linearity oriented toward the telos of inevitable progress. Although progress may occur over time, the manner of arriving at an "elsewhere" may involve cycling back on oneself, or altering the rhythm of time through the alteration of power relations, or loosening the dependence on one's past to free oneself for other opportunities (which may not turn out as "progress" though they are changes).

Space

The third characteristic of the public sphere concerns its sense of space. As with the conception of temporality, spatiality has been undertheorized; it is far more complex than simply having a place in which to talk or take action. As I've suggested in another context, space, like time, is conceived within a modernist frame as an "out there," functioning independently from discourse.[18] However, as it relates to the public sphere, to the places which are acknowledged as "open" for discourse, space functions ideologically; it is fully integrated within the power structures that influence agency. Rather than seen in its simplicity, space can be theorized in terms of a tripartite distinction between and among *spatial practices, representations of spaces and spaces of representations.* Each of these implicates discourse in different ways. Two key terms within the dimensions of *spatial practice* are surveillance and state apparatuses. Through these, the social infrastructure that governs what settings one may speak within and the kind of discourse conventionally accepted is created. This is the most "outside" of the senses of space that one might consider, and the one most complicit with modernist assumptions about the relative importance of space to discursive intent.

The second, *representations of spaces*, has as its key term "mapping"—assessing distance in order to place spaces representationally. This process creates boundaries, what for Pierre Bourdieu is a sense of *habitus*, wherein discourse may be demarcated. As an example, Lisa Flores examines how Chicana women construct a "home" space: "Through their celebration of their culture Chicana feminists begin to transform their space into a home. Creating a home is a necessary step in the building of a Chicana feminist community in that the sense of belonging associated with home is often missing from their lives."[19] As another example, consider the phrase "coming out": It defines, in our culture, a movement from hiddeness to openness, from the darkness of a closet to the lightness of a windowed room. However, it does so much more: it connotes an "outsider/insider" duality, for gays or lesbians "by acting straight . . . can be inside but also watch as outsiders."[20] When bell hooks writes of "the margin as a space of resistance," she highlights the sense of distance from the center.[21] Gillian Rose adds to this the sense that one may inhabit both spaces simultaneously; that is, gays or lesbians, in coming out, may do little more than reverse polarity with respect to margin/center in terms of existence. Once invisible while visible, gays who "come out" reproduce their spatiality as visible while invisible. In the context of *representation of spaces*, they are trapped within the duality of existence; they merely trade one spatiality for another. "Outing," of course, forces displacement without permission, but has the same impact with respect to reversing location in space.

In reversing the terminology to *spaces of representation*, the emphasis shifts from where one is in space, to where one might be represented, hence the key term is "imaginary." The Vietnam Memorial exists as a space of representation: Its placement, its manner of construction, and its history merge to influence spatial politics both as a reminder of our past and as a prologue to our future, without delimiting the representation that might be given that space. The new spaces afforded in the electronic world of "virtual reality" are invitations to the imagination to play in a world of one's own making, where physical rules of spatial geography no longer apply.[22] Hooks gives voice to another, more disturbing sense of spaces of representation: "Feminism in the United States has never emerged from the women who are most victimized by sexist oppression."[23] As the feminist movement began, its white women members articulated a space that was "not" with respect to poor women, women of color, or any other women who were not already interpellated into a spatial politics embracing the nuclear family. Perhaps without intending to do so, the predominantly white-movement discourse in the early years of feminism created a new space for women—a space that excluded women as it embraced them. A decade later, the "spatial politics" and the invidious discourse in which it is expressed takes on a new "covert racism" displacing earlier rhetoric as it delimits the imagination in constructing spaces of representation. As an example in our multicultural society consider code switching, described by a young African-American male:

> My aunts in my family, they all have law degrees . . . and whenever they had [white] people over, I could tell a certain change—snap!—that they would go through . . . the biggest difference was—snap!—she would come up to par, you know, play the part.[24]

As Mark Orbe explains, the switch means that one leaves behind the communication styles of one's community, and adopts "those associated with the dominant European American community."[25] The switch involves more than a simple change in language. It also invokes a spatial politics implicit in the dominant culture: When one is in that "space" (irrespective of geographic location), one adopts the language of the dominant group. As this code switching example illustrates, spaces of representation may move with people, and change the discursive practices within different locales. Furthermore, the example also displays the implicit hierarchy expressed in a spatial politics: even in one's "own" space, change may be necessary as others enter, displacing space in favor of a different order of relationship to one another.

Taken together, these components suggest a far more complex sense of spatiality than that implicated in a purely modernist approach to where one speaks. Temporality and spatiality also impact the potentiality for the next two characteristics to be realized in actual discourse: the composition of the public sphere (thus far, it has assumed an unfortunately narrow monolithic guise in the discussion) and its status with respect to action.

Composition

The fourth characteristic of the public sphere concerns its composition. As noted earlier, several commentators have noted the gendered nature of Jürgen Habermas's conception of the public sphere. Landes's argument is precise: The enlightenment's creation of the public was essentially, not accidentally, gendered. Although that position has been challenged by Bell and Gordon, Landes's argument is clear in suggesting that "at the very least, the post-revolutionary [French] identification of masculine speech with truth, objectivity, and reason has worked to devalue women's contribution to public life to a degree rarely matched in earlier periods."[26] To the extent that other periods of modernity have identified access with the kind of rationality prefigured here, women's roles have been similarly constrained. One could argue that even though women were influential actors during the "salon" period in France, Landes claims they were nonetheless not equal partners with "status as political actors in their own right."[27]

One distinction Habermas makes is relevant to this discussion; he suggests that premodern feudal societies were geared toward "public display"—the king or lord displayed himself in court before others. Thus, there is no true sense of public deliberation or response. However, the sense of display is not always removed from the kinds of public deliberations Habermas favors. For example, when Hillary Clinton visited Orono, Maine, the hockey arena was filled to capacity with "public participants"; the spectacle was complete with large television monitors so that people further removed from the front rows could "see" the speaker and others on the dais. Clinton was present as much for display as for the brief interchange with selected participants in the dialogue on health care.

Habermas has responded to the issue regarding the critical omission of women within the public sphere. Although he is agreeable to the notion that the public sphere was patriarchal, he argues that women and other groups were similarly treated with respect to exclusion and the result of exclusion was "a matter of contingency" with respect to male dominance, even though "its structure and relation to the private sphere has been determined in a gender-specific fashion."[28] Although cognizant of the gendered nature of his initial theorizing, Habermas remains convinced that his original conception contains the flexibility necessary to allow marginalized or excluded groups access to public deliberation:

> Bourgeois publicness . . . is articulated in discourses that provided common ground not only for the labor movement but

> also for the excluded other, that is, the feminist movement. Contact with these movements in turn transformed these discourses and the structures of the public sphere itself from within. From the very beginning, the universalistic discourses of the bourgeois public sphere were based on self-referential premises; they did not remain unaffected by a criticism from within.[29]

His formulation assumes that those in the private realm have access to the public realm. Fraser argues, for example, that the Anita Hill *versus* Clarence Thomas hearings revolved around central questions of "who had the power to successfully and authoritatively define" what was public and private, and "who had the power to police and defend that boundary" once established.[30] If women were already in a public position to define and defend the lines between what constitutes public and private spheres, there would be little need for a "feminist project to overcome the gender hierarchy" that exists.[31] If that were not enough to disqualify the Habermas's optimistic vision of access, it also presumes that the rationality imposed on the sphere is equally shared by its participants. As noted earlier, granting the public sphere a sense of gendered rationality does little to assure access.

Status

The final characteristic concerns the existence of the sphere—either as a singular entity or as present at all. In its initial formulation, the "bourgeois public sphere" operated as a singular entity in matters of social and political concern. It was the successor of a "representative publicity" that was "before" the people, rather than, as in the case of the bourgeois public sphere, "for the people."[32] In a recent essay, Habermas has acknowledged the existence of multiple spheres—a move that commentators and critics had already taken.[33] However, his acknowledgment is conditioned by a clear preference for his initial formulation as the "dominant" sphere—that there may be "competing public spheres" does not, in his view, invalidate the centrality of a "political public sphere" that is "appropriate as the *quintessential concept* denoting all those conditions of communication under which there can come into being a discursive formation of opinion and will on the part of a public composed of citizens of the state."[34] That there is a "procedural rationality" tied to this conception, as the regulative ideal of rationality in such a sphere, is equally clear. In a more recent reconceptualization of the public sphere, Hauser argues for a public sphere that contains within it "multiple discursive arenas" which, taken together, "give the overall Public Sphere a *reticulate* structure."[35] The sense of an ordered structure with boundaries juxtaposed against one another is evident in the choice of "reticulate" as the primary term. Although Hauser suggests that these "boundaries have variable permeability," the sense that the public sphere and its "inhabitants" remains firmly ensconced within a modernist frame is unmistakable.

Others have raised the question as to the existence of the public sphere. Aronowitz, for example, argues against the traditional notion that education and training for citizenship is a necessary prerequisite for the public sphere. In agreement with Lippman, Aronowitz argues for a professional bureaucracy that takes care of the "phantom public."[36] Herbst provides some empirical evidence that the "public" is not convinced there is a sphere. Based on twenty-one in-depth interviews, she concludes: "Informants in this study seemed to think that the free-flowing open discussion, characteristic of the ideal Habermasian public sphere, does not exist. On the contrary, there was much cynicism about the role of polls, media and corporations in warping and limiting America's public space."[37] If this analysis is correct, we are far worse off than even the most cynical among us might imagine. What is clear is that technocracy, to the extent it controls public discussion, serves as the caretaker of the phantom sphere.

This analysis does not go the heart of the existence issue in the same way that current media theory does. G. Thomas Goodnight's analysis of the media's co-opting of the public voice gives rise, in his view, to a need to "recover the public sphere."[38] James Combs and Dan Nimmo argue that "in the modern world of mass communications propaganda . . . may well have become the dominant form of social communication beyond interpersonal discourse."[39] Habermas raises this as an as yet unanswered question:

> [W]hether, and to what extent, a public sphere dominated by mass media provides a realistic chance for the members of civil society, in their competition with the political and economic invaders' media power, to bring about changes in the spectrum of values, topics, and reasons channeled by external influences, to open it up in an innovative way, and to screen it critically.[40]

His question is answered if one accepts Combs and Nimmo's argument: As presented to a consuming public via mass media, propaganda shapes reality for us rather than our shaping it. To the extent that they are correct, the characteristics of the public as defined by Habermas and Goodnight cease to have importance in affecting everyday life. Issues presumably presented to the public by the administration, for example, are so stylized in and through the media presentation, that an open, unfettered discussion of what we should do about health care, the environment, the elderly, or the homeless, is impossible. The "new propaganda," to use Combs and Nimmo's phrase, *is* the public sphere. If we adopt this view, and the pessimism it contains, we consign ourselves to a defeatist attitude and to "the most outmoded form of Enlightenment thinking" imaginable.[41] Rather than "recover the public sphere" in a form envisioned by either Habermas or Goodnight, or bemoan its irretrievable loss, there is another alternative. We can, instead, seek to use the "new propaganda" to advantage in creating a mediated public sphere.

What is *not* clearly represented in the above is the sense of alternative publics—those not privileged with a seat when the public sphere rings the dinner bell. Hauser's examples of those involved in a "reticulated public sphere" are not of this ilk; rather, they are those discrete publics already recognized and accepted within the mainstream culture, with a place at the table already assured should they wish to attend. However, in terms of relative power, there are numerous "enclaved publics" whose special concerns are not deemed critical by the larger, more powerful interests gathered at the dining table of the public sphere. As Nancy Fraser notes, "smaller, counterhegemonic publics . . . generally lack the power to politicize issues."[42] For these enclaves, controversy is not about matters of prudent reasoning—it can be messy, "in your face" talk. For these enclaves, controversy challenges the public sphere's principles of "reasoned discourse" that limit the ability of the disenfranchised to voice their concerns. For these enclaves, the social space within the public sphere does *not* function as "a switch point for the meeting of heterogeneous contestants associated with a wide range of different discourse publics."[43] In short, the characteristics of the public sphere, as identified above, do not represent a hospitable environment for those whose voices remain at the margins.

There is a feature that has been ignored in the consideration of the public sphere's status. Thus far, it has been presumed, by Habermas and others, that the public sphere is an open space in which people act when not operating in their private spheres. What should be stressed is this: The public sphere is a *rhetorical construct* whose existence ebbs and flows with the rhetorical traditions that constitute its presence, or decree its configuration or composition. This is why the feminist articulation of the private/public interplay is critical: Who has the authority to delineate the parameters, and once delineated, who is allowed to enter the sphere? Making these decisions is *not* something that just happens; Habermas articulates to the contrary, the public sphere is not as flexible or amenable to critique that changes its fundamental nature. Rather, it will take a reconceptualization of reason—a sense of reason that is transversal in its operation, and that incorporates the full play of rhetorical proofs and is neutralized with respect to hierarchies of gender, race, class, and sexual preference—as the backdrop against which change in the status of the sphere will occur. So long as "thinking like a straight white professional man" is the response to those wishing access to the sphere, participation will be limited.

Furthermore, a distinction needs to be drawn between the "public sphere" as a time/space for interaction, and the "people." As Michael Calvin McGee notes, when we treat the terms as isomorphic, we lose a focus on the relation between "people" and "power."[44] Reference to the public, in contrast, focuses on the where and when of rhetorical interchange, whereas "people/power" focuses attention on who has the authority to speak in what circumstances. Habermas's focus is *not* on the discovery of power relations, but on the "reconstruction" of the public sphere in which interaction takes place. He assumes a rational process that preexists the instantiation of the public sphere as that place in which democratic argument (with a gendered rationality at its core) takes place. In contrast, the only sense in which the "public sphere" is constituted is in and through an appeal to the people. An analysis of power relations is the only recourse if one is to first understand and then to intervene in the processes whereby a democratically oriented sphere is "opened" to full participation. This requires, without necessarily endorsing a Derridian approach, a "deconstructive" attitude toward relations of power within society. In essence, deconstruction must precede reconstruction.

CONCLUSION

The modern public sphere, in short, is characterized by a preoccupation with prudent reason, ontological time, decisively controlled space, gendered composition and mediated existence. Is it any wonder that, taken together, these characteristics conspire to repress marginalized voices? A rationality that privileges modernist notions of reason is limited in its applicability within the domain of practical discourse. As Lemert advises, "to remain within an essentializing, totalizing vocabulary is to enjoy the passing methodological satisfaction of conceptual leverage at the tremendous expense of a diminished access to the only pervasive reality there is—what people, in concrete settings, learn to say, and do say, about their conditions."[45] Controversy requires one to be open to the possibility of change, and to the potential for other voices to join the community and be heard. Given the dictates of what passes for common sense within a community, public actors may be "prudent" while simultaneously being "smiling and personally empty selves."[46]

The remedies suggested in this essay call for reexamination of the characteristics of the public sphere. To place one of the last points first, the public sphere needs to be conceptualized in the context of the rhetoric that creates it in and through appeals to the people. Second, it requires a deconstructive attitude with respect to the conditions of power that enable persons to achieve status within the sphere. Third, a view of reason as encapsulated within transversal rationality must be in place. Fourth, the sense of time must be altered so as to allow for the rhythms of life to play out their "full significance." Fifth, its sense of space must be clearly articulated in the context of power relations—especially when such space is not "free" to those without means. Sixth, the composition of the sphere, especially in relation to the boundaries of the public and private, must be revised through deconstructive analysis of the power relations that are present. As Fraser suggests, this may mean that one sees not one public as dominant, but several, each with an appeal to the people in its own terms, and each being potentially marginalized by other stronger "subaltern" publics. In the absence of these modifications in the conceptualization of the public sphere, continuing to valorize the public sphere as the site of rational decision making will perpetuate the repression of marginalized voices.

NOTES

1. Dilip Gaonker, "Performing with Fragments: Reflections on Critical Rhetoric," in *Argument and the Postmodern Challenge*, ed. Raymie. E. McKerrow (Annandale, VA: SCA, 1993), 150.

2. Joe Wenzel, "Cultivating Practical Reason: Argumentation Theory in Postmodernity," in *Argument and the Postmodern Challenge*, ed. Raymie. E. McKerrow (Annandale, VA: SCA, 1993), 1–7.

3. Joan B. Landes, *Women and the Public Sphere in the Age of the French Revolution* (Ithaca, NY: Cornell University Press, 1988).

4. Raymie McKerrow, "Corporeality and Cultural Rhetoric: A Site for Rhetoric's Future," *Southern Communication Journal*, vol. 63 (1998): 315–328.

5. Gaonker, "Performing with Fragments," 150.

6. Jürgen Habermas, "Further Reflections on the Public Sphere," trans. T. Burger in *Habermas and the Public Sphere*, ed. Craig Calhoun (Cambridge: MIT Press, 1992), 447.

7. G. Thomas Goodnight, "Generational Argument," in *Argumentation: Across the Lines of Discipline*, eds. Frans H. van Eemeren, Rob. Grootendorst, J.

Anthony Blair, and C. Willard (Dordrecht, Holland: Foris, 1987), 129–144 and G. Thomas Goodnight, "The Rhetorical Tradition, Modern Communication, and the Grounds of Justified Assent." in *Argumentation Theory and the Rhetoric of Assent*, eds. Michael David Hazen and David C. Williams (Tuscaloosa: University of Alabama Press, 1990), 173–195.

8. Goodnight, "Generational Argumentation," 133, 139.

9. Rodolphe Gasche, "Postmodernism and Rationality," *Journal of Philosophy*, vol. 85 (1988): 528–538.

10. Ibid., 60.

11. Raymie McKerrow, "The Centrality of Justification: Principles of Warranted Assertability," in Hazen and Williams, 31–32.

12. Calvin O. Schrag, "Communicative Rhetoric and the Claims of Reason," the Van Zelst Lecture in Communication (Evanston, IL: Northwestern University School of Speech, 1989): 9.

13. Calvin O. Schrag, *The Resources of Rationality* (Bloomington: Indiana University, 1992), 158–159.

14. Calvin O. Schrag, "Transversal Rationality," in *The Question of Hermeneutics,* ed. Timothy. J. Stapleton, (Netherlands: Kluwer, 1994): 61–78, 75.

15. Schrag, *The Resources of Rationality*, 120.

16. Elizabeth Deeds Ermarth, *Sequel to History: Postmodernism and the Crisis of Representational Time,* (Princeton: Princeton University Press, 1992).

17. Raymie McKerrow, "Space and Time in the Postmodern Polity," *Western Journal of Communication, vol.* 63 (1999): 271–290, 286.

18. Ibid.

19. Lisa Flores, "Creating Discursive Space through a Rhetoric of Difference: Chicana Feminists Craft a Homeland," *Quarterly Journal of Speech,* vol. 82 (1996): 142–156.

20. Gillian Rose, *Feminism and Geography: The Limits of Geographical Knowledge* (Minneapolis: University of Minnesota Press, 1993), 152.

21. bell hooks, *Feminist Theory: From Margin to Center* (Boston: South End Press, 1984), 145–146.

22. See George P. Landow, "What's a Critic to Do? Critical Theory in the Age of Hypertext," in *Hyper/Text/Theory,* ed. George P. Landow (Baltimore: Johns Hopkins University Press, 1944), 1–48.

23. bell hooks, *Feminist Theory,* 1.

24. Mark P. Orbe, "Remember, It's Always Whites' Ball: Descriptions of African American Male Communication," *Communication Quarterly,* vol. 42 (1994): 287–300.

25. Ibid., 292.

26. Landes, *Women in the Public Sphere*, 203. For the challenge, see David A. Bell, "The 'Public Sphere,' the State, and the World of Laws in Eighteenth-Century France," *French Historical Studies*, vol. 17 (1992): 912–934. Daniel Gordon, "Philosophy, Sociology, and Gender in the Enlightenment Conception of Public Opinion," *French Historical Studies*, vol. 17 (1992): 882–911.

27. Ibid., 206.

28. Habermas, "Reflections on the Public Sphere," 428.

29. Ibid., 429.

30. Nancy Fraser, "Sex, Lies, and the Public Sphere: Some Reflections on the Confirmation of Clarence Thomas," *Critical Inquiry,* vol. 18 (1992): 569, 595–612.

31. Ibid., 610.

32. Jürgen Habermas, "The Public Sphere: An Encyclopedia Article," trans. S. Lennox and F. Lennox, *New German Critique,* vol. 1 (1994): 49–55.

33. Habermas, "Further Reflections on the Public Sphere," 425.

34. Ibid., 446.

35. Jerry Hauser, "Civil Society and the Principle of the Public Sphere," *Philosophy and Rhetoric,* vol. 31 (1998): 19–40.

36. Stanley Aronowitz, "Is a Democracy Possible? The Decline of the Public in American Debate," in *The Phantom Public Sphere*, ed. Bruce Robbins (Minneapolis: University of Minnesota Press, 1992), 75–92.

37. Susan Herbst, "The Meaning of Public Opinion: Citizens' Constructions of Political Reality," *Media, Culture, and Society*, vol. 15 (1993): 437–454.

38. Goodnight, "The Rhetorical Tradition," 184.

39. James E. Combs and Dan Nimmo, *The New Propaganda: The Dictatorship of Palaver in Contemporary Politics* (New York: Longman, 1993), xi–xii.

40. Habermas, "Further Reflections on the Public Sphere," 455.

41. D. Polen, "The Public's Fear; or Media as Monster in Habermas, Negt, and Kluge," in Robbins (Minneapolis: University of Minnesota Press, 1992), 40.

42. Nancy Fraser, *Unruly Practices* (Minneapolis: University of Minnesota Press, 1989), 167.

43. Ibid., 170.

44. Michael Calvin McGee , "Power to the <People>." *Critical Studies in Mass Communication*, vol. 4 (1987): 432–437.

45. C. Lemert, "General Social Theory, Irony, Postmodernism," in *Postmodernism and Social Theory*, eds. Steven Seidman and D. G. Wagner, (Cambridge: Blackwell, 1992), 17–46.

46. G. Thomas Goodnight, "Formative Rhetorics: On the Limits of Common Sense in the Public Sphere," paper presented at the Temple Conference on Discourse Analysis, Philadelphia, PA.

4 Transversing Dualisms and Situating the Embodied Self in Organizational Theory and Practice

MAJIA HOLMER NADESAN

In this chapter I take up the significance of Calvin O. Schrag's view of the embodied self for the study of organizational communication and, more generally, for the study of organizations. Schrag's ontology of the embodied self provides the grounds for critiquing contemporary organizational practices that invoke modernist dualisms that bifurcate the subject from the object and the individual from the community. At first glance, Schrag's approach to critiquing dualistic thinking may appear similar to other postmodern and critical frameworks. However, an important contribution Schrag's work offers is its emphasis on the individual. Critical and postmodern approaches tend to pit the individual against the "system" or "management" and then address individual agency as resistant forms of bricolage and/or by postulating subversive pleasures. In contrast, Schrag wants to resituate the individual as a responsive and responsible self, but in a way that avoids the modernist fallacy of autonomous individualism. Thus, I believe that the primary significance of Schrag's ontology of the embodied self for organizational communication theory and practice is that it allows us to view individuals as agents endowed with the capacity and responsibility to act ethically in their relation to self and others. By centering the act, the decision to act ethically or not, Schrag extends the role of the subject beyond that of bricolager.

Transversing the philosophy of consciousness and the philosophy of decentered subjects is Schrag's temporalized, spatially situated, embodied self. Yet, for some, Schrag's focus on *subjective* agency may raise suspicion. However, to say that Schrag insists on the importance of the self is not to slide into the modernist aporias surrounding the philosophy of consciousness. Instead, Schrag navigates a careful path between approaches that erase subjectivity and approaches that hypostatize it. As I demonstrate in this chapter, Schrag's concerns over both trajectories are not armchair concerns. The former approaches, those that erase subjectivity, are not restricted to philosophical theorizing but are also invoked in everyday organizational practices. Likewise, those approaches that hypostatize the subject, through assumptions of autonomous individualism, are also invoked daily in the workplace. All of this is to say that although we academics would like simply to shed the subject-object dualism and be done with it, it has bequeathed a legacy of material conditions that we cannot so readily sunder.

Schrag's construct of the self has profoundly shaped my research on individual agency in the enactment of organizational life. Through seminars with Schrag and through the reading of his texts, I developed a profound appreciation for his efforts to retain a phenomenological subject in an era within which the subject has been declared dead. I have struggled with the forces that constrain, control, produce, and enable agency throughout my work. More recently, I have turned to Schrag's reflections upon subjectivity and ethics, particularly the roles of responsivity and responsibility, in my efforts to address a few of the challenges of contemporary organizational life. Accordingly, in order to illustrate Schrag's relevance for organizational theory and practice, I will draw upon some of the applications I have made in my own research.

THE SUBJECT-OBJECT DUALITY IN ORGANIZATIONAL LIFE

In *Communicative Praxis and the Space of Subjectivity*, Schrag critiques the human and natural sciences for generating an artificial dichotomy between spirit and nature, understanding and explanation:

> Both epistemological and metaphysical constructionism, which define understanding and explanation as alternative species of knowledge and install an ontological cleavage of spirit and nature, disfigure the texture of communicative praxis. The hermeneutical project of making sense together, on the part of the human and natural sciences alike, installing the double requirement of understanding and explanation, occasions not the continuation of an epistemological problematic but rather a displacement of it.[1]

These oppositions—explanation and understanding, mind and body—rest ultimately in the subject-object dichotomy that finds its fullest expression in many forms of modernist thought.

The inability to conceive of the mind and body in conjunction, to view consciousness as incarnate, leads, on the one hand, to an "objectivization of the body on the level of ontological construction" inviting "a reductionism of the motility of the human body to an instance of mechanistically determined particles in motion."[2] On the other hand, it leads to a perception of the self as sovereign and autonomous, "whose self-constitution remains impervious to any and all forces of alterity."[3]

The mind-body dualism's ubiquity is not limited to philosophical discourses. The discourses of objectified body and autonomous, rational mind are invoked and enacted in everyday communications and actions. It is my argument that they are invoked so thoroughly in no other place than the contemporary workplace. In the following section I use Schrag's observations to explore how organizational discourses and practices objectify individuals' bodies while, simultaneously, they presuppose and appeal to a disembodied view of their souls. I argue that organizations' responses to the alienation affected by their practices (typically) tend to reproduce the conditions that produced the alienation in the first place. Organizational practices grounded in dualistic thinking cannot be remedied by human resource or leadership programs that also fragment and bifurcate subject and object, individual and community.

Objectivizing Practices

Historically, organizational practices have aimed at harnessing and disciplining the recalcitrant energy of employees. At issue were the physics of employees' effort, force, and bodily mechanics.[4] Frederick Taylor's scientific management and Henry Ford's assembly line illustrate systems of production based on the mechanistic disciplining of and control over the human body. In the contemporary scene, computer surveillance systems that monitor employee keystrokes and/or regimented phone protocol illustrate current applications of this preoccupation with the production of, and governance over, compliant bodies. This process of reducing employees to the energy and mechanics of their bodily productions presupposes an ontology of personhood that Schrag describes as an *idem*-identity.

An *idem*-identity appeals to "objective criteria of identification" and finds "its touchstone in the oneness of numerical identity," thereby securing the "concept of permanence in time, or more precisely, permanence *outside* of time. . . ."[5] Practices and theories informed by an *idem*-identity view individuals as immutable beings, object-like, and subject to objective criteria of identification. In my own research, I have explored how the knowledge and practices of organizational personality testing function to represent individuals using this ontology of personhood.

My research on organizational personality testing was triggered by a phone call from a friend whose job candidacy was rejected based on his personality "profile."[6] His expressed fear that he would be forever barred from meaningful employment based upon the tests' capacity to reveal some inferior, latent, fixed "inner" core triggered memories of Schrag's seminars on existential phenomenology. Accordingly, that moment of fusion of past and present led to an essay within which I implicitly explored the phenomenological relationship between subject and object in this organizational practice for *knowing* employees.

Personality testing is commonly used by American corporations as a hiring and promotion tool.[7] Among the estimated 5,000 to 6,000 corporations that use personality testing are Beatrice Foods, Amstar Corporation, Minolta, Target, Apple, AT&T, Citicorp, Exxon, 3M, Allied-Signal, and Honeywell. For these corporations, personality testing serves as an "objective" representational technique that purports to render the essence—i.e., attitudes, values, motivations—of present and future employees transparent and, most importantly, *calculable*.[8] Many tests are generated and analyzed by specialized computer programs, thereby centralizing, simplifying, and rationalizing selection and promotion processes. From a managerial perspective, personality exams transform information into data by quantifying and formalizing knowledge about the heterogeneous, temporally unstable characteristics of the workforce. Although employee data may not, in fact, render employees more malleable, American management appears convinced about the superiority of this manner of knowing employees.

What strikes me as most significant about personality testing is that it presupposes that individuals possess a fixed inner nature that can be scientifically revealed using primarily quantitative measures. The testing therefore reduces individuals to an *idem*-identity; it reduces them to an invariant essence thought to remain permanent across time.

My first exposure to the idea of an *idem*-identity came in a seminar with Schrag on existential phenomenology. In explaining the foundations of the subject-object dualism, Schrag introduced us to Jean-Paul Sartre's dialectical formulation of being-in-itself and being-for-itself. Ex-istence, Schrag explained, is not defined by a fixed facticity—*being-in-itself*—but rather is produced through the process of its transcendence—*being-for-itself*.[9] However, unlike Sartre, whose tendency to intellectualize transcendence led to unresolved dialectical tensions, Schrag's explanations and illustrations emphasized the subject's grounded, embodied situation. Although acknowledging Sartre's limitations, it is clear to me that Schrag valued his efforts to theorize a subject, who although situated, always/already struggled to exert meaningful agency (not merely resistance). Schrag's admiration for Sartre's struggle to mediate subject and object, transcendence and situation, triggered my own interest in this classical conundrum.

Years later, as I listened to my friend recount his fears, I realized that this conundrum had *material* significance in everyday organizational practices because it is foundational to much organizational theorizing and managerial practice. However, unlike philosophical thought that struggles to mediate the poles of the dualism—subject and object—organizational practices tend to sublate subject to object. In the case of personality testing, the emergent, transcendent aspects of the subject's *being* are reduced to fixed, variable measurements, represented as essential hidden truths that can be revealed only through the technical knowledge of scientifically formulated instruments. In other words, personality testing invokes what Schrag refers to an *idem* articulation of identity that appeals to "objective criteria of identification" and finds "its touchstone in the oneness of numerical identity," thereby securing the "concept of permanence in time, or more precisely, permanence *outside* of time. . . ."[10] According to Schrag, this tendency to sublate or marginalize agency and transcendence is often an outcome of the ascendancy of a particular form of knowledge, *techne*.

In *Communicative Praxis and the Space of Subjectivity*, Schrag takes up Aristotle's tripartite system of practical action, theory, and instrumental activity:

> *Praxis*—"practice," "action," "performance"
> *Theoria*—"knowledge for its own sake,"
> *Poiesis*—"artifactual production," an activity that "produces an object that lies beyond the dynamics of the activity itself."[11]

Praxis has "practical wisdom" or *phronesis* as its form of knowledge, *theoria* has *episteme* as its form of knowledge, and *poiesis* has *techne* as its form of knowledge. *Techne* entails both "calculation" of results and the "mapping of means" to attain an end.

Schrag notes that although *techne* is an indisputably critical form of knowledge orientation, its application has a disturbing tendency to intrude upon the other forms of knowledge. For example, most management research focuses exclusively on improving organizational profitability. As a consequence, almost all organizational phenomena studied—e.g., leadership, culture, climate, ethics, corporate philanthropy—are reduced to independent variables posited in relation to the ultimate dependent variable—profit. Now, although this formulation makes sense (pun intended), its exclusive, almost religious pursuit blinds us to other issues and phenomena that are relevant to employees' work experiences and to community relations. The reduction of all (or most) organizational research to instrumental thought constitutes colonization by *techne*. Life cannot be divided into separate spheres whose logic is dictated exclusively by a particular interest. Yet, organizational theory attempts this division and, further, organizational theory and practice also attempt to colonize all conduct, all praxis, by reducing them to calculuses of quantification. This colonization of praxis is illustrated in a story shared by a student in one of my classes. She recounted how her manager required that all of his subordinates remove candy from their desktops after he conducted time and motion studies of how much time was "lost" due to its consumption. It seemed that the candy facilitated employee dialogue. When organizational theory or practice attempts to engineer every motion, every experience of employees in the pursuit of maximized profit, then we see an intrusion of techne into praxis.

My research on personality testing illustrates how *techne* has colonized both *episteme (theoria)* and *phronesis (praxis)* in organizational knowledge about employees.[12] Increasingly, personality testing serves as the dominant managerial way of accumulating centralized, formalized knowledge about employees. This knowledge is believed to be an important tool that can improve productivity and reduce absenteeism and employee turnover. Yet, the ironic fact is that even the literature on personality testing acknowledges that measurements on personality variables have not been "proven" to predict any measure of organizational success. Although lacking predictive validity, I believe that the reason personality testing and other such instrumental orientations remain popular is because they represent the form of technicism described by Schrag as serving a cybernetic program of social engineering. The quest in the organizational literature is, therefore, to better calibrate the measures rather than to question them because they fit within the language and objectives (i.e., the discourse) of social engineering. In effect, personality testing represents in organizational theory and practice an instance where the interests of *poiesis* have colonized those of both *praxis* and *theoria*.

Even while organizational practices and theories objectify employees by reducing them to quantifiable measures, other approaches to controlling employee behavior appeal to a disembodied view of their soul. In the next section I explore how the subject pole of the subject-object dualism gains ascendancy in recent managerial approaches to organizational spirituality.

SUBJECT–AGENCY

As Schrag explains, efforts to avoid an objectifying view of being often result in a disembodied view of agency, a subject freed from all constraints, from facticity and responsibility. In seminar with Schrag we explored the phenomenological tendency to hypostatize this subject in the pursuit of understanding *experience* and transcendence. Although speculations regarding the foundations and forms of experience and the manner for their transformation might appear inconsequential initially, they are in fact profoundly political. Accordingly, I illustrate how corporate efforts to manage employees' experience presuppose a disembodied view of agency by drawing upon my research on "corporate soul."[13]

Perusing bookstores in search of interesting books, I was struck by how many management texts herald "corporate soul" as the latest and greatest management technique. Titles range from Alan Briskin's *The Stirring of Soul in the Workplace*[14] to T. E. Behr and Lao-Tzu's, *The Tao of Sales: The Easy Way to Sell in Tough Times*.[15] Further research revealed that corporate soul talk is also widespread in the popular media. *Fortune* magazine asks, "Should your company save your soul?"[16] while Chris Lee and Ron Zemke provide empirical examples of "The Search for Spirit in the Workplace."[17] Although the precise meaning of spirituality varies, nearly all accounts view it as a means for simultaneously boosting corporate productivity and for facilitating individual "self-actualization" through work.[18] Accordingly, spiritual attitudes and values are represented as transforming a "mundane task into an artistic mediation,"[19] promoting the form of "self-knowledge"[20] critical for business success, and directly impacting "job performance,"[21] or the "bottom line."[22] As Eric Klein and John Izzo put it, "Corporate Soul is the expression of this primary life-giving energy in work and the workplace. When Corporate Soul is awake, work flourishes, overflows, and manifests as productivity, creativity, innovation, and inspiration."[23] Failure on the part of the individual to express their "deeper more authentic self" is often cited as responsible for depressed corporate soul and, concomitantly, low corporate productivity.[24]

Throughout literature and therapeutic techniques for promoting corporate soul is primarily individualistic orientation and tendency to emphasize personal meditation, authentic self-expression, and karmic accountability. For example, the literature advocates genuine expression of the inner core self:

> Each of us has a core from which our most valuable thoughts and feelings originate. When we're in touch with that center and use it to guide our behavior, we act as genuinely as we can. Unfortunately, most of us take precious little time to reconnect with this dimension of our life, especially at work.[25]

In addition to meditation, proposed strategies for fostering corporate soul include "self-hypnosis, induced altered states of consciousness, and guided visualization" with the intent to change or control thought processes.[26] Corporate soul is proffered as a "solution" to worker stress because it urges employees to shed their "victim mindset" by focusing on the "now" and by acknowledging personal mastery and karmic (i.e., destined) responsibility.[27]

In my essay I argued that corporate efforts to shape individual experience by promoting New Age corporate spiritualism are questionable because they implicate a view of individuals as individualized, autonomous agents who are solely responsible for and empowered to shape their destinies. The discourse's emphases on *individual* experience and transcendence through therapeutic self-reflection are ultimately solipsistic in orientation. Corporate efforts to motivate employees through New Age techniques typically erase employees' material situation and their *communal* responsibilities. For example, New Age corporate spiritualism rarely promotes strategies for fostering community, either within the corporation or between the corporation and its environs.[28] Instead the emphasis is on individual self-actualization. Moreover, the discourse rarely acknowledges that employees have (family) responsibilities outside the sphere of work. Instead, individual employees are exhorted to *self*-actualize exclusively through their work. In demanding that individuals focus on the now while engaged in work, the discourse of New Age corporate spiritualism elides the fact that some work is tedious and physically onerous. In representing individuals as autonomous agents whose work reflects their *karmic* destiny, the discourse depoliticizes the many social and economic factors that limit employment opportunities. In effect, the discourse represents individuals as agents lacking corporeality and commitments whose primary destiny is to actualize exclusively through work (provided magnanimously by the corporation). Accordingly, in response to employee demands for a reduction in the ever-increasing work expectations (e.g., ever expanding hours, tasks, and skill requirements), the discourse of corporate spiritualism promotes a change of attitudes regarding the meaning of work. Rather than addressing the erosion of community and family time, the discourse offers the corporation as a stand-in for community and family. In sum, New Age corporate spiritualism's odd blend of karmic destiny and individual empowerment implicates individuals as solely responsible for their successes and/or failures in the new, increasingly Darwinistic, economic environment.

New Age corporate spiritualism constitutes another instance where *techne* has colonized other forms of knowledge and practice. The process of reducing spiritual thought to a means for motivating employees constitutes a reduction of knowledge to a calculus of quantification guided by the objectified result of increased productivity. Further, the reduction of spiritualism to a feedback control mechanism that serves a program of corporate engineering constitutes the "intrusion of technicism" into the domain of *praxis.*

The point of this critique of corporate spirituality is to demonstrate that organizational practices that sever individuals from their facticity—their embodied situation and their community—by focusing exclusively on their *psyches* are as detrimental as those practices that objectify individuals by reducing their identity to fixed, atomistic attributes or behaviors.[29] The mind-body dualism is ubiquitous in organizational theory and practice because its reductionism simplifies the difficult process of modeling and attempting to control the complexity of organizational life. Yet, the irony is that these approaches often generate cynicism, alienation, and resistance on the part of employees. By attempting to artificially fragment realms of experience that are integrally entwined, dualistic organizational practices/discourses are transparent in their means and ends. Most individuals will not succumb readily to a system of cybernetic control that is both visible and self (i.e., organizational) serving. But while focusing on *organizational* practices, I do not want to imply that individual employees are always virtuous or altruistic in their conduct. One area that critical organizational theorists typically overlook is that of individual responsibility. In focusing on systems of control we tend to deemphasize the importance of *individual* accountability and responsibility. Thus, in the final section of this chapter, I explore how Schrag's efforts to transverse the unwieldy dialectic of subject and object yield a view of agency that is temporally and spatially embedded, yet exerts agency and moral choice.

Reconciling Dualisms: Body and Mind and Individual and Community

Many postmodern thinkers have successfully rethought the subject in ways that avoid dualistic thinking. For example, Michel Foucault, Gilles Deleuze,[30] and Ernesto Laclau and Chantal Mouffe[31] are thinkers whose works exemplify creative and fertile approaches to the problem of subjectivity in social and philosophical theory. Although these thinkers have significantly influenced my work and that of many critical organizational scholars, I would like to address a very important contribution Schrag makes that is not present in other "postmodern" approaches, or that tends to be deemphasized. After developing my account of his contribution, I will draw out how his view of the embodied process of "hermeneutical self-implicature" might inform organizational theory and practices.

In attempting to avoid the aporias of a centered subject, thinkers such as Foucault and Deleuze reject a unified self and they eschew the language of personal experience. Consequently, rather than exploring more traditional existential concerns such as self-constitution and self-understanding, many postmodern thinkers address "competing discourses," "resistance," and "bricolage." Experience, personal ethics and self-development, responsibility, and community are therefore rarely discussed because the vocabulary of much postmodern thought simply does not allow it. In effect, issues surrounding selfhood are primarily left to Lacanians, who tend to emphasize identity rather than selfhood and experience, and feminist/cultural studies scholars who primarily address these phenomena from the localized vantage point of gender, race, or class. Although these approaches are insightful and productive, what is typically lost is a more generic discussion of the self, its implicature in facticity, language, and community, its quest for self-understanding, and its moral responsibilities. Some readers might argue that my choice of the word "generic" is in itself problematic because it implies transcendentalism. Transcendentalism has a bad name these days but surely we must have some kind of quasi-transcendentalist framework if we require that our formulation of the self be always/already indebted and obligated in relation to its environmental others. Schrag's "quasi"-transcendentalism avoids the pitfalls of essentialist constructions of facticity and consciousness while it *transverses* the equally problematic poles of existential relativism and moralistic dogmatism. I wish to stress that I am in *no* way implying that postmodern, Lacanian, feminist, or cultural studies approaches suffer from either existential relativism or moralistic dogmatism. Rather, my point is that the localized nature of much of the current work on selfhood and experience tends to impinge against development of a more generalizable framework for exploring personal ethics and responsibility. It is my belief that such a generalizable framework is needed because the effects of localized practice always/already ripple outward, affecting the lives of countless *others*. Accordingly, I will sketch Schrag's formulation of the situated self, the *who* of which is implicated through decision and action, before developing organizational applications.

Schrag takes subjectivity as a starting point but his subject is not *centered* in the metaphysical, modernist sense. His experiential, corporeal subject is always/already situated in time, space, language, community, and has the capacity for "transcendence."

Schrag's phenomenological subject lives in an ever-emergent present that fuses the horizons of past and future. Wise to the problems that bedeviled Edmund Husserl and George Herbert Mead's formulations of this living present, Schrag existentializes the concept through his articulation of the subject's emergence through temporal-spatial action and communication. For example, In *Communicative Praxis and the Space of Subjectivity* Schrag describes the subject as *process*, as an "event of temporalization" *achieved* within a fusion of past, present, and future.[32] Rejecting transcendental consciousness and a transparent representation of time, Schrag's past is not represented—i.e., it is not representational—and his subject is not unified or one-dimensional, and the locus from which it operates is "shifting" because of its continual emergence.

This very Heideggerian formulation of the subject's temporality is complemented with insights about the subject's motility and spatiality derived from Maurice Merleau-Ponty: "The presence of the subject is a *bodily* presence. This immediately shifts the emphasis away from a preoccupation with an elusive seat of unification and mental contents and a fugitive epistemological point."[33] Schrag's use of spatiality is not geometrical or concerned with a "locality of position."[34] Rather, Schrag argues that "bodily presence is an event rather than a position."[35] In developing this account, he adopts Merleau-Ponty's "spatiality of situation"—a spatiality of bodily gestures and motilities that is expressive of the subject's immediate experiences and intentionality as well as his or her cultural embeddedness. Schrag's appropriation and elaboration of Merleau-Ponty's work enables him to avoid over-intellectualizing the subject while, simultaneously, it enables him to address the subject's corporeality and expressivity without lapsing into the problems of behaviorism.

For Schrag, the subject's temporality and spatiality are expressed/performed through his/her action and communication, though *praxis*. Through the initiation of action, the subject, the *who* as Schrag puts it, is called into being. The who is implicated by the experience of making a "decision," a decision to act and/or communicate.[36] Each act is always a response to a prior action, thus the who implicated through the decision, through the act, is

> neither a sovereign and autonomous self, whose self-constitution remains impervious to any and all forces of alterity, nor a self caught within the constraints of heteronomy, determined by

> forces acting upon it. The self as the who of action lives *between* autonomy and heteronomy, active and reactive force, pure activity and pure passivity.[37]

Each decision/action/communication implicates the past and the future. The past encompasses the subject's own personal past but also his or her community and culture.

Schrag refers to this rich understanding of temporality as "narrative temporality."[38] Schrag uses the idea of narrative to capture not only the speech acts and language games that make up discourse, but also the stories that provide the horizons of interpretation within which speech and language acquire *sense*. Narrative is always imprinted by the past and anticipates the future. It is temporal in its form and in its sedimentations but it is always/already subject to transformation through its iterations. Through narrative, the subject is fundamentally situated within his/her community.

For Schrag, community means more than customs or norms because it encompasses cultural narratives and "integrating purpose."[39] Consequently, community is a process, an ongoing achievement, rather than a fixed state. It requires a particular manner of being with others. Although Schrag discusses many ways of being with others, I focus on his conception of an "ethics of a fitting response."[40] At an ontological level, Schrag argues that the relation between oneself and an other is not one in which the other is for-me; rather, the other constitutes an exteriority that stakes a claim on my own subjectivity. In this sense, Schrag follows Emmanuel Levinas in positing a fundamental alterity that infuses self-other relations. Thus, although community encompasses the narratives that unite individuals historically and culturally, it is not totalizing because it is, in part, constituted out of relations of alterity, exteriority. Accordingly, Schrag's formulation of the (communal) integrating purpose cannot be considered to be a dialectical one whose purpose is to sublate difference. Difference, as constitutive of the other, poses an ontological claim on me, for me. The fitting response to this claim requires responsivity and responsibility, the latter of which Schrag defines in relation to the call of conscience, which always directs one to the "voice and face of the other."[41] Schrag does not catalog the characteristics of a fitting response because that would deny the situated nature each claim. Individuals, the *whos* implicated through their praxes, are not ethical because they are characterized by certain virtues but because they heed *others* through their communicative and practical decisions.

It seems to me that Schrag's articulation of the relationship between the self, others, and community has vital significance for organizational theory and practice. On the one hand, his account of the self as temporally and spatially embedded provides an approach that transverses the theoretical and material pitfalls of dualistic organizational thinking and practices. On the other hand, his view of the self's implicature through its decision and the moral/ethical/transcendental implications of that decision provide a framework for addressing organizational ethics and individual responsibility.

As organizational communication scholars and practitioners, we must address the self's temporal, spatial, and communal embeddedness. Let me provide some brief illustrations of how researchers and practitioners might address these dimensions of experience. First, few organizational scholars have explored how individuals' temporal positioning in terms of chronological age impacts their organizational experiences. And yet, the media frequently provides examples of how age bias has become more prevalent, as illustrated by *Fortune*'s article, "Finished at 40."[42] Chronological age (and its phenomenological experiences) is constructed within organizational narratives as an important identity marker and yet we as academics have largely ignored it. Another temporal issue that could be addressed by scholars concerns the temporal and spatial dislocation that many employees experience as they are forced to manage multiple jobs simultaneously in order to make ends meet and/or because of conflicts between family and work commitments. By exploring these pressing temporal issues from an *experiential* or phenomenological lens, we as researchers "legitimize" employees' experiences as salient organizational communication issues and we may help promote dialogue (and even solutions) by providing rich, thick descriptions.

Spatiality and corporeality, as constitutive dimensions of organizational life, require further investigation. Although there are endless ways of approaching these phenomena, I would begin with the question of embodiment. How do job requirements, tasks, and expectations in the new computer-mediated workplace constrain and enable individuals' bodily involvement in their work and, concomitantly, how do individuals experience/interpret their bodily involvements? How do they conform, resist, or actively transform them? An example that highlights the integral role of tacit (i.e., bodily situated) knowledge in the workplace is provided by Cigna's (an HMO) failed attempt to centralize its appointment scheduling services in Phoenix. In an effort to systematize its geographically dispersed and relatively autonomous clinics, Cigna designated one office building as a centralized locale for handling all patient requests for appointments in Phoenix. Patient representatives at the central office were trained to use a new expert computing system that was designed to plan and coordinate all scheduling. Receptionists in the geographically dispersed clinics were required to have patients call this central office to make appointments. Cigna felt that this system would be more rational, efficient, and transparent. It was not. In fact, Cigna soon found its scheduling capacity to be severely compromised. Enamored with complex "solution systems," Cigna had overlooked the ability of each clinic's receptionists to *make time*, actively and creatively, for patients and doctors to connect. Each receptionist's tacit knowledge, their ability to circumvent the restrictions of their clinic's computerized schedules, was vital to operations, yet it could not be replicated by a computerized solution system nor by the centralized, but spatially disconnected (i.e., disconnected from the everyday life of the clinics) service representatives. After patients complained in droves about hour-long waits for scheduling appointments that were unavailable for months, Cigna reverted to its previous, decentralized system.

In addressing embodiment in the workplace, scholars should also address issues pertaining to the (bodily) management of a "professional" identity. Corporate employees are becoming increasingly diverse in terms of ethnicity, gender, national origin, and age. Simultaneously, corporations are becoming ever more sensitized to the role of image and are increasingly requiring (implicitly and explicitly) that their employees perform carefully engineered bodily and etiquette protocols. In effect, workplace diversity is met with dictates for conformity. What are the experiential effects of this clash? Angela Trethewey's work illustrates an embodied approach to organizational identity that addresses how control operates to discipline "unruly" bodies, that is, bodies that signify *otherness*.[43] She explored how "professional" decorum and dress constrain women in the workplace, causing them to experience bodily alienation and "leakages." Her work looks at the intersections between individual experience and institutional relations, as they are enacted through bodily performances. More research, that addresses other points of view on bodily involvement in the workplace, is called for.

In addressing management, system, and structure, however, we must not overlook the role of *individual* accountability and responsibility, the role of the everyday *who* implicated through praxis. Individuals have an ontological, transcendental responsibility to *exist ethically* in their relations with others in their lifeworld.[44] Too often, critical and postmodern scholars seem, by default, to affirm lower-level employees simply by virtue of their subordinate positioning. At least, I know that my own research has been complicit with this tendency. Yet, employee resistance or bricolage can often have harmful consequences for coworkers, families, or those in their community. Indeed, in a study in which I focused on service-workers, I found that employee resistance was often directed at other low level employees, effectively undermining the kind of solidarity needed for these employees to have greater negotiating power with management.[45] Postmodern and critical celebrations of resistance must be tempered by deeper scrutiny of the *effects* engendered by such resistance.

Schrag's model of a "fitting response" nicely complements critical and postmodern organizational celebrations of resistance by foreground the effects for the *other* engendered by both routine and unorthodox organizational decisions and praxes. In exploring the ethics of a "fitting response," it becomes necessary to expand our horizons for understanding ethics beyond those of community values, norms, rules, and laws. A decision is not ethical in the sense described here merely because it conforms to some normative framework. History has demonstrated most persuasively that normative frameworks can naturalize oppression just as easily as they can protect against it. In exploring the relations of ethics in the call to action that requires some response, Schrag comments

> the criteria that are called upon in decisions induced by the existential doubt in a praxis-rooted either/or are not antecedently defined and legislated in advance of the investigative process. They are the progeny of the discernment and deliberation that accompanies the contrastive comparisons at play in the lifeworld of human interactions. Criteria are as much constituted by the events and process in the lifeworld as they are a judge of them, attesting to a continuing dialectic of constitution and evaluation.[46]

Schrag's point in this passage is that ethical criteria cannot be reduced to codified or readily memorized decisional heuristics. The process of engaging in a fitting response requires an openness to the (future) environmental impacts of decisions, both routine and momentous, and a willingness to reflect actively upon the effects of prior decisions so that the criteria implemented in the present reflect the lessons learned from the past.

Efforts to study decision making in organizational communication have typically focused retroactively on "what went wrong" with decision processes that ultimately resulted in catastrophic situations. Using Schrag's ethics of a "fitting response," the research goal would be to develop models for helping employees/managers learn to expand their decisional criteria to include *effects* for multiple-stakeholders. This process requires that decisional criteria be expanded beyond the interests of *techne* and it requires that employees of all levels be empowered to evaluate decision-processes and be made accountable for their effects.

Stanley Deetz's work is exemplary in its efforts to develop a model and process for organizational decision making that fulfills these objectives.[47] However, the project has only begun and requires considerably more work, the work of communication praxis.

NOTES

I wish to express my deep gratitude to Professor Schrag for awakening in me a love of philosophy and for giving his students the *gift* of his knowledge, support, and charm. He lives his philosophy of *praxis*, of responsivity, and responsibility. I would like to acknowledge the careful editorial assistance Jnan Blau provided me.

1. Calvin O. Schrag, *Communicative Praxis and the Space of Subjectivity* (Bloomington: Indiana University Press, 1989), 75.

2. Calvin O. Schrag, *The Self after Postmodernity*, (New Haven: Yale University Press, 1995), 58.

3. Ibid., 59.

4. Michel Foucault, *Discipline and Punish,* trans. Alan Sheridan (New York: Vintage Books, 1979).

5. Schrag, *The Self after Postmodernity*, 35.

6. Majia Nadesan, "Constructing Paperdolls: The Discourse of Personality Testing," *Communication Theory,* vol. 7 (1997): 189–218.

7. See, for example, Judith H. Dobrzynski, "Want a Job? Take a Test," *Arizona Republic*, vol. 4 Sept. 1996, sec. A1, p. 8; or Daniel P. O'Meara, "Personality Tests Raise Questions of Legality and Effectiveness," *Human Resource Magazine*, vol. 39:1 (1994): 97–100.

8. Nikolas Rose, "Calculable Minds and Manageable Subjects," *History of the Human Sciences*, vol. 1:2 (1988): 179–200; and Nikolas Rose, *Governing the Soul: The Shaping of the Private Self* (London: Routledge, 1990).

9. Jean-Paul Sartre, *Being and Nothingness,* trans. Hazel E. Barnes (New York: Pocket Books, 1956).

10. Schrag, *The Self after Postmodernity*, 35.

11. Schrag, *Communicative Praxis and the Space of Subjectivity*, 18–19.

12. Majia Nadesan, "Constructing Paperdolls: The Discourse of Personality Testing," 189–218.

13. Majia Nadesan, "The Discourses of New Age Corporate Spiritualism and Evangelical Capitalism," *Management Communication Quarterly,* vol. 13 (1999): 3–42.

14. Alan Briskin, *The Stirring of Soul in the Workplace* (San Francisco: Jossey-Bass, 1998).

15. T.E. Behr and Lao-Tzu, *The Tao of Sales: The Easy Way to Sell in Tough Times* (San Francisco: Element, 1997).

16. "Should Your Company Save Your Soul?" *Fortune*, vol. 123:1 (1991): 25–29.

17. Chris Lee and Ron Zemke, "The Search for Spirit in the Workplace," *Training*, vol. 30:6 (1993): 21–28.

18. Christopher Neck and J. F. Milliman, "Thought Self-Leadership: Finding Spiritual Fulfillment in Organizational Life," *Journal of Managerial Psychology*, vol. 9 (1994): 10.

19. Eric Klein and John B. Izzo, *Awakening Corporate Soul: Four Paths to Unleash the Power of People at Work* (New York: Fairwinds Press, 1998), 24.

20. Andy Cohen, "The Guiding Light," *Sales and Marketing Management*, vol. 149:8 (1997): 46.

21. Neck and Milliman, "Thought Self-Leadership: Finding Spiritual Fulfillment in Organizational Life," 10.

22. Tom McDonald, "Getting in the Spirit," *Successful Meetings* vol. 46:6 (1997): 22.

23. Klein and Izzo, *Awakening Corporate Soul: Four Paths to Unleash the Power of People at Work*, 8.

24. Ibid., 46.

25. McDonald, "Getting in the Spirit," 22.

26. C. Mitchell, "New Age Training Programs: In Violation of Religious Discrimination Laws?" *Labor Law Journal*, vol. 41 (1990): 410.

27. Klein and Izzo, *Awakening Corporate Soul*, 31.

28. For exceptions see Philip H. Mirvis, "'Soul Work' in Organizations," *Organization Science*, vol. 8 (1997): 193–206; and the special issue of the *Journal of Organizational Change Management*, vol. 7 (1994).

29. This tendency to free the subject from facticity and responsibility haunts New Age thought, humanistic psychology (e.g., Maslow), as well as existential phenomenology. It is an ironic legacy for thinkers who aimed to promote more reflexive individuals capable of participating more directly in transforming their surroundings and communities. Despite this limitation, I would argue, the quest for self transformation is worthy. It must, however, be pursued cautiously to avoid solipsism, narcissism, or instrumental appropriations.

30. Gilles Deleuze and Claire Parnet, *Dialogues*, trans. Hugh Tomlinson and Barbara Habberjam (London: Athlone Press, 1987); and Gilles Deleuze, *Negotiations 1972–1990*, trans. Martin Joughin (New York: Columbia University Press, 1995).

31. Ernesto Laclau and Chantal Mouffe, *Hegemony and Socialist Strategy*, trans. Winston Moore and Paul Cammack (London: Verso, 1985).

32. Schrag, *Communicative Praxis and the Space of Subjectivity*, 146.

33. Ibid., 152.

34. Ibid., 153.

35. Ibid., 155.

36. Schrag, *The Self after Postmodernity*, 59.

37. Ibid., 59.

38. Ibid., 36.

39. Ibid., 87.

40. Ibid., 92.

41. Ibid., 100.

42. Munk, N. "New Organization Man," *Fortune* 16 Mar. 1998, vol. 137, issue 5, 50.

43. Angela Trethewey, "Disciplined Bodies: Women's Embodied Identities at Work," *Organization Studies,* vol. 20 (1999): 243–250.

44. Schrag, *The Self after Postmodernity*, 102.

45. Majia Holmer-Nadesan, "Organization, Identity and Space of Action," *Organization Studies,* vol. 16 (1996): 49–81.

46. Schrag, *The Self after Postmodernity*, 106–107.

47. Stanley Deetz, *Democracy in an Age of Corporate Colonization* (Albany: State University of New York Press, 1991).

Part III ❧ On Giving and Suffering

5 The Gift of Acknowledgment

MICHAEL J. HYDE

In his most recent book, *The Self after Postmodernity*, Calvin O. Schrag speaks of the genuineness of gift-giving as something that must be taken seriously if humankind is to cultivate a temperament of grace.

> A gift, to be genuinely a gift, is given without any expectation of return. There can be no expectation of a "countergift," for such would place the giving within the context of a contractual rather than a gift-giving relation. Certainly, if there is to be any countergift, a species of "gift exchange" if you will, the same gift that was given cannot be returned without annulling the very conditions of gift-giving, and in the end amounting to a refusal of the gift. . . . Mutatis mutandis, from the side of the gift-reception, the receiver of a gift in accepting the gift needs to be freed from any obligations to reciprocate, for such would transform the gift into an incursion of a debt that requires repayment.[1]

Schrag would thus have us understand that the genuiness of the gift comes from "outside the economy, both economy in the narrower sense of monetary management and in the broader sense of motivating forces and requirements of reciprocity and exchange in the culture-spheres of scientific, artistic, ethico-moral, and religious-institutional endeavors."[2] Human beings are gifted with the capacity to be gift-givers, but the power (*dynamus*) of this capacity, according to Schrag, draws its authenticity from the even greater and related capacities of *caritas* and *agape* and the fundamental expression of "love" that they make possible—"a love that issues from a power to love in spite of rejection, a love that loves for the sake of loving," and hence a love that "is construed as freely given and nonpossessive in nature."[3]

Love is a gift that should be given with no catches and caveats. Schrag draws support for this claim by turning to such religious thinkers as Saint Augustine, Søren Kierkegaard, Paul Tillich, and Emmanuel Levinas. Might it thus be said that the gift of which Schrag speaks is one that is best understood by turning to the Holy Scriptures where it is told how a loving God, who at times could become quite angry, called us into being with a "Word"? The Word at work here was the ultimate *avowal*, coming as it did from One uttering declarative speech ("Let there be light!") whose function was "to bring and show forth" (*epideixis*) at the "appropriate moment" (*kairos*) the truth of what was on One's mind. God is the Great Avower: The One who declares most assuredly, openly, bluntly, and without shame. Such an open declaration or avowal is, of course, also known as a type of "acknowledgment."

By way of a most glorious gift of acknowledgment—love—God created the place wherein all other such gifts could be given by creatures with the capacity to do so. Schrag never explicitly states that he wants us to be godlike when it comes to giving gifts; although he would have us use "the measure of the gift of love" when determining how best to craft a "fitting response" to the exigencies of life. Hence, he tells us that the "fitting response, using the measure of the gift of love, responds by excavating a space for that which *can be done*, concretely expressed in random acts of kindness, in which one exemplifies the virtuous deed of a Good Samaritan, as well as in collaborative projects of selfless charity (such as, for example, the Habitat for Humanity and the Mennonite Relief Agency)."[4] Recalling his reading of Philip Hallie's *Lest Innocent Blood Be Shed: The Story of the Village of Le Chambon and How Goodness Happened There*, Schrag also emphasizes the example of "sacrificial love" that the people of the village performed during World War II as they risked their own lives in order to help hide and thus save thousands of Jews from the Nazi horde. As Schrag puts it: "In this isolated village in Southern France there was a display of a gift that required no reciprocity—not even that of being acknowledged as a gift." Schrag then goes on to note: "The story of Le Chambon, and others like it, stands as a reminder of the need to consult case studies and local narratives to illustrate how the gift can be given and received, and how goodness can happen and justice be done within the economy of our civil societies. What stories of this sort teach is that there are indeed motivations of ethical attitudes and actions that transcend all expectations of return."[5]

In this essay I discuss and analyze a case study whose local narrative tells a story that I believe speaks to the importance of Schrag's remarks and directives on the related matters of the gift, acknowledgment, and love. These are the things that Schrag is famous for as a teacher, scholar, and friend. I say this with twenty-seven years of personal experience behind me. As a graduate student of Schrag, I was continually in a state of needing reassurance about my worth—a state, I would add, that is not uncommon with most, if not all, graduate students—and the professor never disappointed. Being the perceptive and sensitive "hermeneut" that he is, he knew how to read his students like he would a much cherished book: with care and devotion. We students were never left on the shelf but were always opened with gentle hands and studied with wideawake eyes and a loving heart. That was a grand gift to give us: Our presence called out for help: "Where art thou?" Schrag was always there to say "Here I am!" and thus to share with us the life-giving gift of acknowledgment. It is, indeed, an honor, to once again have the opportunity to try to return the favor.[6]

Be aware, however, the case study I present is not as "straightforward" as the examples offered by Schrag. I am interested in the rhetoric of public moral argument and the case in question is part of a major controversy happening in this country today: the debate over the justifiability and social acceptability of euthanasia. This debate is to a large extent about people whose well-being is in jeopardy and who are thus in desperate need of acknowledgment. Whether they want to live in peace or to die in peace, these people call out "Where art thou?" and wait to see who might reply "Here I am!" Although the specific case I relate is not a happy one, I nevertheless hope it will shed further light on both the importance and complexity of our topic—the gift of acknowledgment and the love with which it is *sometimes* shared. I introduce the case with some brief remarks about the existential nature of this gift.[7]

THE NATURE OF THE GIFT

What would life be like if no one acknowledged your existence? This question, of course, confronts one with the possibility of being isolated, marginalized, ignored, and forgotten by others. The unacknowledged find themselves in an "out-of-the-way" place where it is hard for human beings, given their social instinct, to feel at home. The suffering that can accompany this way of being in the world is known to bring about fear, anxiety, tears, anger, and sometimes even death in the form of suicide or retaliation against those who are rightly or wrongly accused of making one's life so lonely, miserable, and unbearable.

Acknowledgment provides an opening out of such a distressful situation, for the act of acknowledging is a communicative behavior that, if only for a moment, grants attention to others and thereby makes room for them in our lives. With this added living space comes the opportunity for a new beginning, a "second chance," whereby one might improve his or her lot in life. There is hope to be found with this transformation of space and time as people of conscience opt to go out-of-their-way to make us feel wanted and needed, to praise our presence and actions, and thus to acknowledge the worthiness of our existence. Offering positive acknowledgment is a moral thing to do. Granted, such acknowledgment may embarrass us, and it might even makes us feel guilty if we know that our presence and actions have something deceitful about them or, at least in our humble opinion, are not really that great. But generally speaking, positive acknowledgment makes us feel good as it recognizes something about our being that is felt by others to be worthy of praise and perhaps even remembrance after we are gone. Indeed, have you ever thought about your own death, your funeral, and who might show up to pay their respects? And when thinking about this last matter, have you ever become upset with those people who you believe should have attended the ceremony but did not? Even when we have passed to the most out-of-the-way place there is, we still crave the goodness of positive acknowledgment—the way it brings us to and keeps us in mind and "alive."

Of course, not all acknowledgment that comes our way is positive. For example, in a certain situation hearing someone say to you "Looking good!" may rightly be understood as a compliment. In a different situation, however, these same words, coming from one who you have never gotten along with, might also be legitimately heard as a sarcasm, a slight, an articulation whose tone of voice speaks ridicule, disrespect, and dislike. Such negative acknowledgment is also at work whenever we call people "stupid" or "worthless," thereby opening and exposing them to the further ridicule of others. Like its opposite, negative acknowledgment creates a place for recognition. But the space provided here, even if it is given with the best of intentions—as when a parent, trying to provide careful guidance, scolds a child for being "naughty"—more often than not makes us feel bad.

Acknowledgment is a significant and powerful form of behavior, one that can bring joy to one's heart and also drive a stake through it. Acknowledgment functions as both a life-giving gift and a life-draining force. Moving from its positive to negative form and then to a state of no acknowledgment at all, we find ourselves in a place that is hard-pressed to support life because it is so barren of the nourishment provided by the caring concern of others. Institutionalized forms of negative acknowledgment such as racism, sexism, and ageism expose people to this fate. Certain rituals of culture, on the other hand, are meant to protect us from it. Proper decorum dictates, for example, that we say "hello" and "goodbye" to people so that they feel noticed; that we make them feel important and respected by holding open a door and saying "after you"; or that we send them a birthday or condolence card so to assure them that, at a moment of great joy or great distress, they are in our thoughts and perhaps our prayers. The presence of people in need of acknowledgment sounds a call of conscience: "Where art thou?" Good manners encourage us to say "Here I am!" Knowing or at least believing that this response truly "comes from the heart," we are likely to feel better than if we know or believe that what we are receiving is mostly some ritualized behavior steeped in the shallows of unthinking behavior rather than in the depths of genuine care.

This last point receives much emphasis in the euthanasia debate. Wanting to live on despite one's illness or disability, and having the sense that those who assist you feel more burdened than anything else, certainly defines a horrendous existential situation. The situation also materializes when a patient who wants to "die with dignity" receives assistance from people (e.g., family members, physicians, nurses) whose obliging compassion is perceived to lack the appropriate amount of sincerity and genuine emotion.[8] In both cases, the patient is situated on a path leading from negative acknowledgment to no acknowledgment at all. What a horrible way to be; what a horrible way to go. Yet, these things happen. The following case study admits as much. As I hope to show, however, the case is still quite educational: its rhetoric works in a "deconstructive" sort of way to evoke a sense of awe for the gift of acknowledgment.

IS THAT ANY WAY TO SAY "HERE I AM!"?

In the March 1996 issue of *Harper's Magazine*, B. J. Nelson writes about his "Mother's Last Request," which he subtitled "A Not So Fond Farewell."[9] With his opening paragraph Nelson gives us a sense of why this subtitle is appropriate:

> Marie wanted to die. She'd been wanting to for most of her life, I think, and wasn't it time? She was asking me. She'd been thinking about how to kill herself for months, years, especially the last few weeks. Now she knew how she would do it and was simply focusing on when. She was eighty and a couple of her teeth had recently fallen out, her stomach was swollen, food made her sick; she was in pain all over, the worst pain she'd ever had, she said, though every pain throughout her whole life was always the worst. Over the years, the hundreds of times she was

> sick, each time she was "deathly sick." Each pain for decades had been "the most horrible pain" she'd ever felt. You never knew. She'd turn the least matter into melodrama, managing her life neurotically, even from the beginning, I've come to believe, by pretending, by living in a world of pretense. (P. 35)

Have you ever known a person like Marie, someone whose very presence is discomforting and whose typical behavior makes this presence all the more irritating if not maddening? Have you ever wondered why people act this way? Have you ever tried to "reason" with such people in an attempt to have them see what is "wrong" with them? Did they finally see their problem and realize that by being more presentable and genuine they perhaps could receive more positive acknowledgment from others? Did you feel good about what you had accomplished? Did you tell the story to friends and acquaintances in an attempt to be the recipient of such acknowledgment? Wouldn't it be a bit depressing to find out that some of the good people who listened to your story were irritated and much annoyed by having to listen to what you had to say about yourself?

Sometimes what goes around comes around. Nelson's story about his mother—who is only referred to as Marie throughout the narrative—is, among other things, a tale that illustrates the oftentimes tragic reality of this existential way of being. Authors like the late Anatole Broyard write about death and dying by putting the best face possible on the entire matter.[10] Nelson's story, however, is dark, sad, tragic, and, according to one reader, "repugnant."[11] When all is said and done we know that Marie is dead and that her son assisted her in committing suicide. The way in which Nelson reveals this state of affairs is evocative from beginning to end. Nearly every line is given over to producing a vivid picture of Marie's horrible life and thus the story lacks any well defined philosophical argument that justifies the author's action. Nelson, it seems, is of the school that believes that an argument, no matter how intellectually rigorous it is, has much less persuasive force than the vivid evocation of an experience, and that such an argument becomes relevant only after this emotional stage of storytelling has been completed.[12]

Marie's son admits that he told her that suicide "had to be up to her, no one else" and that she would ask: "But didn't I think she might as well? What did she have to live for?" (p. 35). Continuing with a description of Marie's existence, Nelson immediately notes:

> She had terrible noise in her ears and couldn't hear, she'd disconnected her phone, no one called anyway, she had no friends.

> She had lived for fifteen years as an almost total recluse, and other than a sister she hated and another son she hadn't heard from in thirty years, there was only me. She couldn't see her soap operas except as a blur, she was shaking, trembly, she got out of breath walking from her room to the front of the house, so before being too helpless, while she could still manage, wasn't it time? (P. 35).

We are being told about a woman who is bothersome, who lives in a world of pretense, who seems quite ill, and who is certainly alone, although there is still Nelson, the son who has to hear Marie ask for a reality check given what she wants to do. When those who are suicidal make such a request they present a classic example of people in need of the life-giving gift of acknowledgment—a gift given by a self answering "the call of conscience" coming from someone whose well-being is rapidly declining. Where art thou? Here I am! We are being told a story about this call, about an other (a mother) who sounds it and a self (a son) who hears it.[13] The son reports what his mother has told him: "You don't know how many times I've prayed I wouldn't wake up. Every night I go to sleep praying, dear God, please, just let me die and not wake up. So I'm going to do it. But I can't by myself. You'll have to help me" (p. 36).

A request for assisted suicide made by a mother to a son—two people who share a "blood bond" that is greater (at least biologically) than any other bond that can form between human beings. The plan was simple. Marie had saved a stash of one hundred Xanax, a sedative. The pills would put her right to sleep, then all Nelson would "have to do was slip a bag over her head and wrap it airtight around her neck with a scarf. No rubber bands. They might leave telltale lines." Nelson explains how Marie had "already tried the bag on to be sure it wasn't too big. She said it wasn't. A large bag would retain too much air and take longer. She'd read that in a book from the Hemlock Society." Marie would call Nelson later that night when she was ready. Another admission is made: ". . . was there anything I needed to consider? Feelings, emotions? No. My feelings for Marie were fairly reconciled. I came into this world out of her body, or the physical me did, . . . but I didn't like her as a person. I was ashamed of her as a mother. I wouldn't miss her" (p. 36).

The scene is as chilling as Nelson is cold-hearted. He feared that "Marie would struggle, even zonked on Xanax, and she would be clawing the thing to get free, to breathe. The Hemlock Society book said that this was common. I could see myself trying to hold her hands down or, frozen, just standing there, watching" (p. 36). The event would take place in a room in Nelson's house, the room were Marie had lived for the past two and a half years. In all of that time she had never left the house. Nelson shopped for her and secured whatever medicine she needed. The two never had a good conversation. Rather, as Nelson details, Marie typically took charge by airing one complaint after an other.

> The arthritis in my hand is so bad, I took four of those pain pills, they didn't help a bit, I don't know what I am going to do. . . . Those ratty kids next door were playing so loud, hollering and carrying on, I couldn't hear myself think. I wish that family'd move away, they're nothing but white trash. I saw the woman out in her yard yesterday wearing shorts, with big ol' fat legs, I'd be ashamed. (P. 37)

Nelson is remembering Marie, a woman who "didn't like herself," probably "hated herself, and the way it showed was depressing" (p. 37). The illness that she had "was probably a consumptive heart condition," although this fact is never clarified by the author beyond his telling us that, according to Marie, her condition, as described in her "medical book," would lead to serious lung, stomach, kidney, and liver problems. Eventually one becomes "bedridden," unable to "go to the bathroom or feed yourself—you couldn't eat anything anyway—and you'd just lie there in agony and finally die" (p. 37). We also learn that Marie knew that she had "messed up" her kids because of her reckless lifestyle. She left her children, married several times, was trying "to have fun" and, at the same time, find a home for her kids, "but it never turned out, she never got what she wanted, which was just to be happy and for us kids to be happy, but she couldn't help any of that now, she couldn't go back" (p. 37).

Nelson has no good memories of Marie. Let us take a moment to consider how tragic this is. Earlier I asked if you had ever given some thought to your own death—how you might die, how it would feel, who would be around at the end, and who would attend the funeral. I also asked if you had ever gone further with your thinking as you pictured those folks who "should" have but did not attend your funeral and thereby warranted your anger. Why would a "rational" person conceive of such a bitter situation? Why not be more optimistic or at least more laid back? Why not leave well enough alone and rest in peace?

Although answers to these questions might lead one to conclude that the person in question is somewhat neurotic, I submit that there is something more positive going on when we think this way: We are creatures who need the acknowledgment of others; and even after death we want to be remembered as someone who was worthwhile and who will be missed. The acknowledgment that comes with fond memories at least keeps our "spirit" alive; it thereby provides a way to satisfy what Ernest Becker terms a human being's "urge to immortality." This urge "is not a simple reflex of the death-anxiety but a reaching out by one's whole being toward life . . . a reaching-out for a plenitude of meaning. . . . It seems that the life force reaches naturally even beyond the earth itself, which is one reason why man has always placed God in the heavens."[14] Indeed, and here is where we can seek help when no one else will acknowledge our existence. It is a wonderful and awesome (symbolic) construction—the perfect place to find One who, at least according to the Bible, is also in need of the acknowledgment that we pray for.[15] What would your life be like if no one acknowledged your existence? Without acknowledgment, even being immortal would not mean much.

At the heart of the case before us lies an existential paradox. Marie asked Nelson for the gift of life of acknowledgment: say "here I am!" and help me to die. This paradox is a staple of the euthanasia debate. It comes about when people whose final chapter of life has become a "living death" and who do not want to be remembered for dying this way. Yet, as indicated above, Marie's request was not always straightforward; it sometimes included a question: Didn't Nelson think that she was right in wanting to die? As he shares his memories with readers, Nelson tells a story of a person who he took in when nobody else would and who he would not miss when she died. Marie's life was becoming ever more a living death for both her and her son. Marie spoke of God; Nelson did not. Marie wanted a second opinion about the worth of suicide and all that Nelson had to go on were horrible memories of a woman who inspired no compassion or love. So when for the last time she said "I can't think about it anymore . . . I want to just go on and do it, is that all right with you?" Nelson would only say, "If you're ready" (p. 39).

Was Marie hoping for more acknowledgment than this? If she was, neither she nor Nelson would admit it. Instead, Nelson goes on to discuss in great detail how he assisted Marie with the pills, the bag, and the scarf. During this discussion Nelson admits that:

> A terrible feeling came over me, a weight of darkness. Here was this old, lonely woman actually going to die, killing herself. This was the last moment she would ever know, a worthless, measly last moment in a dismal, cluttered room in central Texas. She would never again see the two squirrels in the tree outside her window. Or the sky, the sun, the rain. This earth, this great beautiful earth around her would be no more. She was going to die and nothing would be all. I had no words for what I felt, except pity. Poor old woman. (P. 39)

Nelson hugged Marie and she patted his arm. He told her he loved her. "I love you, too," she said. The words were "perfunctory." There was "no clutch of emotion." The pills began to take effect. The bag and scarf were at hand. "Poor Marie, I thought, your whole life so damned unhappy. I felt sorry for her. I snugged at the scarf to be sure it was trapping the air." After approximately two-thirds of his story is completed, Nelson reports Marie "died at 7:25 in the evening, April 19, 1995" (p. 40).

In developing his theory of "the call of conscience," Levinas contends that the "mortality of the face [a dying person's presence] . . . commands me to not remain indifferent to this death, to not let the other die alone, that is, to answer for the life of the other person, at the risk of becoming an accomplice in that person's death."[16] In the euthanasia debate this way of thinking comes into play when arguing about whether an assisted suicide was an act of "murder or mercy." I suspect that Levinas would allow the point to be made *only after* a patient's loving "caress" of the other was no longer of any use to the other because, due to physiological complications, he or she had gone beyond the point of ever being able to experience its heart-felt emotion. This certainly was not the case with Marie. Nelson, however, is not yet done telling Marie's story. He continues to remember:

> Marie had been a dirt-poor country girl, her parents sharecroppers from Alabama who moved to Texas. She claimed she graduated from high school, I think maybe she got to the tenth grade. . . . Growing up, she'd worked in the fields like a man. . . . She married Charlie, she said, to get away from home. She had my bother and me by the time she was nineteen. . . . She married six times, well, seven, if you count the one she married twice, the one who regularly beat her. . . . Marie's most articulate aspiration was "just to be happy, that's all I ever wanted." This was her litany. She never learned that happiness is a matter of degree, not a permanent condition. . . . To hear her tell it, most of her life was occupied with "getting a man." . . . If she could attract a man, get a man to want her, this had to mean that she had some value, didn't it. On the other hand, by being so easy that any man could screw her and did—"screwing" is what she called it—didn't that really prove she was of the least value, a throwaway? Being little more than a fuck is being little more than faceless. (P. 40–41)

Nelson continues to tell a story about a person who long ago lost what for someone like Levinas is an essential existential feature of life: a "face" whose presence and "otherness" sounds a call of conscience.[17] Marie was but a "throwaway," a disposable creature of little if any value. Nelson's memories of Marie made it impossible for him to see the humanity of her face beyond *his* rhetorical construction of its miserable existence. "After all," writes Nelson, "when you have children of your own, you find out that you don't just up and leave them after a few years and make an X for them in your life, not if you care. You don't leave your kids with a hole in their heart" (p. 43).

Nelson concludes his story by telling how he cleaned up the scene, had a drink to calm his nerves, and called the police. "I told the coroner my mother had deteriorated rapidly in the last week. . . . He took a cursory look at her, pronounced her dead from natural causes, and called the mortuary." Nelson told the "mortuary man" that he wanted Marie cremated. "How about a service? No, none of that, I said, just the simplest, quickest way." And finally he remarks: "My mother, I thought, the one person I'd known my whole life, she'd given me life. But I always only knew her as Marie. I never called her mother and she never called me son" (p. 43). Sad words, to be sure, but no sadder than the ones that, as quoted above, reveal what perhaps is the most telling admission by the author: He is a person whose mother left her "kids with a hole in their heart."

The ailment being noted here, especially when considered in light of the teachings of the Old Testament, warrants the diagnosis of being a severely impaired conscience.[18] This is an illness that attacks the person more than the body, for it makes one uncaring and unreceptive to a call that sometimes, as in the case of Marie, can only be heard as an irritating question concerning the worthiness of one's life. Marie transmitted this illness to Nelson, who returned the favor: What was left of his conscience allowed him to remember nothing good about his mother, nothing that deserved being acknowledged as inspiring and worthy of continuation. One reader of Nelson's story saw this to be its primary "message": When it comes to "the achievement of some sort of understanding between a difficult mother and her son," we need merely "put on a 'clinical' face, write about it in a matter-of-fact style, relate the facts of death without any reference to loss, and generally let loose the little Kevorkian in us before the real emotional work is done."[19] I must disagree with this interpretation, for it is philosophically and rhetorically naive.

Unlike many "academic" rhetoricians who have entered the euthanasia debate, Nelson opts to tell an evocative story that avoids the strain of intellectual abstraction.[20] The story is not written by one who has "put on a clinical face"; rather, it comes to us from a son whose mother never called him by his name and whose fate it was to struggle with an emotional and moral ailment that took hold when he was but a kid. The euthanasia debate is not just about the problem of medical and technological zeal that may be counseled by well-defined intellectual arguments. "Mother's Last Request" helps to make that clear. The debate over the morality or immorality of assisted suicide is rooted in the lives of people, in person stories whose characters have many different histories, lifestyles, dreams, and nightmares—all of which come into play as the characters assume the burden of having to face up to the challenge of freedom of choice and ethical responsibility. Marie and Nelson took on this challenge. What is missing from their story, however, is a more nuanced appreciation of how human beings exist not only "with" but also "for" others. One reader made the point this way: "New glasses, a home health aide, and antidepressant medication might have made [Marie's] last months far less miserable. . . . [A] phone call to the doctor by her son, stating her problems and asking for exclusively home-based care, may have been all that was necessary. After all, she was depressed, not terminal."[21] Yes, but again, I must stress that the case is not that simple.

Nelson's story offers an account of conscience: How it calls through sickness and misery, how it may itself become ill, and how such an illness can affect one's memory and acknowledgment of others. The story is tragic; its characters bear faces that are repugnant and that perhaps remind us of others whose hearts are cold and crippled because of life's circumstances. Perhaps we are even reminded of ourselves—creatures who, like Broyard, tell stories in order to bring some coherence to what illness or accident has made incoherent. The activity is therapeutic and rhetorical. Isn't Nelson engaged in this activity? Hasn't he reconstructed from memory a scene that is as educational as it is horrible? Doesn't Nelson's story sound a call of conscience that is heard as a confession about his illness? Doesn't "Mother's Last Request" speak to us of things that, for the sake of humanity, we cannot afford to forsake? Nelson's story is a reconstruction of events of deconstruction—of heartbreak, choices gone wrong, bad memories, illness, and death. He offers readers a picture of persons whose faces, I suspect, are not for most people objects of envy. Who would want to be remembered like Marie? Who would want a son like Nelson? But it wasn't all his fault! Does that matter?

What if Marie wanted the type of acknowledgment that Nelson was incapable of giving? What if Nelson proved capable of giving this gift? What if mother and son eventually healed each other's heart through loving conversation and understanding? Would Marie still have wanted to die? Would her son still have been willing to assist her? Would that have been death with dignity? It certainly would have been a better way to end the story. Two people being with and for each other; two people making a sacrifice for the other. Marie would no longer be a burden and would leave her son with some good memories. Nelson would be able to say that he finally gave back to his mother a gift that she desperately wanted, that granted her reprieve from a living-death, and that both she and her son knew was given and received with much love. If such a story were told in as an evocative way as is "Mother's Last Request," one might read it to be a story of heroism, as well. The rhetoric of the right to die is filled with such stories.[22]

As it stands now Nelson's story, of course, is not about heroes. His remembrance of Marie constitutes a rhetorical construction of a "faceless fuck." His confession of assisting in a suicide makes him out to be what, for the most part, is a creature without much of a conscience. But still there is a call of conscience at work in this confession. If you don't have a big hole in your heart you should be well enough to notice it. My interpretation of this call has emphasized how it speaks to us (albeit at times indirectly but still forcefully) of matters that play an important role in the euthanasia debate: acknowledgment, personal histories, fond memories, faceless souls, and why it is so important to cultivate caring relationships with family, friends, and neighbors. The particular way that Nelson treats these concerns in his story may be nothing more than an attempt to clear his conscience. No matter, though; the story still functions as what I have termed elsewhere "a rhetorical interruption" of our moral consciousness: Nelson's reconstruction of Marie's and his own face presents a story that, in being as depressing and repugnant as it is, begs for deconstruction; by which I mean that "Marie's Last Request" was made to remind us of how certain things that are at work in the euthanasia debate need to be *called into question*.[23] Nelson tells a story that is in no way an argument for the right to die; it is too antiheroic. Death with dignity requires more than what Nelson and Marie had to give: the gift of positive and loving acknowledgment.

CONCLUSION

At the beginning of this essay I noted how Schrag would have us "consult case studies and local narratives to illustrate how the gift (of acknowledgment) can be given and received, and how goodness can happen and justice be done within the economy of our civil societies." My analysis of Nelson's essay was meant not only to provide such an illustration but also to further Schrag's assessment of the matter by offering a closer reading of how the workings of rhetoric can play a role in the giving and the withholding of the gift of acknowledgment. Nelson's rhetoric is disturbing and evocative; it sounds a call of conscience that opens readers to the related issues of life, death, memory, human relationships, hearts with holes in them, and the importance of remedying this terrible ailment with the help of a loving gift. Hence, the call at work here constitutes what I take to be a sad yet fitting response to the euthanasia debate. After reading "Marie's Last Request," who would not be moved to think at least about the "good" that needs to be done in this world? Nelson's disturbing narrative speaks (albeit indirectly) to the heroic capability of human beings—a capability that, with enough hermeneutic charity from his readers, might at least be perceived in Nelson's decision *to go public* with his confession.

This said, however, there still remains a small problem between Schrag and myself. Recall that Schrag speaks to us of a gift that ought to be given "without any expectation of return." With the Old Testament in mind, I must admit that I have a difficult time accepting this prescription. For as Rabbi Abraham Joshua Heschel reminds us with his reading of this holy text, it is not only God who acknowledges us, but we who, in turn, must acknowledge God.[24] From the very beginning, if you will, the loving gift of acknowledgment was given with an expectation of return. The gift brings with it an obligation to reciprocate. Schrag would have us see matters otherwise. The *giving* of the gift of acknowledgment defines an asymmetrical operation: The only thing that counts is the self saying "Here I am!" to those who call out "Where art thou?"[25] My much loved and respected teacher, Schrag, is known for his belief that, when all the teaching and writing are done, "it is our students that should matter the most." As a student, however, I submit that those who have devoted themselves to their calling as much as this generous soul certainly deserve at least some small gift in return. Heroes warrant heart-felt acknowledgment and remembrance, for that is how we keep them alive such that their wisdom and courage can educate future generations of students.

NOTES

1. Calvin O. Schrag, *The Self after Postmodernity* (New Haven: Yale University Press, 1997), 139–140.
2. Ibid., 140.
3. Ibid., 141–142.
4. Calvin O. Schrag, "On the Ethics of the Gift: Acknowledgement and Response," 19. This essay is scheduled for publication in a collection honoring philosopher Gary B. Madison.
5. Ibid., 19–20.
6. I say "once again" because I have written another piece honoring Schrag. See my "The Interruptive Nature of the Call of Conscience: Rethinking Heideg-

ger on the Question of Rhetoric," to be published in a *Festschrift* edited by William McBride and Martin Beck Matustik. The reader should notice with this act of "reciprocity" I am going against Schrag's understanding of what a genuine gift is. I deal with this problem in the conclusion of the present essay.

7. I have also utilized this case in my *The Call of Conscience: Heidegger, Levinas, Rhetoric, and the Euthanasia Debate* (Columbia: University of South Carolina Press, forthcoming). In that book the case in presented in chapter six ("Reconstruction: Emotions, Definitions, Arguments, and Stories").

8. For an extended discussion of this point, see Timothy E. Quill's *Death and Dignity: Making Choices and Taking Charge* (New York: W. W. Norton, 1993), and *A Midwife Through the Dying Process: Stories of Healing and Hard Choices at the End of Life* (Baltimore: John Hopkins University Press, 1996).

9. B. J. Nelson, "Mother's Last Request: A Not So Fond Farewell," *Harper's*, 292 (March 1996): 35–43. Further references to this essay will be cited in the text. The essay was also published as a chapter in Nelson's *Keepers: A Memoir* (New York: W. W. Norton, 1998).

10. See his *Intoxicated By My Illness and Other Writings on Life and Death* (New York: Ballantine Books, 1992).

11. Barry L. Nelson, "Letters," *Harper's*, 292 (June 1996): 81–82.

12. For an excellent treatment of the position, see Raphael Demos, "On Persuasion," *The Journal of Philosophy*, 29 (April 1932): 225–232.

13. The notion of "the call of conscience" mentioned here draws from Martin Heidegger's and Emmanuel Levinas' respective treatments of the topic. For an extensive discussion and critical treatment of these philosophers' thinking on the call, see my *The Call of Conscience*, especially chapters two through four.

14. Ernest Becker, *The Denial of Death* (New York: The Free Press, 1973), 152–153.

15. See, for example, Abraham Joshua Heschel, *God in Search of Man: A Philosophy of Judaism* (New York: Farrar, Strauss and Giroux, 1955). More is said about this point in the conclusion.

16. Emmanuel Levinas, *Time and the Other*, trans. Richard A. Cohen (Pittsburgh: Duquesne University Press, 1987), 109.

17. Levinas has a very robust appreciation of "the face." He defines it as "the expressive in the Other (and the whole human body is in this sense more or less face)." See his *Ethics and Infinity: Conversations with Phillip Nemo*, trans. Richard A. Cohen (Pittsburgh: Duquesne University Press, 1985), 97. For a detailed discussion of the relationship between the face and the call of conscience, see my *The Call of Conscience*, especially chapter four.

18. For a discussion of the relationship between the "heart" and "conscience" in the Old Testament, see R. J. Zwi Werblowsky, "The Concept of Conscience in Jewish Perspective," trans. R. F. C. Hull, in *Conscience*, ed. the Curatorium of the C. G. Jung Institute, Zurich (Evanston: Northwestern University Press, 1970), 81–109.

19. Barry L. Nelson, "Letters," *Harpers*, 292 (June 1996): 82.

20. For one who does not avoid this strain but still writes an excellent essay, see, for example, Leon R. Kass, "Death with Dignity and the Sanctity of Life," in

A Time to Be Born and a Time to Die, ed. Barry S. Kogan (New York: Aldine De Gruyter, 1991), 117–145.

21. Libby Cone, "Letters," *Harper's*, 292 (June 1996): 81.

22. I make much of this point in my *The Call of Conscience*, chapters seven and eight.

23. Michael J. Hyde and Kenneth Rufo, "The Call of Conscience, Rhetorical Interruptions, and the Euthanasia Controversy," *Journal of Applied Communication Research* (forthcoming).

24. Hence, the title of Heschel's famous work, *God in Search of Man: A Philosophy of Judaism*.

25. This position is especially crucial to Levinas. For his discussion of this asymmetrical operation, see, for example, *Totality and Infinity*, trans. Alphonso Lingis (Pittsburgh: Duquesne University Press, 1969), 194–216.

6 Awaiting the Year of the Donkey

STEPHEN PLUHÁČEK

ON GIVING THANKS

There is to be a feast of words—that is, hospitality and gift. There is to be celebration and commemoration of the fine work that has been shared, of the good that has been bestowed, of the beauty that has been brought into the world. There is to be thanks given for expanding the horizons of so many students, colleagues, and friends, for providing the time and space in which to develop thoughts and projects—often divergent from one's own, for working tirelessly for others, for nurturing intellectual growth, for guiding so many spirits on countless journeys, for attempting to humanize the (inhuman) process of professionalization, for listening—with an open door and a welcoming smile. And, of course, there is to be thanks given for all the stories that have been shared. One is to be honored—for the inspiration that has touched so many lives in such incalculable ways.

ON GIVING THANKS?

There is to be a feast of words—that is, hospitality and gift. Who is to be invited? In other words, to whom is credit to be extended? To be sure, to the one who is to be banqueted with fine words, feted for the gift of words already given. For it is time to give back—although it will never settle accounts—to the one to whom much is owed. In this case, Calvin O. Schrag. It is time to give back not just for the intellectual and spiritual gifts given, but for the cultural, academic, and even economic capital acquired. So an invitation must also be extended to those who are to give the feast of words. And this raises the question of who is to be given the opportunity to give. For there is more than one gift of words before the gift of words. Before the giving of words, credit is extended to those who will be allowed to speak or to write. Of course, this credit is not extended to just anyone nor is it given without qualification. This gift of words situated within academic space is not without relation to the circulation and accumulation of academic capital. Within academic space, capital breeds capital. Thus, those to whom credit will be extended, and academic power depends upon such credit, will have already acquired certain reserves to which an invitation to give might be added. For those who look to give a gift without return this feast of words thus presents a problem. Caught up in advance in the circulation of academic capital, having turned a profit in the give and take of the academic market, they will most likely profit again from their speculations. Looking to give a gift, they may not only pay back the one they honor, but perhaps pay themselves well in the process. Looking to give a gift, they circulate (symbolic) capital. Thus is academic capital distributed across generations. Furthermore, of those to whom credit is extended, there is an expectation to give back—that is, to speak or to write—according to certain protocols. The models of propriety call for good taste. There is an expectation that those invited to give thanks will obey the protocols of giving; that they will pay homage to the one to be honored. Such implicit restrictions no doubt raise certain difficulties when the love of wisdom requires us to honor truth above protocol.

TO GIVE: THE GIFT

One, two. . . . When is the third? When is the time of the gift?

For there to be a gift it seems necessary that someone give something to someone other. In other words, that A give X to C. Involved in this giving also seems to be a certain *intention* on the part of the one to give something (a gift) to the other. Absent this intention to give, there would be no gift. There would be no gift given by accident, given indifferently, given in response to force (be it natural or cultural). And yet things are not so simple. For a present cannot be made of the present. To present the gift is to annul the gift in exchange. The gift as the impossible ought not appear as gift, its simple identification serving to destroy it *as gift*—its identification serving as a countergift that pays back the gift. And it matters little whether this identification occurs by the one who gives or the one who receives. In either case, the gift is annulled in the counter-gift. For if the donee accepts and recognizes the gift, the acceptance and recognition serve to pay back the donor. Yet if the donor identifies the gift as gift, again, the gift is annulled. This simple identification of the gift serves to pay the donor back at the threshold of giving, to give back symbolically the value of what is to be given. At the threshold of giving, the giver stays within economy. Giving begins with keeping—keeping the gift through identification, keeping close to the home, to property, keeping what is mine even if to give it to the other. Consciousness, which would be a condition of giving, would serve to appropriate the gift, keeping what is to be given. If this is the case, how, within consciousness, can the right hand give without the left hand knowing, and appropriating, it? (How) can consciousness be kept from (re)appropriating the gift? How to give without return?

How to suspend the time of the gift? How to forestall the moment in which the gift appears and disappears in its appearance? If the appearance of the gift, its being (a) present, serves to annul the gift, then the gift must never appear as such. How then to give? And who (is) to give? And to whom? If the temporalization of time serves to annul the gift, if the recognition (and/or acceptance) of the gift as gift (by either the donor or the donee) serves to annul the gift, how then to give, and to whom?

ON SOUNDING TRUMPETS IN THE SYNAGOGUES AND IN THE STREETS

In giving the gift, the giving needs to recede in order that the gift as such can have a chance. If the giving itself does not recede, it threatens to overwhelm the gift, drawing attention and focus to the giving and the giver rather than to the gift or the donee. If this recession or withdrawal is necessary for the gift as such to have a chance, a number of difficulties arise. How much withdrawal is enough? Can the withdrawal be measured? Is there a proper limit here? Furthermore, who gives? If, insofar as the giving and the giver—the "I," the person, the ego, the subject of the giver—do not withdraw, the gift as such has no chance, who, or what, gives the gift? And finally, how to give?

How to think, to speak (and, perhaps more importantly, to live) this relation, this "encounter" between the giver and the recipient, between donor and donee, this appearance that disappears in its appearance, this identification of an object that is never present as such? It cannot be comprehended. The gift is on neither the plane of representation nor the plane of conceptual relation. It is not a matter of empirical observation. The world of experience does not reveal the gift anywhere within its limits. It cannot be totalized by a concept of relationship. Nor can it be thought on the basis of a phenomenological horizon within which a *cogitatum* can be recognized and understood by a *cogito*.

THE TIME OF THE GIFT

Does the gift call for another time? Or for time's other? Might the gift not call for *kairos* rather than *chronos*? Might kairos be the third, the time of the gift? Perhaps. Kairos, as the lived time of human existence, would offer an alternative to the objectively measured time of chronometers, clocks, and calendars. The gift as kairos would characterize the extraordinary times and places for gift giving, the right moment for a gift to be given and to be received. Kairos, as the moment of decision, would signal the *right* time, the *opportune moment* for executing a plan of action. In the kairos there would be an invitation to a fitting response—a fitting response in discourse and action that keeps the gift as its measure.

And yet, is not the difference between chronos and kairos still *a difference within the economy of time itself*? Is not the gift as kairos still the gift as economic object—no longer or not yet unconditional, but defined as much as defining? Can the gift be presented any better by phenomenological-existential time than by cosmological time? If the gift cannot be comprehended, grasped, without being annulled in an economic taking/keeping, (how) does a turn to phenomenological time help? Do not both chronos and kairos presuppose and impose an order, an economy, an *oikos* and a *nomos*, that would annul the gift?

If so, kairos, as the moment in which time is transfigured (by eternity), in which the (eternal) *meaning* of temporality as it is lived is *apprehended*, would signal the destruction of the gift as gift. To hold the gift, to apprehend its meaning, to grasp its (eternal) significance would be to lose the gift—to suspend the suspension of time, of the time of the gift, if there is any, in a holding-apprehending-grasping that would bind the gift in a temporal, economic synthesis.

AN ECONOMY OF MEANING

The (re)appropriation of the gift in discourse and action serves to annul the gift and to compensate (economically) for the excessiveness of the gift. In attempting to render the gift meaningful, graspable, utilizable within the restricted economies of discourse and action, the gift is annulled. A discourse oriented in advance by restricted economic concerns (of an existential and phenomenological nature) would attempt to impose the (unjustified, destructive) demand that everything, including the gift, be situated or situatable within that economy. The demand that the gift be situated within a horizon of meaning, of sense—a horizon it may both limit and exceed—annuls the gift in a reduction of the gift to exchange.

To call into question the orientation of this discourse, as well as the attempted (re)appropriation of the gift within (restricted) economy, is to open the gift to the insecurity, the risk without which there would be no gift. The gift, insecure through and through, open to risk without limit, far from providing a sheet anchor against (semantic, conceptual, ontological, or existential) drift, would solicit any security it was thought to secure.

A "NEW" MODALITY

(How) can one be certain that a gift has been given; that there is gift? The price of such certainty would be the annulment of the gift in exchange. Because the simple intention to give serves to annul the gift in the return of recognition, because the simple identification of the gift serves to pay back the donor (at the threshold of giving), it would seem that the gift, if there is any, points toward a new modality as well as different "relations" than those between (conscious) subjects, or between (conscious) subjects and objects.

Translating the account of creation in hymn X.129 of the Rg Veda into the idiom of the gift:

> Who really knows? Who will proclaim it?
> Whence the gift? (Whence) was it given?
> The gods came after-words.
> Who then knows whence it was given?
> Whence this gift has been given—
> perhaps it gave itself, or perhaps it did not—
> the one who looks down on it, in the highest heaven,
> only he knows—
> or perhaps he knows not.

THE TIME OF THE GIFT?

Is there another third? One that does not come after the first two—time, eternity—bringing them together in the moment, but that solicits them—both calling them forth and causing them to tremble—in advance of their being there. Is this the time of the gift? Perhaps a past that was never present. Or a future always to come—even when it has arrived. The gift, coming from a past that could not be recalled or from a future always to come, not because it would be situated very far behind or ahead, but because it would not be "made" for the present, would remain heterogeneous to any temporal synthesis that would signal the unbinding of the gift in exchange.

Is such a gift possible?
Or is it the impossible itself?

SITTING WITH THE BUDDHA

Why all this talk of the gift? What is being pursued? At what does one grasp? Can words express it?

Words cannot express it.

Why then all these words? What is to be gained? What is to be gained by distinguishing gift from economy? Is it any better to crave, to desire the impossible than to desire the possible; to desire the gift rather than economy? Is this not to have renounced the forest of desire, yet to run back into it?

There is desire in either case. Cut down the whole forest of desire, not just a tree. To hold that the gift is eternal or to hold that it is not, or to agree to any other propositions regarding the gift, is the forest of theorizing, the bondage and the shackles of theorizing; it conduces not to detachment. Proceed with the mind which neither grasps nor rejects, the mind unconcerned with name or gain.

Why this concern—this anticipation, this expectation—for the moment (of the gift)? Is any one moment more momentous than any other?

The fullness of time does not occur at a particular time in history. Any moment of history, if there is any, "is" the fullness of time.

Is any acquisition whatsoever made in the fullness of time?

Then Subhuti asked Buddha: World-Honored One, in the attainment of the consummation of incomparable enlightenment did Buddha make no acquisition whatsoever?

Buddha replied: Just so, Subhuti. Through the consummation of incomparable enlightenment I acquired not even the least thing; wherefore it is called "consummation of incomparable enlightenment."[1]

There is no (time for the) gift (of incomparable enlightenment).

There is to be a feast of words—that is, hospitality and gift. In the year of the donkey.

NOTE

1. *The Diamond Sutra and the Sutra of Hui-neng* (Boston: Shambhala, 1990), 43.

7 On Hearing the Call

From the Pain of Affliction toward Healing

DAVID JAMES MILLER AND
MICHAEL J. MILLINGTON

> But can you prevail (*peisomen*) upon us if we refused to listen?
> —Plato, *The Republic* (327c)

OCCASIONING THE GIFT

Foreshadowing his forthcoming book in the interview that accompanies this volume, Calvin O. Schrag turns to a notion of the gift as a means of elaborating the content and measure of the fitting response as the ethicopolitical moment of the transversal dynamics of communicative praxis.[1] The gift, or rather the event of the gift, as the content and measure of the fitting response draws upon but is by no means reducible to the transversal dynamics of communicative praxis. Rather the event of the gift, and so the fitting response itself, is occasioned within the transversal dynamics of communicative praxis, but it is an occasioning that cannot be generalized to communicative praxis as such. This remains the case, even if the occasion for the fitting response confronts us constantly today, may in fact always confront us. Consequently, the occasioning of the gift as such becomes a critical moment in the elaboration of the fitting response. It is this occasioning, a moment which, as it now stands, is in need of further clarification, that we would like to address in this essay.

A CALL TO COVENANT

Drawing in part upon the work of Emmanuel Levinas, the occasion for the fitting response, the occasioning of the gift is understood as the call that issues from the visage and voice of the orphan, the widow, and the stranger. To speak here of the call as issuing forth from the countenance of the orphan—in the Hebrew, the "fatherless," the widow, and the stranger—or again to follow the Hebrew, the "sojourner," is, of course, to speak figuratively. The triad serves as a metaphor for the disenfranchised in general—the afflicted, as we will come to use the term. In considering this, however, it is useful to recognize that the force of the figure—already symbolic in parts of the Hebrew canon—is derived from an historical event first narrated in the book of Exodus, namely the communal commitment commonly termed the Sinai Covenant and covenant code.

Often misconstrued legalistically as a set of commandments demanding obedience, the tenets of the Covenant and the covenant code—written in the future imperative—articulate a set of expectations that serve to constitute the people of Israel as a community. Among these expectations are specific provisions concerning care for the sojourner—those living among you who are other, different, alien. As is the case here, the sojourner is commonly associated with the widow and the fatherless, as well as with the poor (also singled out for special treatment in the covenant code), each of whom can be and, as with the widow here, are at times characterized as sojourners.

Each of these groups is singled out for special concern not only because of the suffering that attends their unique circumstances and their particular vulnerability. But they are also singled out because these circumstances have been, and are at the time, cause for social denigration with its attendant consequences. Their members are, in effect, social outcasts. As such, their suffering is compounded, may in fact be produced and doubled by this alone.[2]

In this entreaty, the people of Israel are asked to recall their own sojourn, the sufferings visited upon them in Egypt as well as the suffering that attended the status they enjoyed as an oppressed people. And they are asked to recall the deliverance from their oppressors, a deliverance freely given. They are called upon to turn their gaze, illuminated by this recollection, to their own community and its actions, both as it is and as it is to become.

Thus the expectation articulated here can be construed as twofold. There is the expectation that the community as such care for those within its midst who suffer and are in need of special protection. And there is the expectation that the community as such will not needlessly cause pain: that those who suffer will no longer be burdened by further suffering—unnecessary suffering—through the actions of a community that stigmatizes them.

Considering this, it would seem appropriate to say that the call that issues forth occasioning the gift, and, as such, occasions the fitting response, issues forth from suffering. To be more precise, it issues forth from the unnecessary suffering the community itself inflicts upon those it sets apart without justification. To speak in more general terms, this amounts to saying that the call speaks to us of and by means of pain.

But we must ask ourselves a number of questions here. Specifically, how can pain communicate itself to us? And what of the specificity of the pain that seeks to communicate to us in occasioning the call? Finally, what is it this pain seeks in seeking to be heard? These are the questions that will guide us in attempting to clarify the occasioning of the gift and so the fitting response.

TURNING

It is surprising how often another's pain fails to move us in any appreciable way. It is equally surprising that when it does manage to move us—to concern, to care, even, at times, to action—how quickly we grow weary within that movement. It is a weariness that seems to grow, albeit unevenly, in proportion to the duration and the intensity of the suffering. Tiring of the seemingly endless protestations, much like Job's impatient friends, concern and care can turn inside out, twisting and distorting until only indifference, or worse, disdain, remains.

How are we to account for this? Although it is evident that there is much time for such suffering in our world, there seems to be little time for those who suffer. It would appear that either this suffering is incapable of sustaining our attention or that we ourselves have forsaken our ability to attend to it.

If the former is the case, perhaps attention is simply incapable of focusing upon suffering, that underlying its flight lies the fundamental inexpressibility of pain, an inexpressibility that by depriving attention of an object, turns it, by necessity, to other matters. Have we not convinced ourselves that pain is the elusive secret of the other, the final refuge of inwardness—interior and inaccessible—which if revealed, would bear the other's soul to us? Is it not all but an article of faith for us that we cannot share another's pain? Alternatively, perhaps suffering is so overwhelmingly mundane, the repetitiveness of complaint so banal that it inevitably overtaxes our patience, forcing our attention to flee almost as a matter of self-preservation.

If, however, the latter is the case—that is, that we have forsaken our ability to attend to suffering—then the inability of suffering to sustain our attention would be but one of its consequences. The reasons offered only excuses masquerading as justifications for a practiced, paradoxically vigilant, inattention. In this case, to accept the notion that suffering is incapable of sustaining our attention is for us to resign ourselves—and condemn others—to the necessity of what is unnecessary. It is an acquiescence equivalent to saying: "There is nothing to be done here." or, perhaps put more truthfully, "There is nothing I will do here."

AFFECTIVE COMMUNION

If pain cannot sustain our attention, then we cannot reasonably expect the call to be heard. Consequently, we must attend to the first two possibilities proffered above, namely, that the fundamental inaccessibility of pain offers attention no object for consideration, or that attention can hold fast to pain only until its grip becomes so fatigued by the repetitiveness of complaint that it slips away.

With respect to the former, Elaine Scarry, in what is nonetheless an impressive analysis, discusses what she takes to be our inability to communicate pain, its ultimate inexpressibility, in terms of its resistance to language. "Whatever pain achieves," she writes, "it achieves in part through its unsharability, and it ensures this unsharability through its resistance to language."[3] Or again: "Physical pain does not simply resist language but [in extremis] actively destroys it, bringing about an immediate reversion to a state anterior to language, to the sounds and cries a human being makes before language is learned."[4]

Yet, language as such is not our only means of communication.[5] Nor is lived language without a highly developed affective component (evident in intonation, volume, facial, and bodily comportment, etc.—a component also made manifest in various ways in written language). The different cries made by an infant—cries of frustration, cries demanding attention, cries of distress, and others—are readily discernable by caregivers. Likewise, there are the nonlinguistic sounds that lovers make—sounds of enticement, of pleasure, of urgency, and so forth. The affective communication by means of which lovers reciprocally guide one another, often communicates in a manner that is not only more immediate but communicates more fully in the circumstances than any linguistic utterance could. If and when pain displaces language, it may well give way to a more fundamental form of communication, an affective communication wrongly characterized as regression.[6]

The claim that another's pain is simply inaccessible to us and as such cannot be communicated, stems from what Schrag refers to, and what has commonly come to be referred to, as the metaphor of the "interior" set over against the "exterior." It is an insidious metaphor that has infiltrated our thinking in ways we are still uncovering.[7] The figure stems from the tenets of modern epistemology following in the Cartesian wake in which mind and body, the former interior and inaccessible to others, the latter exterior and accessible, are, as incommiscible substances, necessarily incommunicado. Here a divide is constructed between the "feeling" or "sensation" of pain as an interior event (or event-state) and its external "expression" manifest in language or behavior in terms of which the interior event must, by some slight of hand, be inferred or intuited or something kindred.

Within the context of these constraints, the communication of pain as pain becomes impossible. However, as one of the present authors has argued elsewhere, given the context of these constraints, *all* communication becomes impossible.[8] The basic assumptions of the position when considered thoughtfully make this obvious. Since mind and body are construed as fundamentally incommiscible substances, the chasm opened between them simply cannot be crossed, crossed by any means whatsoever. The fact that we communicate at all is enough to prove the assumptions faulty.

Yet with respect to the issue of pain in particular we may be too eager to blame René Descartes for this problem, too rote in our interpretations, even careless in our reading. In *Meditations on First Philosophy*, Descartes has difficulty dealing with affect in general. It fails to fit neatly on either side of the rift he creates between mind and body and so goes largely unaddressed.[9] Only at Elizabeth's behest some eight to nine years later, does Descartes return to the question. And in the resulting work, *The Passions of the Soul*, published shortly before his death, Descartes prefers to take a physiological approach to affect, all but abandoning the language and distinction of mind and body.[10]

It is largely within the context of the ensuing rationalist and empiricist traditions that the problem of pain—and the pain of the problem—is raised within the context of the mind/body distinction. All told, the problem is that pain is abstracted from the lived context within which it occurs. The concrete experience of pain is divided against itself. Here pain is present only to the person experiencing it. Pain is a personal, private affair incapable of being communicated as such.

By contrast, when Descartes does deal with the issue of pain in the *Meditations*, he does so in the service of reintegrating what he had earlier torn asunder. There is a passage in the Sixth Meditation worth quoting here: "There is nothing that this nature [bestowed by God] teaches me in a more clear-cut way than that I have a body that is ill-disposed when I feel pain. . . . By means of these feelings of pain . . . nature also teaches that I am present to my body not merely in the way a seaman is present to his ship, but that I am tightly joined and, so to speak, mingled together with it, so much so that I make up a single thing with it. For otherwise, when the body is wounded, I, who am nothing but a thing that thinks, would not sense the pain. Rather, I would perceive the wound by means of the pure intellect, just as a seaman perceives by means of sight whether anything in the ship is broken."[11] In order to deal with the experience of pain, Descartes returns to the concrete reality of lived pain, a reality that precedes the abstractions dividing the experience of pain and preventing its communication.[12]

And something else of great value is to be found here. Namely, that pain is not some abstract thing unto itself but is always someone's pain—in this case, Descartes' own.

FORSAKEN

So perhaps it is not the inaccessibility of pain but rather the repetitiveness of complaint that forces our attention to flee. But if the repetitiveness of complaint forces others from us when we most need them, what possible logic could underlie such excessive rumination where a stoic silence, a noble resignation, would serve us better?

A story told by Aulus Gellius is telling here. During a storm at sea, the passengers were so curious to see the eminent Stoic philosopher Aristippus growing paler and paler with fear, that they forgot they themselves were in peril. Following the storm, one passenger asked why a Stoic should show fear when he himself had shown none, to which the Stoic responded: "You had no cause for anxiety for the life of a miserable profligate, but I had reason to be alarmed for the life of Aristippus."[13] We typically do not suffer in silence. To force someone to do so can only be construed as sadistic, to force ourselves to do so, masochistic.[14] Although there may be many noble things for which one suffers, there is nothing noble about suffering itself, nor is there anything noble in suffering.

Perhaps what we hear in complaint is only what we are not hearing: lament, the poetry of everyday pain, in a culture that no longer comprehends or has a place for it.[15] We have ceased to understand the need for lamentation and what its positive function is. To lament is to put the pain of one's situation into words or something analogous to words. This is essential if one is to move forward, to take positive steps, to affirm or reaffirm one's life. Thus the duality of lamentation: at once pain and hope. But to speak alone is not enough. It does little if there is no sense of acknowledgment, no sense of communion. In other words, it does little if one is left with the sense of being alone, of remaining alone. So there is repetition, even ritual, again seeking acknowledgment, again seeking communion. Lamentation is fundamentally dialogic. And in dialogue—with the sense that another has acknowledged, has shared one's pain—lamentation is a step toward the affirmation or reaffirmation of life, the first glimmerings of hope, an initial movement from a psalm of sorrow toward a psalm of joy.[16] So too, the immeasurable damage done by our misconstruing it as complaint, by our turning away.

And so we are left with our practiced, paradoxically vigilant, inattention.

PAIN IN BEING

We have been somewhat lax in our use of language to this point. Up to this point, we have used different terms for pain as they are used in common parlance and as context has dictated.[17] But it is important, in order to continue, for us to delineate our terms.

We will use the term "pain" in a general sense, encompassing the "types" of pain we typically distinguish in terms of "physical pain," "psychological," or "emotional pain," and though other terms are perhaps more prevalent, "social pain." When psychological or emotional pain is bound up with physical pain or its equivalent, as it must be, or when social pain is tied to the two (since without psychological or emotional distress the latter can scarcely be termed pain), we will use the term "suffering." More importantly, when the latter involves some manner of social denigration or the fear of it, we will use the term "affliction."[18]

The term "affliction" translates the French "*malheur*" as Simone Weil—whom we will be following in part—uses it.[19] We should note with her translator that the French "*malheur*" bears a sense of inevitability and doom not captured by the English "affliction."[20] In light of this, perhaps "afflicted and forsaken" comes closer to the French, more adequately capturing the sense in which we wish to use it here.

Presumably, these distinctions are clear enough, with the exception of our speaking of the "equivalent of physical pain." To speak here of the "equivalent of physical pain," is to acknowledge Weil's critical insight that psychological or emotional pain, and therefore social pain, which lacks physical pain or something analogous to it is at bottom little more than what she terms "romanticism or literature."[21] Sorrow over the absence or death of someone we love, for example, inhabits and possesses our body, taking hold of it in a harsh, unshakable grip. "The irreducible part of the sorrow," she writes, "is akin to physical pain, a difficulty in breathing, a constriction of the heart, an unsatisfied need, hunger, or the almost biological disorder caused by the brutal liberation of some energy, hitherto directed by an attachment and now left without a guide."[22] Or again, "Humiliation is also a violent condition of the whole corporal being, which longs to surge up under the outrage but is forced, by impotence or fear, to hold itself in check."[23] This caveat is essential because only physical pain or something akin to it is capable of tying our thoughts and actions to it, cutting off any route of escape.

This is true of affliction as well, perhaps more so, since the attention and comfort generally afforded physical pain and suffering (so long as they do not become chronic, in which case they often become affliction) are rarely afforded the afflicted. As Weil writes:

> As for those who have been struck by one of those blows that leave a being struggling on the ground like a half crushed worm, they have no words to express what is happening to them. Among the people they meet, those who have never had contact with affliction in its true sense can have no idea of what it is, even though they may have suffered a great deal. Affliction is something specific and impossible to describe in any other terms, as sounds are to anyone who is deaf and dumb. And as for those who have themselves been mutilated by affliction, they are in no state to help anyone at all, and they are almost incapable of even wishing to do so. Thus compassion for the afflicted is an impossibility. When it is really found we have a more astounding miracle than walking on water, healing the sick, or even raising the dead.[24]

Yet for Weil such miracles do happen, beyond gravity there is grace.

NECESSARY PAIN

We will experience pain throughout our lives solely by virtue of being human, beings at once fragile and limited, pain that is born of and borne by this finitude. There is, for example, the pain that attends physical harm to the body, the pain we experience in injury or in disease. Similarly, there is the pain that accompanies the body pushed beyond the limits of what it is capable of or used to enduring—evinced, for example, in the contortions and cries of a difficult and prolonged childbirth.[25] Or again, there is the pain that comes from an awareness of our own limitations, the pain we suffer in self-doubt or in watching possibilities dissolve in the difficult decisions we find ourselves forced to make. Or again, there is the pain that results from our separation from others, the pain we suffer in loss or in the inevitable conflicts we face, both interpersonal and social.

Although these "modalities" of pain may be analytically distinct, even existentially distinguishable, they articulate in such a way that while one or another may come to the fore, the others are often implicated—perhaps are always implicated—to a greater or lesser extent. This is the case because it is always we, ourselves, who are in pain. It is always someone who is in pain: it is you or I, he or she. And as someone, we are always in relation to the world, in relation to ourselves through some measure of self-awareness, and in relation to others. We exist not as a concatenation of disjointed relata, but as the ongoing moment in which these relations, relations that are only relatively autonomous, converge and, at times, collide.

Understood in this sense, we can say that the experience of pain is constitutive of being human, part of what it means to be human. Amidst necessity and chance, within our awareness of actuality and possibility—conditions for the bounded freedom we enjoy—we are wed to one another, beyond all difference, through the shared experience of pain. This is not equivalent to saying we are tied to one another through the experience of a given pain, that this bond is forged by a common experience we find equally painful (though, of course, it cannot be construed as precluding this eventuality either). It is simply to say that the experience of pain attends the human condition as such. It haunts and inhabits our lives, an ever-present specter. Pain in this sense is unavoidable and inescapable, something before which we must and will acquiesce. Our willingness or unwillingness to accept this speaks only to the manner in which we relate to the inevitable. Although acceptance or nonacceptance may in some measure alter our experience of pain when it arrives, it does not, nor can it displace it. Were we to somehow displace pain altogether in the sense we have delineated it here, we would at the same time cease to be human, as we understand what it means to be human.

HEALING THE WOUND

The terms we have employed in describing the experience of pain—"attend," "result," "come from"—terms common enough, can be misleading insofar as they suggest a causal division, whether linear or nonlinear, within the experience of pain and so an internal scission separating the experience from itself. This is part of the residue of modern epistemology as we characterized it above. Understood in this way, the experience of something—of loneliness, for example—serves as a cause that gives rise to pain as its effect. Often we regard pain in this way when we consider it a symptom, as we must at times in seeking to alleviate it. But we should be clear that in considering pain as a symptom, even if we understand our investigation of it to be to be a matter of determining a cause, we are in fact looking to pain to disclose the larger phenomenon of which it is part. The experience of pain is at one with, a defining feature of the experience it helps to characterize. In terms of our example, pain is not an effect of loneliness. Rather, loneliness is a painful experience. And if I ask "Why are you in pain?" And you answer "Because I am lonely," it is not the case that your pain is an effect of the loneliness that causes it, but rather that loneliness itself is a way of being in pain. This is not of course to claim that we can experience pain without some agent or agency being involved, which in fact there always is. Rather, it is to say that the experience of pain is never the experience of pain per se—which can only be an abstraction. Pain is always the pain of something, an affective modality of greater or lesser intensity characterizing the experience of our being in pain.

UNNECESSARY PAIN

Insofar as it is bound to finite being, the experience of pain, at once unavoidable and inescapable, is such that, without displacing our individual differences, transcends those differences, binding us together as human beings. However, within the necessity of pain as such there is also another kind of pain that is unnecessary, a pain that makes use of our finitude but is in no other way bound to it. Rather than gathering us together as human beings, we are torn apart by it. It is added pain, pain that, rather than transcending difference, results from the divisive use of it, a misuse of difference that is at best contingent, if not arbitrary.[26] It is an experience of pain that is shared, but shared only by those who, in one way or another, are set apart and in being set apart, whether intentionally or thoughtlessly, are set upon, are beset. This is the pain of affliction. The unnecessary pain of social degradation—pain compounding suffering, suffering affliction alone may have brought about—pain we needlessly inflict upon one another. Or put more accurately: We take part in inflicting this pain upon others, or we are among those upon whom it is inflicted (although these cannot always be regarded as mutually exclusive categories).

As Weil puts it: "There is not real affliction unless the event [or series of events] that has seized and uprooted a life attacks it, directly or indirectly, in all its parts, social, psychological, and physical. The social factor is essential. There is not really affliction unless there is social degradation or the fear of it in some form or another."[27] Elaborating the latter, this deeply religious young woman writes:

> Men have the same carnal nature as animals. If a hen is hurt, the others rush upon it, attacking it with their beaks. This phenomenon is as automatic as gravitation. Our senses attach all the scorn, all the revulsion, all the hatred that our reason attaches to crime, to affliction. Except for those whose whole soul is inhabited by Christ, everybody despises the afflicted to some extent, although practically no one is conscious of it.[28]

Pain or suffering, unless chronic, typically receive both our attention and care. But the pain of affliction (which often includes chronic pain or chronic suffering), since it is inflicted pain, usually garners neither. For this reason, the pain of affliction specifically occasions the call. And for this reason as well, the call is usually neither heard nor heeded.

The pain of affliction, to draw upon Scarry's analysis of pain, is the pain of negation, negation in the sense of denying the complete value or worth of the individual identified as a member of the stigmatized group.[29] Yet, insofar as the pain of affliction is unnecessary pain, we can also work to overcome it, but we can do so only if we allow ourselves to hear and heed the call that issues from it.

AFFECT-BEING AFFECTED

Earlier we spoke of pain as an affective modality. It may seem odd to speak of pain as affective, accustom as we are to understanding it in terms of physical sensation. And under certain circumstances, there are advantages to speaking of pain in terms of sensation or sensate experience. In medical diagnosis, for example, semantic differentials ("Is your pain throbbing, shooting, stabbing, sharp, burning, stinging, dull, etc.?") have proven to be of some value. However, as we noted above, we are looking here to pain to disclose the larger phenomenon of which it is part. Again, pain is at one with, a defining feature of the experience it helps to characterize.

No doubt the uneasiness we experience in hearing pain described as an affective modality stems, in part, from the degree to which the tenets of modern epistemology along with its impoverished view of the human body (with its own history) have insinuated themselves into our common sense notions of pain. But it is also the case that from the time of Aristippus (435–356 BCE) and the founding of the Cyrenaic-Socratic school, pain as the deprecated other of pleasure has been discussed in large measure within the context of the economy of hedonism. Various formulations of hedonism and the debates surrounding it—which have ensued to the present—have set considerations of pain apart from discussions and the numerous tabulations of the affects historically in the West.

In speaking of pain as an affective modality, we do not wish to be misunderstood. We inhabit the world in a way that is at once sensate, sensual, and sentient. Although concretely these are of a piece, it is possible, at least analytically, to discern certain features characteristic of each. In considering pain, our concern here lay with the second, the affective moment of this inhabitation (using the term "sensual" to emphasize the embodied character of this moment). Our purpose in emphasizing this moment is not to discount the others, but to elaborate the means by which pain is capable of communicating itself.

Our choice of the term "affective" is deliberate. Of the various English terms we might have employed here, it permits us, by blurring the passive and active senses of the term "affect," to speak of a single movement.[30] It is a movement consisting of "being affected" as a material effect on the body, a bodily happening, and "affection" the simultaneous bodying forth or embodiment of that happening. The language of "being moved" testifies to the fundamental inseparability of these two senses—something Aristotle clearly understood when (despite its apparent passive sense in Greek) he took up the issue of the *pathe* in the *Rhetoric* in considering the manner which the rhetor might move an audience to action.

By way of their common root, the relation of the term "affective" to "affectation" has, by way of the latter, the added advantage of reminding us that we are never without this affective moment, otherwise affectation would be unnecessary. And although we can in many circumstances disguise or minimize the particular manner in which we are affected, we do so only through the affectation of affective difference or indifference.

The affective moment of our inhabiting the world is at once the manner or character of experience as it happens to us (being affected) as well as the character of our comportment in that experience (affection/ affectation).

A PASSION PLAY

The call that issues forth from the visage and voice of sojourner, the fatherless, the widow—the afflicted and forsaken—must be allowed the material force the pain occasioning it is capable of having when we turn toward rather than turning away from that pain. We cannot distance ourselves from the pain that occasions the call, presuming to understand without entering that pain. There is no communion with the afflicted without touching and being touched by pain.[31]

When there is a deep and loving bond with a child on the part of a parent, and the child is in great pain, the parent does not experience pain for the child, the parent experiences the child's pain as their own. It is from this shared pain, that comfort and healing proceed.

There is a difference between "weeping for" and "weeping with." The first scourges visited upon Job are bound to finite being, the second, which make him an outcast—something inflicted upon him by the community—put him among the afflicted. Transcending divisive difference, yet maintaining their individual differences, Job's friends act out of a common capacity for compassion. They do not weep for him. They weep with him. They do not experience pain for him. They share his pain.[32] It is only when the author turns to theological matters in an effort to assign blame for Job's pain that the friends are made to act as though they had shared nothing, are used to perpetuate, even compound his affliction through their accusations. Job's pain is bound up first with his own finitude and with finite being, and then with the inhumanity of the community, an inhumanity his friends are made to participate in. In a sense, we are Job's friends with one important difference: we have the ability to use or misuse our freedom, are the authors of that freedom.

We must assert as fact the possibility of an affective sharing not premised on a cognitive sharing, a direct communication that does not, at least in the moment, require the mediation of language. Any notion that I cannot share another's pain beyond the assertions of modern epistemology, which we contend cannot be maintained, trades on an equivocation in the senses of sharing, substituting the fact that I am not the other for the possibility that in sharing I might understand and be moved. Or rather, that I might be moved so become capable of understanding. If an understanding of affliction is to take place at all, the former must precede the latter. Since without the former, the perspective required for the latter is lacking.

At the outset, we suggested that the call that issues forth occasioning the gift, and, as such, occasions the fitting response, issues forth from suffering. Further, that this amounts to saying that this issue speaks to us of and by means of pain. We asked how pain could communicate itself. We asked about the specificity of the pain that seeks to communicate to us in occasioning the call. And we asked what pain seeks in seeking to be heard.

To return to these questions we are now in a position to say that the pain that occasions the call communicates through compassion in the sense of its Latin root *compati* (*com* + *pati*): to bear or suffer together. It is to allow oneself to be gathered into an affect, to take part—if only for a moment—in the pain of affliction, which is the specificity of the pain occasioning the call. To be gathered into this pain is to share that pain, to become one with it such that the voice and visage of the afflicted becomes that of the unafflicted. And when it is truly shared, the pain of bringing another into one's own pain pains the afflicted. In this moment, each knows the other has understood, not at a cognitive level, but at an affective level. Affective understanding that acknowledges the pain of affliction, that bears that pain with the afflicted, if only for a moment, is the beginning of healing. And it is the beginning of healing that this pain seeks in seeking to be heard.

Yet, although the pain occasioning the call always proceeds from someone as a member of an afflicted group to someone, it is to someone as a member of a community. And the call itself, though individuated, is the call of a chorus. The call is always to the community since the community is ultimately responsible for affliction, the community that has the ability and the resources to respond to affliction. The call requires community. It calls out to and for a community. Where there is no community, the call can only fall into the vacuous space of what Michel Foucault has called "excluded speech" and which we have termed a practiced, paradoxically vigilant, inattention.[33] Yet even within this space, the call, or rather the chorus of calls, echo and the echo may yet be heard. And when someone, anyone, hears the call and responds, it can lead to community, create community, a community that deserves to be called compassionate.

A PASSIONLESS GAME

Too often, we allow abstractions to take the place of real human beings. So, we speak of affliction in terms of the evils of discrimination, of oppression, of domination, and the like. Yet, we forget that it is someone who is discriminated against, someone who is dominated, someone who is oppressed. And we believe that by talking with one another we are acting. Talk can be costly when speaking is a matter of acting. Too often, though, it is cheap, accomplishing little other than posturing as a surrogate for acting. But it allows us to sleep well, drowning out the call through the din we make. We should not sleep well. We should sleep with difficulty, sleep restlessly, kept awake by the call ringing in our ears, the pain occasioning it causing us to toss and turn. The call issuing from the visage and voice of the sojourner, the fatherless, and the widow, a call occasioned by the pain of affliction, is all about us. And if we would listen, we would be hearing the call.

But can we prevail if you refuse to listen?

NOTES

We have distanced ourselves from the subject matter of the present essay, choosing to discuss the possibility of sharing pain, in particular the modality of pain we have called "affliction," from a fairly conventional philosophical standpoint. Strictly speaking, however, the subject matter is part of what we like to call a "lived philosophy": The central thesis grew out of a shared experience—a moment in Kierkegaard's sense of the term—in which the two of us lived the "affective communication" described in section XI below. Cf. Søren Kierkegaard, *Either/Or* Vol. II (New York: Anchor Books), 116.

In that same section, we speak of the "compassionate community." So it is important here to speak of the community of individuals who participated in shaping this essay. We would like first to thank Dr. Patty Sotirin and Dori Ashton both for their support as well as for the substantial contributions they made to the ongoing dialogue that underlies this essay. We would also like to thank Dr. Anthony Holzgang, M.D., and Tom Collins, CPC, CSW, CAC, for taking time to discuss many of the ideas that found their way into the piece. Credit is due Elizabeth Bancroft for her critical insights in the revision process and to our reviewers at SUNY Press for pointing out the need for clarification at several points. We would also like to acknowledge Bruce Houghton, P.C., for his encouragement and selfless offer of aid in a time of need. And finally, but by no means least, to Calvin O. Schrag: Our appreciation is beyond words.

1. We are relying here on the foreshadowing of that book, entitled *God as Otherwise than Being: Toward a Semantics of the Gift* (Evanston: Northwestern University Press, forthcoming) as it is articulated in the interview "From the Loving Struggle to the Struggle to Love" included in this collection.

2. Until it becomes necessary for the sake of precision to delineate different modalities of pain in a more specific manner (cf. Section VI, *below*), we will use the different terms for pain as they are used in common parlance and as context dictates.

3. Elaine Scarry, *The Body in Pain: The Making and Unmaking of the World* (Oxford: Oxford University Press, 1987), 4.

4. Ibid., p. 4.

5. Scarry seems to waiver in her position regarding the sharability of pain, sometimes, as here, appearing to take the position that pain is absolutely unsharable. Elsewhere, however, she seems to moderate this stance, appearing to take the position that pain is relatively unsharable, or, put more simply, that pain is difficult to share. For example, she writes: a "dimension of physical pain is its ability to destroy language, the power of verbal objectification, a major source of our self-extension, a vehicle through which the pain could be lifted out into the world and eliminated" (Scarry, p. 54). What is significant here is that language, while a "major source" of "self-extension," that is, a means of moving from "inside" to "outside," is not the only source of such extension. She tacitly illustrates this when she draws examples from artistic depictions of pain, notably the face contorted in a "silent" scream (cf. Scarry, pp. 52–53).

By saying that she waivers in her position, we do not wish to detract from what we consider to be a brilliant analysis of pain (cf. Scarry, pp. 52–56). We would, however, contest the epistemological presuppositions that tend to find their way in and out of her analysis. Insofar as she waivers with respect to the sharability of pain, we view this wavering as her inability to strictly maintain these presuppositions. But, from our point of view, it is to her credit that, when necessary, she sacrifices these presuppositions to the phenomenon at hand.

The logic of her position seems to be as follows:

1. physical pain, as it is commonly understood, is the exemplary instance of pain;
2. there is a radical separation between "inside" and "outside" (that is, she accepts the epistemological division and its entailments);
3. however, the division is not absolute (in physical pain, the boundary between the two can be "dissolved," the two can be "conflated," "inverted," and can "merge");
4. normally, language ("a major source of our self-extension") is the fundamental bridge between the two; 4) with the destruction of language, pain becomes all but impossible to share. (cf. Scarry, pp. 52–56)

There is, however, an interesting caveat in her position regarding the latter, that is, it is possible for others to speak for us when we are unable to speak for ourselves.

> Because the person in pain is ordinarily so bereft of the resources of speech, it is not surprising that the language for pain should sometimes be brought into being by those who are not themselves in pain but who speak *on behalf of* those who are. Though there are very great impediments to expressing another's sentient distress, so are there also very great reasons why one might want to do so, and thus there come to be avenues by which this most radically private of experiences begins to enter the realm of public discourse. (Scarry, p. 6; cf. pp. 6–11)

6. We would be remiss were we not to mention Martin Heidegger here. Discussing mood (*Befindlichkeit*), Heidegger writes: "mood is a primordial kind of Being for Dasein, in which Dasein is disclosed to itself [finds itself and is found] prior to all cognition and volition, and beyond their range of disclosure." Martin Heidegger, *Being and Time*, trans. John Macquarrie and Edward Robinson (New York: Harper and Row, 1962), 175.

7. Cf. Calvin O. Schrag, "Being in Pain" in *The Humanity of the Ill: Phenomenological Perspectives*, ed. Victor Kestenbaum (Knoxville: University of Tennessee Press, 1982): 101–124. This piece should be considered in any discussion of pain.

8. Cf. David James Miller, "The Philosophy of Communication" in the *Encyclopedia of Phenomenology*, eds. Elizabeth A. Behnke, Lester Embree, David Carr, J. Claude Evans, José Huertas-Jourda, Joseph J. Kockelmans, William R.

McDenna, Algis Mickunas, Jitendra Nath Mohanty, Thomas M. Seebohm, and Richard M. Zaner (Boston: Kluwer Academic Publishers, 1997), 526–530. For a more detailed analysis, cf. David James Miller, "Edmund Husserl and the (Im)possibility of Communication: A Prolegomenon to a Philosophy of Communication," Unpublished Dissertation (West Lafayette: Purdue University, 1991).

9. René Descartes, *Meditations on First Philosophy*, trans. Donald A. Cress (Indianapolis: Hackett Publishing Company, 1979).

10. René Descartes, *The Passions of the Soul*, trans. Stephen H. Voss (Indianapolis: Hackett Publishing Company, 1989).

11. Descartes, *Meditations on First Philosophy*, 50.

12. Again, we would be remiss not to mention Maurice Merleau-Ponty here, who in his *Phenomenology of Perception* would seem to have put this division to rest. Shaking the fist, for example, is not the external expression of anger as some interior event, but rather anger itself. Cf. Merleau-Ponty, *The Phenomenology of Perception*, trans. Colin Smith (Atlantic Highlands: Humanities Press, 1981).

13. Cited in H. M. Gardiner, *Feeling and Emotion: A History of Theories* (New York: American Book Company, n.d.), 70–71.

14. Compare this with Dorothee Soelle's discussion of theological sadism and theological masochism in her work, *Suffering*, trans. Everett R. Kalin (Philadelphia: Fortress Press, 1984), 9–32.

15. We are building here upon the work of Dorothee Soelle in *Suffering*, 70–77.

16. Compare this with Ramsey Eric Ramsey's discussion of dissatisfaction and utopian longing in *The Long Path to Nearness: A Contribution to a Corporeal Philosophy of Communication and the Groundwork for an Ethics of Relief* (Amherst, NY: Prometheus Books, 1998). See especially chapter 3.

17. Cf. footnote 2 above.

18. The point here is not to conflate different modalities of pain, denying the significance of what can and should be experientially differentiated. For example, the bodily experience of myofascial pain is different from the bodily experience of the pain of chronic anxiety and both are different from the bodily experience of the pain of the mundane humiliation that attends being identified with a stigmatized group, though it is important to note that the three are not mutually exclusive. Rather, we are attempting here to establish a vocabulary, albeit a nascent one, that shows both the continuities and the discontinuities of these different modalities of pain. In the end, our purpose is to delineate the modality of pain that occasions the call. (We are indebted to Dr. Patty Sotirin for the phrase "mundane humiliation.")

19. Simone Weil, "The Love of God and Affliction" in Simone Weil, *Waiting for God*, trans. Emma Craufurd (New York: Harper and Row, 1973), 117–136. Also see Simone Weil, "Additional Pages on the Love of God and Affliction," in Simone Weil *Gateway to God*, ed. David Raper (New York: Crossroad, 1982), 77–91.

20. Weil, *Waiting for God*, 117, translator's note.

21. Ibid., p. 118.

22. Ibid., pp. 117–118.

23. Ibid., p. 118.

24. Ibid., p. 120.

25. Dr. Patty Sotirin suggested the striking example of childbirth here.

26. Tom Jackson, a colleague from Crewe, England, has suggested the apt phrase "added sorrows."

27. Weil, *Waiting for God*, p. 119.

28. Ibid., p. 122. The sense that pain is a punishment somehow deserved goes back to its Greek root *poine*, a sense that carries through the Latin *poena*, the Old French *peine*, into Middle and Modern English. Again we would note Soelle's discussion in *Suffering*, pp. 9–32.

29. Scarry, *The Body in Pain,* 52.

30. The term "passion" would serve as well if the passive sense of the term—as in the passion of Christ—were as well preserved in English as its active sense.

31. Michael Martin deserves thanks for pointing us to a literary parallel in the poignant "Ragman" by Walter Wangerin Jr. in *Ragman and Other Cries of Faith* (New York: Harper and Row, 1984), 3–6.

32. The vigil of Job's friends is extraordinary. In his commentary, Marvin Pope notes that it is: "An impressive demonstration of sympathy and grief. Seven days and nights [the length of their vigil] are devoted to mourning for the dead." *Job*, trans. Marvin H. Pope, *The Anchor Bible*, vol. 15 (New York: Doubleday, 1965), 25, note 13.

33. Michel Foucault, "Madness, the Absence of Work," trans. Peter Stastny and Deniz Sengel, *Critical Inquiry,* vol. 21 (Winter 1995): 290–298. This piece has not received the attention it deserves.

Part IV Philosophizing the In-between

8 Feminism after Postmodernity

Some Places of Narrative and Communicative Praxis

DENNIS K. MUMBY

Given this context, the title of this essay may, at first blush, appear rather incongruous. No one who is familiar with Calvin O. Schrag's work would make any serious claims about his status as a feminist scholar (including, I am sure, Schrag himself), and I am not interested in positioning him as such. Instead, I want to argue that his philosophical project and that of contemporary feminist thought converge in several rather important ways. To borrow one of Schrag's own phrases, there is a "convergence without coincidence" between these two projects. Such a convergence throws both projects into sharp relief and suggests ways in which each can take on new and significant qualities.[1]

The balance of this essay therefore examines three principal ways in which this process of convergence can be articulated. First, both contemporary feminism and Schrag's work have explicitly addressed the tensions between modern and postmodern forms of thought. In different ways, both have questioned the continued epistemological viability of modernity, interrogating and critiquing the "metaphysics of presence" on which much of that project implicitly rests. At the same time, however, neither is prepared to accept postmodernism *in toto* and unproblematically as a viable alternative to the problems created by modernist foundationalism. In this sense, both projects can "be construed as an exploration of rationality *between* modernity and postmodernity."[2] That is, how does one articulate a model of rationality and truth that neither relies on the security and comfort of a purported "objective" world, nor succumbs to the temptations of postmodern nihilism and relativism? Part of this essay, then, will explore the various ways in which the "betweenness" of these two projects gets played out.

Second, and relatedly, both projects jettison "the despised logos"[3] in favor of a discursive, communicative, and narrative model of reason and rationality. For Schrag, reason and meaning are fundamentally communicative achievements. In a similar vein, many feminist theorists have turned to discursive models of meaning and identity to explore the gendered dynamics of institutional forms.[4] Schrag's claim, "we no longer search for meaning in the representations of isolated acts of cognition but rather within the play of social practices,"[5] can be applied equally well to both projects. In this essay, we will be particularly interested in narrative as the discursive embodiment par excellence of a communicative model of reason.

Finally, both projects are committed to some notion of praxis that, in different ways, signals a critique of the project of modernity. For feminists, the focus on praxis is simultaneously a rejection of the patriarchal privileging of (transcendental) reason, and a clarification of the material, political consequences of ways of knowing. Thus, the claim that "the personal is political" is an explicit attempt to reconfigure the patriarchal, modernist separation of spheres, and to transform—by reconnecting—the relationship between theory and practice. Although Schrag's notion of praxis is not as overtly political as that articulated by the feminist project, it nevertheless stands as a move beyond the "theory-grounded, subject-centered, epistemological-criteriological paradigm of modernity."[6] Praxis, for Schrag, signals a move beyond reliance on either a transcendental ego or an a priori system of rules that dictates the status of knowledge and rationality. Instead, praxis forms the context for a new model of critical rationality "that finds its resources in the dialogic transactions and institutional forms that make up the fabric of our socio-historical existence."[7]

It would appear, then, that the intersection of Schrag's philosophical project and the work of many contemporary feminists has much to offer.

INTERSTITIAL THEORIZING: BETWEEN MODERNISM AND POSTMODERNISM

The "crisis of representation"[8] fomented by postmodernism has both rejuvenated previously moribund areas of theory and practice, and generated serious concerns about the status of knowledge in the social sciences and humanities. Subject to criticism from both the left and right wings of the political spectrum, postmodern thought elicits both cautionary tales about the slide down the slippery slope of relativism and nihilism, and hopeful stories of escape from the "tyranny of consensus" and apodictic forms of truth. The fact that postmodernism has been characterized as both radical and conservative suggests no easy answers to its role in addressing issues of knowledge, power, meaning, and identity.

Perhaps more than any other body of theory and practice, feminism has the most tension-filled relationship with postmodernism. Born of the modernist, Enlightenment project, feminism nevertheless stands in opposition to the grand narrative of patriarchy, but in solidarity with the grand narrative of collective enlightenment and emancipation from the oppressive features of patriarchy. Postmodernism, then, is both friend and foe for many feminists. On the one hand, its critique of modernist metaphysics and foundationalism suggests that alternative ways of knowing (such as feminism) are taken seriously and recovered from their position of marginality in modernist thought. On the other hand, the rejection of any foundationalist epistemological position would appear to undercut feminism's privileging of women's experience as the prime instrument of critique of patriarchal power.

Nancy Hartsock nicely encapsulates the suspicion with which many feminists view postmodernism when she states:

> Why is it that just at the moment when so many who have been silenced begin to demand the right to name ourselves, to act as subjects rather than objects of history, that just then the concept of subjecthood becomes problematic? Just when we are forming our own theories about the world, uncertainty emerges about whether the world can be theorized. Just when we are talking about the changes we want, ideas of progress and the possibility of systematically and rationally organizing human society becomes dubious and suspect.[9]

Given these apparent contradictions between a feminist and a postmodern agenda, Anne Balsamo asks, "Are we being seduced . . . by the frenzy of postmodernism?"[10]

This characterization of the relationship between feminism and postmodernism as being one of "seduction" appeals to a model of sexual conquest that unintentionally situates feminism as the innocent and pristine victim of a predatory postmodern sensibility. More appropriate, perhaps, is Seyla Benhahib's characterization of feminism and postmodernism as existing in an "uneasy alliance."[11] Such a notion recognizes the inherent tensions between the two traditions, but at the same time acknowledges the potentially fruitful products of its union of equality.

Some feminist theorists argue that the conjuncture of feminism and postmodernism has allowed for an expansion of feminist concerns beyond issues of political practice and consciousness and into the realm of epistemology. Nancy Fraser and Linda Nicholson, for example, argue that the relationship between feminism and postmodernism is useful for both enterprises because each mitigates the other's respective weaknesses.[12] Although postmodern thought has paid particularly close attention to the critique of the foundational, metaphysical tendencies of much of Western philosophy, such critique tends to lack grounding in political practice. On the other hand, feminist thought has tended to privilege politics and social transformation, but with an attendant suspicion toward arcane philosophical debates and grand theorizing. At a most general level, then, feminism and postmodernism provide counterbalances to tendencies in each to neglect the relationship between theory and politics. In short, postmodern feminism represents the intersection of politics and epistemology.

Linda Singer characterizes the conjuncture between feminism and postmodernism as one rooted in a fruitful tension and strategic interplay between the two discourses that resists any simple unification (and hence potential reduction of one to the other):

> The "and" therefore keeps open a site for strategic engagement. The "and" is a place holder, which is to say, it holds a place open, free from being filled substantively or prescriptively. The "and" holds/preserves the differences between and amongst themselves.[13]

One way to explore this fruitful tension between feminism and postmodernism is to take up a central theme of postmodern discourse, variously referred to as the "death of man," or the "decentering of the subject." For postmodernism the notion of an essential, natural human being that can be defined a priori is a humanist fiction that obscures the extent to which human identity is constructed through various discourses of power and knowledge. For someone like Michel Foucault, "man" is a fictive character who exists only through the functioning of certain epistemes that define objects of knowledge.[14]

This theme of the decentering of the subject has become a central one for postmodern feminists. In particular, the notion of "woman" as a category that describes a stable, coherent, female identity has been "subject" to extensive critique. Such a notion is seen as problematic for two reasons. First, it positions women as defined in terms of, and subordinated to, men, and thus as "the second sex."[15] Second, the notion of a stable category of woman suggests a universal basis for feminism, invoking an identity politics that is exclusionary in its vision of resistance and empowerment. Thus, postmodern feminists argue that any feminism built upon an essentialist,

Enlightenment conception of subjectivity inevitability reproduces the attendant limitations of such thinking. Second-wave feminism, for example, with its strongly middle class, white, heterosexual conception of women's liberation is inevitably built upon the acceptance of patriarchal definitions of identity, autonomy, and participation in the good life.

If the notion of a centered, rational, autonomous subjectivity is problematic for postmodern feminists, what alternatives do they suggest? Judith Butler argues that the idea of decentering the subject is not the same thing as completely negating the very concept and possibility of a subject. She suggests that postmodern feminism focus on analysis of the processes by which particular forms of subjectivity are privileged; that is, whose interests are served by the construction of one form of subjectivity over another?

> To deconstruct the subject of feminism is not . . . to censure its usage, but, on the contrary, to release the term into a future of multiple significations, to emancipate it from the maternal and racialist ontologies to which it has been restricted, and to give it play as a site where unanticipated meanings may come to bear.[16]

Thus, postmodern feminism does not reject the category of the subject but rather interrogates its construction according to particular foundational premises. Such a move is clearly consistent with Jacques Derrida's attempt to situate rather than destroy the subject.[17]

For feminists like Jane Flax, this decentering of the subject leads to a fundamental shift in thinking about the feminist project. Rather than locating emancipation in a "grand narrative" like "women's experience" or in some other unitary notion of "woman," Flax argues that feminism should be concerned with gender relations and the processes through which masculine and feminine subjectivities are jointly constructed in the context of relations of power. In this sense, both women and men are "prisoners of gender" in their subordination to patriarchal constructions of subjectivities.[18] Following from this, Flax sees the principal goal of feminism as one of introducing more instability, complexity, and disorderliness into our conceptions of reality than currently exist. It is through such a process that we can begin to unfreeze the stability of the gender categories that, postmodern feminists argue, are articulated through patriarchal discourses that shape our understanding of difference.

Like Butler, Flax does not view the feminist project as one of the complete negation of the category of the subject. Instead, she suggests that feminist theorists "have a special interest in constructing concepts of self that do justice to the full complexity of subjectivity and the spaces in which it is likely to find itself. It is possible and more desirable to construct such concepts of subjectivity than to 'repress our intuitions of it' or abandon the subject altogether."[19]

At the center of the postmodern feminist project, then, is the deconstruction of gender as a stable, taken-for-granted category for organizing experience. This deconstructive process involves "stepping back from the opposition of male and female in order to loosen the hold of gender on life and meaning [thus] rendering gender more fragile, more tenuous, and less salient both as an explanatory and as an evaluative category."[20]

How does this deconstructive project unfold? How, from a feminist perspective, can we both preserve the agentive subjectivity that undergirds feminism, and articulate a vision of self that is contingent, fragile, and communicatively grounded? Furthermore, how can we avoid the kind of pantextualism that is redolent of much postmodern thought, and preserve the material, politically vibrant impetus of the feminist project? In the next section, we turn to an examination the discursive, narrative model of self, or agency, that is a centerpiece of Schrag's philosophical project. As such, we attempt to address the following question posed by Schrag: "After all the postmodern dust has settled, what traces remain of the self in discourse, the self in action, the self in community, and the self in transcendence?"[21]

THE "WHO" OF DISCOURSE: NARRATIVE AGENCY AND FEMINIST STUDIES

As was mentioned in the introduction to this chapter, the discursive/linguistic turn has posed some important challenges to the metaphysics of presence that characterizes much modernist thought. In contrast to the monadic model of mind as the "mirror of nature,"[22] the linguistic turn relocates meaning and rationality within a discursive model of being. The most dramatic consequence of this shift is that self and world, mind and body, subject and object, are no longer seen as separate, preformed, sovereign entities, but rather as coconstructed through the ongoing dynamics of human interaction.

Part of Schrag's intervention in this important shift involves the articulation of a robust conception of self and rationality that navigates between the Scylla of universalism (modernity) and the Charybdis of particularism (postmodernity). In such a model the "who" of discourse (as Schrag puts it) takes on a particular resonance and texture:

> The presence of the who is not that of a self-identical monad, mute and self-enclosed, changeless and secure prior to the events of speaking. . . . The who of discourse is not a "thing," a pre-given entity, a ghost in a machine, or whatever. . . . The who

> of discourse is an achievement, an accomplishment, a performance, whose presence to itself is admittedly fragile, subject to forgetfulness and semantic ambiguities. But in all this there is still a unity and a species of self-identity, secured not by an abiding substratum but rather by an achieved self-identity, acquired through a transversal extending over and lying across the multiple forms of speech and language games without coincidence with any one of them.[23]

Within such a framework, "the task of rationality is to discern and articulate how our own discursive and nondiscursive practices hang together, however loosely, within the texture of everyday life. Its business is to track the assemblages of thought and action within the chronotope of our communicative interactions."[24]

This focus on the search for meaning within the "play of social practices" resonates closely with the postmodern feminist agenda discussed in the previous section. For feminists, obviously, the texture of everyday life is heavily gendered, and it is the discernment and critique of these gendered practices that is their central task. As such, we need to address the possible points of articulation between Schrag's work and that of a postmodern feminism, particularly in regard to issues of self/identity and discursive practices.

One significant and fruitful point of articulation is the focus on the role of narrative as a pivotal, constitutive, feature of everyday life. Indeed, the field of communication writ large has seen the emergence of what Walter Fisher has termed a "narrative paradigm."[25] In this view, human beings function *qua* humans insofar as they make sense of the world via narrative. Such a perspective has had a significant impact in areas such as organizational communication,[26] performance studies,[27] and interpersonal communication.[28] Perhaps the most important point to make about such work is that it takes narrative to be not merely the representation or expression of an already constituted and coherent identity that speaks about an objective, fixed world. Rather, narrative "is a form and dynamics of the self as life-experiencing subject."[29] In this sense, narrative is positioned as ontologically structuring human experience.

However, we must be careful here not to slide inexorably into the kind of postmodern "text positivism" that Schrag and others have warned against. Self and world are not exhausted by the narrativizing of human experience; rather, narrative provides the discursive context through which discourse and action are articulated. Thus, in adopting a narrative perspective on social practices and processes, we are interested in the extent to which the relationship between self and world is realized through communicative praxis. In other words, the narrativized self is always already situated within the discursive and nondiscursive context of habits, social customs, and institutional structures.[30]

Furthermore, narrative is not simply textual; it exists as both discourse and action. At its simplest level, narrative has to be told by a speaker or writer to an audience in order to be considered a story. Such a view does not reassert the priority of the rational, modernist subject, but rather recognizes the multiplicity, flux, and becoming of meaning. Consistent with the postmodern turn, the author(ity) of such narratives is decentered, becoming part of a network of interdependent systems of meaning that include readers, listeners, and reinterpreters of such narratives. As Schrag states, "Discourse becomes narrative; the logos as "word" is taken up into the logos as "story."[31]

What, then, of feminist studies? In what ways can we articulate Schrag's narrative model of self and rationality, and feminist concerns with issues of gender, identity, discourse, power and resistance. That connection, one can argue, lies in Schrag's work itself (although not in a fully explicated manner). Invoking Julia Kristeva's "politics of marginality,"[32] with its focus on the micropolitics of marginalized groups, Schrag argues that:

> any effort to sketch a portrait of the human self needs to move away from purely semiotic or linguistic investigations to a psychology of motivation and action, and then to the wider economy of a polis in which the production and exchange of signs and the performance of individuated action first find their proper context for understanding and explanation.[33]

From a (postmodern) feminist perspective, such a vision implicitly captures the ways in which gendered identities unfold in the communicative praxis of everyday life. Gendered identities are storied/narrated, but these narratives are always partial, contested, and situated within the larger economy of signs, material practices, and sedimented structures of power and domination.

In order to make these issues more concrete, I explore two extended examples of narrated identities. I am interested in each as exemplifying the processes through which the (gendered) self is constructed within the political economy of communicative praxis.

NARRATIVE, THE [RACED] SELF, AND COMMUNICATIVE PRAXIS

Patricia Williams—an African American critical legal scholar—relates the following story:

> Buzzers are big in New York City. Favored particularly by smaller stores and boutiques, merchants throughout the city have installed them as screening devices to reduce the incidence of robbery: if the face at the door looks desirable, the buzzer is pressed and the door is unlocked. If the face is that of an undesirable, the door stays pressed and the door is locked. I discovered [these buzzers] and their meaning one Saturday in 1986. I was shopping in Soho and saw in a store window a sweater that I wanted to buy for my mother. I pressed my round brown face to the window and my finger to the buzzer, seeking admittance. A narrow-eyed white teenager, wearing running shoes and feasting on bubble gum glared out, evaluating me for signs that would pit me against the limits of his social understanding. After about five minutes, he mouthed "we're closed," and blew rubber at me. It was two Saturdays before Christmas, at one o'clock in the afternoon; there were several white people in the store who appeared to be shopping for things for *their* mothers.[34]

In many ways this story fits our conventional understanding of narrative: it has an identifiable storyteller (Williams), protagonists (Williams and the teenager), a sense of temporality (it recounts a past event), an implied audience (the reader), and a plot structure with a surprising denouement (a black woman's desire to purchase a Christmas gift for her mother is unexpectedly thwarted by a white, teenage sentinel). Most significantly, the narrative has embedded within it what one can regard as a distinguishing feature of this trope—a moral imperative. Narratives distinguish themselves from other forms of discourse to the extent that they lead us to make particular value judgements about the nature of the world and our role in it. In this particular instance, the moral imperative has to do with the daily injustices of racism. This story brings into sharp relief the stark, day-to-day realities of living in a world where "whiteness" is the discursive system of representations through which all "others" are interpellated and made sense of—it is a world that those of us with white skin do not have to confront.

This narrative, then, exemplifies the politics of marginality as they get played out at the intersection of various discursive and nondiscursive practices. Although identities of race and gender are discursively constructed, they are also reinforced by, and reproduce, such material realities as buzzers, locked doors, and the white male objectifying and evaluative gaze. But physical structures such as buzzers and locked doors are also signs, existing as signifying micropractices within the larger political economy of race, class, and gender. That is, they not only control space, but *signify* the ability of the powerful to limit access to the space that they control. Similarly, narratives are material in their structuring of meaning systems that have practical consequences for individuals and social groups. For example, in Williams' story, the "grand narrative" that positions African Americans as poor and criminal looms large in the sense-making processes of the teenager, literally and physically positioning Williams as marginal and disenfranchised.

Narratives, however, do not exist in isolation; indeed, their meaning(s) are derived from their positioning in the larger network of discourses and actions. In the case of Williams' story, its meaning is inseparable from other narratives that provide the context for our interpretive processes. Indeed, exploration of these embedded narratives reveals complex and contradictory signifying practices. In addition to the grand narrative of race, the story also draws on and critiques the larger narrative of commodity capitalism. For example, the store to which Williams was denied access was Benetton, a company that has consistently appropriated images of racial harmony and social and political progress as part of its marketing strategy. Thus, a contradiction emerges between the careful privatization of and controlling of access to commercial space for "desirable" customers, and the public articulation of an image based on the celebration of difference and a philosophy of inclusion and social change. In this instance, Benetton's postmodern aestheticism is confronted, deconstructed, and contradicted by a narrative account that highlights the intimate connection between racism and the privatization of public space for commercial profit.

We can see, then, that Williams' narrative needs to be made sense of within the multiple and contradictory discourses of race, gender, commodity capitalism, and patriarchy. Although ostensibly it is a personal story of racism, any reading is inseparable from the wider political economy (production and exchange) of signs within which it is situated and from which it draws. Such an analysis helps to bring to life Schrag's claim that we need to look for meaning "within the play of social practices"—that is, as an achievement of communicative praxis. However, one must recognize that such meaning making processes are born of processes of contradiction and overdetermination. In this sense, the "who" of discourse is always contingent, decentered, and fragmented—a condition that is highlighted in my second example.

NARRATING [GENDERED] SELVES

Doreen Kondo's magnificent ethnography, *Crafting Selves*, is a rich and textured account of everyday life on the shop floor of a small, family-owned Japanese company in the Shitamachi area of Tokyo. This book is an important piece of scholarship for a number of reasons, but two are particularly significant for our purposes.

First, Kondo's ethnography deconstructs and undermines the Western (particularly the United States) image of the Japanese "economic miracle" and its success through strong corporate culture, loyalty, harmony, and lifetime employment. This dominant "orientalist"[35] model of the Japanese self, employed by western observers to explain the challenge to U.S. economic and political hegemony, is shown by Kondo to be "based almost entirely on large industry, on elite government bureaucracies, and on the lives of Organization Men in elite firms."[36] Indeed, Kondo shows that less than 20 percent of the labor force is employed in such organizations, which constitute about 1 percent of the total number of businesses in Japan. The vast majority of Japanese workers are employed with small, family-owned businesses (defined as less than 300 employees for manufacturing businesses, or less than fifty for wholesale and retail businesses), many of which struggle to remain profitable. The workers in such companies are frequently poorly paid, female, part-time employees with little opportunity for advancement. In this sense, Kondo's ethnography takes as its focal point the politics of marginality, and brings to light a narrative that is heavily obscured by the political and economic exigencies of U.S. economic and cultural imperialism.

Second, the principal focus of Kondo's study is the interrelationship of power, gender, and discourses of identity as they are articulated together in the communicative praxis of everyday life. Most significantly, her account challenges Western notions of a stable, unitary, pregiven identity that is relatively transparent to self and others. In contrast, she shows how Japanese self-identity is shifting, fragmentary, and contradictory, and heavily contingent on issues of class, gender, cultural context, and language. Although it is not possible to do justice to the broad range of issues that Kondo addresses, there is one particular example from her study that speaks eloquently to narrative as "a form and dynamics of self as life-experiencing subject."[37] Furthermore, this example illustrates the self as the narrative expression of complex and contradictory relations of gender, class, and power.

Kondo's ethnography is conducted in a family-owned pastry company. In her account, two of the principal sets of protagonists are the male, highly trained artisans who are responsible for designing and creating the confections and pastries that the company sells, and the female, part-time, poorly-paid workers whose job is to mass produce the items designed by the artisans. In Harry Braverman's sense, we see here the classic capitalist separation of conception and execution of labor, divided along gender and class lines.[38] However, what is particularly fascinating about this example is Kondo's analysis of the narrative construction of identities that occurs among these two different groups. For example, Kondo spends an entire chapter discussing a life narrative that Ohara-san, a male artisan, told to her. Kondo analyzes this narrative as a means of self-construction for Ohara-san, showing how it is a "paean to his artisanal aesthetic" and how it self-constructs him as the embodiment of "traditional" craftsmanship. However, Kondo mitigates this rather romantic reading to show how, in addition to articulating an aesthetic artisanal identity that ties Ohara-san to a long tradition of craftsmanship, this narrative is also implicated in—and reproduces—larger systems of power relations:

> [T]he discourse on artisanal identity, when contextualized within the workplace, reveals itself as a way of creating and legitimating hierarchy, by partially excluding all part-time workers, almost all of whom are women. Cultural meanings are not free-floating and disembodied, but are implicated in systems of power relations.[39]

Thus, the artisan's romantic narrative that constructs his craft identity, is also shown by Kondo to be a narrative of exclusion, *once it is situated within the larger context of the political economy of the workplace, and the play of social practices*. Thus, the narrative reveals its more complex meaning(s) only when examined as a moment of communicative praxis embedded within, and expressive of, the larger system of discursive and nondiscursive practices.

However, the artisan's narrative of identity/exclusion is not hegemonic in the sense of producing a "sutured totality" of meaning.[40] Alternative narratives also exist on the shop floor which Kondo studies. In describing the stories told to her by the female part-time employees, she states the following:

> Their narrative production of work identity—far from single, seamless performance delivered to a rapt audience—were pervaded by a sense of fragmentation, both in the circumstances of the telling and in the narrative line, as the women simply moved from one part-time job to another, without a teleology to satisfy desires for totalizing narrative closure, a ready sense of progress, or some easily discernible way to perceive continuity. . . . The narrative conventions shaping their work histories seem contingent and noncumulative, a series of episodes that focus less on the joys of work itself than on the general value placed on adding a bit to the family income and doing something other than sitting at home.[41]

One of the most fascinating aspects of this account is the degree to which, structurally speaking, the women workers' narratives are a discursive manifestation of their marginal, contingent position in the political economy of the workplace. Although the narrative voice of the artisan (described by Kondo as a "commanding, masterful performance of a coherent, familiar story") is singular—an embodiment of the modernist vision of knowledge and progress—the narrative voices of the women workers are fragmented, incomplete, and decentered. Such a recognition highlights an important but often neglected feature of the everyday power relations that undergird communication processes. That is, the "who" of discourse frequently has a problematic relationship to that discourse, particularly in terms of their opportunities for articulating self-identities. In this sense, one important indicator of power has to do with the opportunities for self-expression that a particular institution affords. The political economy of the workplace allowed these women room only for the articulation of an identity in the interstices of existing structures of discourse and action.

As Kondo shows, however, this interstitial self is simultaneously marginal and resistant. By drawing on traditional conceptions of gendered identities, these women workers on the one hand ensure their marginality within a strong masculine ethos of heroic hard work and artisanship, while on the other hand they situate themselves as indispensable to the everyday life of the factory by bringing their roles as mothers to the shop floor. Indeed, Kondo shows how the women workers, by invoking their obligation to *Uchi* (home), are able to undercut the masculine values of punishing endurance on the job.

Schrag's claim that the "who" of discourse is an achievement, a performance unfolding in everyday life, is perhaps never better borne out than in Kondo's analysis of the fragmented, contingent, and ironic selves of the Japanese workplace. However, as an empirical illustration of the processes underlying this "who," Kondo is able to illustrate vividly the extent to which such a performance is shot through with contradictory issues of class, gender, and race. As such, "the texture of everyday life" is an uneven texture made up of rips, knots, and flaws, and not everyone is equally included in its weaving.

CONCLUSION

The juxtaposition of elements of Schrag's philosophical project with recent developments in postmodern feminism brings to light a number of important issues for contemporary communication scholars. Most significant, perhaps, is the insight that the "speaking subject" of communication (Schrag's "who" of discourse) is not the coherent, unitary, unproblematic subject of Cartesian modernity, but is rather contingent, fragmentary, and imbued with possibility. Such a recognition does not undercut the very raison d'être of communication studies; instead, it reaffirms its significance. Although much of our field has framed communication as the externalization of mental representations of an objective world, both Schrag's project and that of postmodern feminism takes the relationship among self, communication, and world as precisely that which must be understood. In this sense, decentering the speaking subject of modernity recenters communication as the ontological condition for human becoming and community.[42] In the spirit of Derrida's work, decentering the subject does not mean getting rid of it, but rather of "knowing where it comes from and how it functions."[43] Such a project is radically communicative in its assumptions.

Finally, as intellectuals operating in the interstitial space between modernity and postmodernity, both Schrag and postmodern feminism articulate a model of rationality and meaning that "is transversal to the multiplicity of our discursive and nondiscursive practices."[44] Both recognize that it is neither through an appeal to some metaphysical conception of universal experience, nor to a notion of meaning rooted in "the rhapsodic play of *différance* and a rampant pluralism"[45] that human self-understanding lies. Rather, it is only through a thoroughly praxis-oriented conception of self, rooted in analyses of the moment-to-moment exigencies of discursive and nondiscursive practices, that we can come to understand and appreciate the nuances of human being-in-the-world. It is in such a model that we can recognize systems of marginality and inclusion, resistance and domination, and moments of possibility and closure. For the moments of possibility that—through his writings—Schrag has opened before us, we are in his debt.

NOTES

1. It is a distinct honor to be a part of this celebration of the work of Calvin Schrag, and to have the privilege of addressing the work of a philosopher who, in the course of his career, has contributed much to the field of communication. Indeed, one might argue that, despite calling philosophy his disciplinary home, Schrag has taken the problematic of human communication more seriously than many of us who are trained in this field. Even a cursory examination of his work will quickly establish that almost his entire oeuvre has been devoted to a systematic examination of the connections among communication, reason, meaning, self, and praxis. In fact, more than most philosophers or communicologists, Schrag is

a philosopher of everyday life who is profoundly interested in the processes through which human beings engage in the complex and precarious task of meaning making. His is a communo-philosophical project that enhances significantly our understanding of the human communication condition.

2. Calvin O. Schrag, *The Resources of Rationality: A Response to the Postmodern Challenge* (Bloomington: Indiana University Press, 1992), 7.

3. Ibid., 17–23.

4. See, for example, Jane Flax, *Thinking Fragments: Psychoanalysis, Feminism, and Postmodernism in the Contemporary West* (Berkeley: University of California Press, 1990); Susan Bordo, "Postmodern Subjects, Postmodern Bodies," *Feminist Studies,* vol. 18 (1992): 159–175; Judith Butler, *Gender Trouble: Feminism and the Subversion of Identity* (New York: Routledge, 1990); Dorinne K. Kondo, *Crafting Selves: Power, Gender, and Discourses of Identity in a Japanese Workplace* (Chicago: University of Chicago Press, 1990); Chris Weedon, *Feminist Practice and Poststructuralist Theory* (Oxford: Basil Blackwell, 1987).

5. Calvin O. Schrag, "Transversal Rationality," in *The Question of Hermeneutics*, ed. T. J. Stapleton (Amsterdam: Kluwer Academic Publishers, 1994), 71.

6. Ibid., 69.

7. Schrag, *Resources of Rationality*, 57.

8. Fredric Jameson, "Foreword to J-F Lyotard," in *The Postmodern Condition* (Minneapolis: University of Minnesota Press, 1984), vii–xi.

9. Nancy Hartsock, "Foucault on Power: A Theory for Women?," in *Feminism/Postmodernism*, ed. Linda J. Nicholson (New York: Routledge, 1990), 75.

10. Anne Balsamo, "Un-wrapping the Postmodern: A Feminist Glance," *Journal of Communication Inquiry,* vol. 11 (1987): 64.

11. Seyla Benhabib, "Feminism and Postmodernism: An Uneasy Alliance," *Praxis International,* vol. 11 (1991): 137–150.

12. Nancy Fraser and Linda Nicholson, "Social Criticism without Philosophy: An Encounter between Feminism and Postmodernism," in *Feminism/Postmodernism*, ed. Linda Nicholson (New York: Routledge, 1990), 19–38.

13. Linda Singer, "Feminism and Postmodernism," in *Feminists Theorize the Political*, ed. Judith Butler and Joan Scott (New York: Routledge, 1992), 475.

14. Michel Foucault, *The Order of Things: An Archaeology of the Human Sciences* (New York: Vintage, 1973).

15. Simone De Beauvoir, *The Second Sex*, trans. E. M. Parshley (New York: Vintage, 1973).

16. Judith Butler, "Contingent Foundations: Feminism and the *Question* of Postmodernism," *Praxis International,* vol. 11 (1991): 160.

17. Calvin O. Schrag, *The Self after Postmodernity* (New Haven: Yale University Press, 1997), 14.

18. Flax, *Thinking Fragments*, 179–183.

19. Ibid., 219.

20. Kathy Ferguson, *The Man Question: Visions of Subjectivity in Feminist Theory* (Berkeley: University of California Press, 1993), 4.

21. Schrag, *The Self after Postmodernity*, 28.

22. Richard Rorty, *Philosophy and the Mirror of Nature* (Princeton: Princeton University Press, 1979).

23. Schrag, *The Self after Postmodernity*, 33.

24. Schrag, *The Resources of Rationality*, 94.

25. Walter R. Fisher, "Narration as a Human Communication Paradigm: The Case of Public Moral Argument," *Communication Monographs*, vol. 51 (1984): 1–22.

26. See, for example, Dennis K. Mumby, "The Political Function of Narrative in Organizations," *Communication Monographs*, vol. 54 (1987): 113–127; Robin Patric Clair, "The Use of Framing Devices to Sequester Organizational Narratives: Hegemony and Harassment," *Communication Monographs*, vol. 60 (1993): 113–136; James Helmer, "Storytelling in the Creation and Maintenance of Organizational Tension and Stratification," *The Southern Communication Journal*, vol. 59 (1993): 34–44.

27. Kristin M. Langellier, "Personal Narratives: Perspectives on Theory and Research," *Text and Performance Quarterly*, vol. 9 (1989): 243–276.

28. William K. Rawlins, *Friendship Matters* (New York: De Gruyter, 1989).

29. Schrag, *The Self after Postmodernity*, 42.

30. Ibid., 26.

31. Schrag, *Resources of Rationality*, 93.

32. Schrag, *The Self after Postmodernity*, 72.

33. Ibid.

34. Quoted in Candace West and Sarah Fenstermaker, "Doing Difference," *Gender and Society*, vol. 9 (1995): 31.

35. Edward Said, *Orientalism* (New York: Pantheon, 1978).

36. Kondo, *Crafting Selves*, 50.

37. Schrag, *The Self after Postmodernity*, 42.

38. Harry Braverman, *Labor and Monopoly Capital: The Degradation of Work in the Twentieth Century* (New York: Monthly Review Press, 1974).

39. Kondo, *Crafting Selves*, 231.

40. Ernesto Laclau and Chantal Mouffe, *Hegemony and Socialist Strategy: Towards a Radical Democratic Politics*, trans. Winston Moore and Paul Cammack (London: Verso, 1985).

41. Kondo, *Crafting Selves*, 260.

42. Greg Shepherd, "Building a Discipline of Communication," *Journal of Communication*, vol. 43 (1993): 83–91.

43. Quoted in Schrag, *The Self after Postmodernity*, 14.

44. Schrag, "Transversal Rationality," 68.

45. Schrag, *Resources of Rationality*, 9.

9 Epistemology, Tropology, Hermeneutics, and the "Essence of Language"

LENORE LANGSDORF

> Philosophy emerged out of rhetoric. We thus seem to become spectators of a rather remarkable homecoming.
>
> —Calvin O. Schrag, "Rhetoric Resituated at the End of Philosophy"[1]

> The recovery of the space of communicative praxis places us on a new terrain and provides us with a new beginning. . . . We enter the hermeneutical space in which . . . the dialogue between rhetoric and philosophy first begins.
>
> —Calvin O. Schrag, "Rhetoric Resituated at the End of Philosophy"[2]

The notion that the end of philosophy is a rebirth of rhetoric is promulgated in a variety of implicit and explicit ways in contemporary theory. It receives a mixed reception that seems to depend upon how we understand philosophy and rhetoric and whether we welcome the "linguistic turn" that both Euroamerican and analytic philosophy took in the middle years of the twentieth century. The effect of that reorientation of philosophical attention was to engage philosophers with material—language—that was largely ceded (or, left to) rhetoricians, after the division of labor wrought by Plato and Gorgias. After a long period of separate and sometimes contentious development, often marked by strikingly different disciplinary-sanctioned readings of the same texts, contemporary interest in devising alternatives to modernist conceptions of the subject, object, and process of inquiry encourages taking up this shared interest in language for clues to such an alternative.

I take up that theme here by focusing on the interpretive dimension of language in use—that is, in communicative praxis—and on the very nature of language itself. To this hermeneutic phenomenologist, the very divergence in how philosophy and rhetoric go about the use and investigation of language suggests that the homecoming of philosophy that Calvin O. Schrag discerns may benefit from discussion of what language—"the thing itself"—is, as well as how it actually functions in the communicative praxis of everyday life. I take my clue for the first topic from Martin Heidegger's thesis "that the essential being of language cannot be anything linguistic."[3] My focus in regard to the second topic—how language functions in everyday life—is directed toward how communicative praxis uses that "essential being."

In the first section of the chapter, I sketch traditional notions of philosophy and rhetoric in order to emphasize the different directions they took since their origins in classical scholarship, and the extent to which both endeavors ignored or denied their interpretive dimension. The second section takes up Heidegger's observation on the recursive nature of the builder's task and Paul Ricoeur's call for "reinterpretations and reappropriations" of "philosophies of the past,"[4] in order to discern, despite their self-descriptions, the interpretive dimension within both endeavors. Heidegger's conception of interpretation as ontological, along with Ricoeur's conception of discourse as distinct from language and Schrag's conception of communicative praxis, are vital to this section's "excavation" (in contrast to "deconstruction") of the subject, object, and process involved in philosophy and rhetoric. In the third section, I turn to interpreting certain cryptic remarks on the "essential being of language" and the nature of messages in *On the Way to Language*. Heidegger's insistence upon reminding us that he adhered to Husserl's goal of "disclosing the things themselves"[5] suggests reading those remarks as clues for a path that both rhetoric and philosophy take in coming home to "a new terrain" of hermeneutical space that "provides us with a new beginning." Rather than analyzing language as a virtual system of signs, Heidegger's investigation began from the actual presence of language in saying—that is, in communicative praxis. I recognize this starting point as a response to Husserl's call for a phenomenology of the life world.[6] It's from that starting point that he sought to discern "the essential being of language," which he maintained, "cannot be anything linguistic." If we take this starting point as the site for the convergence that Schrag discerns as a resituation of rhetoric at the end of philosophy, we find that this convergence is of a philosophy and rhetoric quite different from those that parted in classical thought.[7]

PART ONE: THE LEAVETAKING

> The theory that philosophy is rhetoric, or worse still, that rhetoric is philosophy, causes scandal. In traditional philosophy we look for objectivity, in other words, what the object is for itself. We look therefore for non-subjectivity, for ahistoricity. This has resulted in the rejection, on the part of traditional metaphysics, of everything that can 'disturb' rational access to the object; that is, any rhetorical language linked to time and place or influenced by emotion which distracts from man's proper logical processes.
>
> —Ernesto Grassi, "Why Rhetoric is Philosophy"[8]

> Rhetoric is the counterpart of Dialectic. . . .Rhetoric may be defined as the faculty of observing in any given case the available means of persuasion.
>
> —Aristotle, *Rhetoric*, Book One

Any talk of "philosophy" or "rhetoric" in the singular form relies upon tacitly drawn threads of connection between the many varieties of philosophical and rhetorical thinking in our history. In other words, there is no single definition that would suit any and all of the practices designated by those names since Socrates, Gorgias, and Aristotle turned their attention to delineating their nature, relation, and difference. The brief and highly selective sketch of traditional philosophy and rhetoric that I develop in this section begins with the identification of domicile and action suggested in the remark by Schrag that serves as epigraph for this paper: "Philosophy emerged out of rhetoric." The suggestion—with which I agree—is that of a part distinguishing itself from the whole; which is to say, that rhetorical practices potentially or actually included philosophical practices, but practitioners—people who used both forms of thinking in their communicative activity—gradually differentiated them and came to consider them as separate endeavors. As is often the case when distinct entities emerge from a social process, the results become reified, so that later practitioners take as fixed and natural what was a fluid and social process of identification by delineation. Thus, my characterizations of "traditional philosophy" and "traditional rhetoric" in this section focus on what made those practices distinct from one another. In the following section, I focus on the implicit hermeneutic dimension of both practices.

Ernesto Grassi's identification of traditional philosophy's focus on objectivity reminds us of a locus that persists throughout a tangle of implicit assumptions that have changed significantly throughout philosophy's history. Surely, the object of inquiry for Plato was the form, not the things or events that instantiate it. In other words, the object of dialectic—of philosophy, in contrast to rhetoric—was analysis of ideas or concepts, rather than investigation of things and events, which Plato took to be intrinsically imperfect manifestations of their forms. The evident distrust of multiplicity and diversity in Plato's political philosophy and ethics is equally evident in his metaphysics and epistemology: We find throughout the dialogues a persistent effort on Socrates' part to shift his interlocutors' attention from the multiplicity of appearances and things to the singular ideas that they manifest. This effort rarely succeeded: The class system proposed in *Republic* III.415, and the need for philosopher-kings (dialecticians who excel in both "pure" and "practical" reasoning), emphasized in *Republic* V.473d, document Plato's low opinion of most citizens' epistemic abilities.

In contrast to that orientation, Aristotle's *Metaphysics* opens with the observation that "[a]ll men naturally have an impulse to get knowledge," and immediately adds this evidence: "A sign of this is the way we prize our senses. . . ." ("We" here does not seem to include those who follow the Platonic injunction [most clearly advocated in *Republic* VI.510–VII.518] to turn from knowledge sought through use of the senses to that achieved through dialectic.) Aristotle's empirical turn, however, did not rest with simply reporting information gained in experience. Nor was it directed upon the diverse and even contradictory systems of belief about objects that could be found as one traveled to the ends of the then-known Earth. Rather, observation was the first step toward categorization, which enabled discerning the nature of any object in terms of genus and species and then, within those typologies, investigating all things in terms of their material, efficient, formal, and final "causes."

These conceptually- and empirically-oriented strands of classical philosophy were taken up into the Christian synthesis of late antiquity and the medieval period, for which the object of inquiry became God and His works. Desacralization of the universe in early modern philosophy retained that focus on "works," but now with a strongly empirical turn toward how the universe itself (including the objects within it) works, which is to say that Divine authorship was no longer pertinent to the metaphysical and epistemological mainstream of philosophy. The assumption that was retained, however, was that both conceptual and empirical modes of inquiry were properly focused on objects that await human investigation. Perhaps as a result of reasoning analogously from the impressive results of natural-scientific inquiry, desacralization intensified dehumanization. In Grassi's phrase, inquiry (as advocated within the empiricism of Francis Bacon and John Locke) focused on "what the object is for itself," or (within Kantian rationalism) on how objects must be known in terms of the forms and categories employed by any thinking being whatsoever. More methodologically-oriented modern philosophy would add: known by anyone equipped with the appropriate techniques of instrumentation or logic. The very proliferation of those techniques may well have necessitated the increasing focus on method that characterized modern philosophy, and the almost exclusive attention to logic and language—the "tools" of philosophical method—in late modernity. Early postmodern philosophy intensifies the focus on language, and often does so in isolation from the sociopolitical environment of a text. In other words, it focuses on language as a game that is of interest because of its structure or rules; or, as a space in which words play. For other philosophers, language—theorized as discourse—is of interest because of the systems of power that are discerned as the producers of texts.

This contemporary preoccupation with text and systems of power/knowledge may seem quite distant in content as well as time from classical philosophy's focus on conceptual and empirical objects. Yet there is one tacit assumption that persists throughout this (admittedly sketchy and selective) history of traditional philosophy: The proper task of philosophy is epistemology and metaphysics, aimed at knowing the nature of objects, whether empirical (spatiotemporal things and events that may be observed) or conceptual (ideas, essences, concepts, propositions, systems of power, or language games that may "come to mind" at any time or place). Correlatively, the proper task of philosophy has not been investigation of the communicative praxis of actual human beings; of questions about how humans effectively articulate their experience with empirical or conceptual objects. Those questions have been of interest to rhetoric, but rhetoric's response to them, as Schrag notes, "congealed into a formalized body of procedures and principles" in which "method is construed as mere technique."[9] It will be useful to sketch that history before turning to the neglected hermeneutic presence within both endeavors.

Traditional rhetoric began in the oral/aural culture of ancient Greece. Even as it increasingly concerned itself with written as well as oral communication, it remained engaged with the actual effects of language use in daily life as well as in special contexts such as judicial proceedings and legislative assemblies. This concern with *how* language *works* (rather than with what words *mean*), and how it works differently in different contexts, encourages an instrumental rather than epistemological focus. In other words, rhetoric's focus on how particular attitudes, beliefs, practices, and values come to be adopted by particular people in particular circumstances presupposes an interest in using language as a tool (instrument) to bring about changes in the lives of those people. Speakers/authors are audience-centered insofar as they are responding to listeners' questions and needs. But they must also be speaker/author centered, insofar as they access their own experience to provide those responses. Rhetors seek to effectively articulate ideas by construing what is at issue as meaning this, rather than that; as calling for this action, rather than that. Thus rhetoric provides a bridge between the interests of the speaker/author and those of the listener/reader that is constructed by the former, to influence the latter, but is only effective insofar as it responds to what is of issue to the latter.

There is a sense in which traditional rhetoric has no more need of hermeneutic than does traditional philosophy, for the rhetor aims to provide responses to the audience's (implicit and explicit) questions that will be readily understood, which is to say, will require little interpretive effort from the listener/reader. Yet, rhetors must put interpretive effort into their own understanding of the interests of their audiences (which often are not, or not only, what they immediately seem to be) and the contexts from which those interests emerge. The rhetorical activity which was a topic of contention for Socrates and Gorgias occurred in a primarily oral/aural context, among people who lived within a relatively cohesive culture that provided stable rules for public discourse, and so interpretive effort was minimized. As Gorgias says in response to Socrates' query, "persuasion is the chief end of rhetoric," and that goal involved performances tailored to influencing specific audiences operating with relatively stable procedures: "the judges in the courts, or the senators in the council, or the citizens in the assembly" (*Gorgias* 452). The rhetoricians were, in effect, the lawyers of ancient Greece, for since citizens had to present their own positions and cases in the courts, council, and assembly, they had to learn (from rhetoricians) the rules and conventions specific to each of those places, and how to effectively articulate their interests within the relevant constraints. Both hermeneutic's concern for multiple interpretations and philosophy's concern for truth were neglected by rhetoric's primary concern for effective strategy. It's not surprising, then, that rhetoricians' nasty reputation (as documented by Plato) came to be shared, to a great extent, by lawyers (as documented by popular discourse, and especially jokes).

Aristotle systematized the rhetorical practices that the Sophists had taught, and so emphasized a method that would establish probability through deliberation, rather than (as in Plato's method) certainty through dialectic. "All men naturally have an impulse to get knowledge" (*Metaphysics* 1.980a) certainly indicates a broadened conception of the category of those interested in knowing, in comparison to Plato's mistrust of the many's abilities.[10] A reconception of knowing accompanied this revision of expectations in regard to who belonged in the category of knowers. Along with seeking probable rather than certain knowledge, there was a change in method from analysis of ideas (forms) in order to explain things, to observation, categorization, and deliberation concerning things and events, in order to discern their causes. Aristotelian rhetoric traveled from Greece to the Hellenistic world and then to Rome, but declined with the growth of the Roman empire. In that changed polity, the senate controlled the empire on the basis of economic and military power, and so need for deliberation in the courts and assemblies declined.

A synoptic look at the history of rhetoric from the first century onward reveals an almost uninterrupted growth in the importance of declamation and style in influencing audiences, in opposition to deliberation that would inform, and even enlighten, rhetors and their audiences. There were two exceptions. The first was in the fifth century, with St. Augustine's call for deliberation in order to achieve wisdom in spiritual, in contrast to political, affairs. That goal necessitated emphasis on clarity (rather than eloquence) in order to direct attention to the truth revealed by the rhetor's words, rather than allow attention to be diverted to the display of those words. The primary object of attention in Augustinian rhetoric, therefore, was Divine Truth; once that was grasped, the rational abilities of each listener/author could be relied upon to devise correct action. The second exception was in the fifteenth century, as the Renaissance humanists revived attention to wisdom combined with eloquence, in the service of communicating virtue. But Peter Ramus' explicit transfer of the most epistemic of the traditional tasks of rhetoric—invention and arrangement—to philosophy in the sixteenth century simply ratified the dominant belief of preceding centuries: Rhetoric was a matter of style and delivery, whether employed in the service of grasping Divine Truth or of moving the audience to action in accord with the rhetor's purposes.

The rise of observational science in the seventeenth century denigrated style as likely to interfere with simple reporting of observations. Plain speech (which was taken to be the absence of style) was extolled for enabling clarity—not, as for Augustine, so that spiritual truth could be revealed, but so that words would directly re-present observed things and events. The Protestant Reformation reinforced what the Scientific Revolution preached: Clear thinking and plain language would do away with (in Grassi's words) "anything that can 'disturb' rational access to the object." The Enlightenment relied upon a variety of impressive arguments from authority: Aristotle's conviction that all human beings "naturally have an impulse to get knowledge"; Descartes' provision of a method that would allow access to "clear and distinct ideas" of things, and so allow knowledge of the spatiotemporal environment comparable to the certain knowledge attributed to mathematical and logical deduction; Locke's new job description for philosophers (appropriate in an age that would replace kings, rather than attempting to make them philosophers), which would set them to clearing away the "underbrush" that obscured men's path of inquiry. The overall direction was clear: Influence, reaching into persuasion, was an inappropriate way for rational beings to come to conclusions about themselves and the things in their environment. Philosophy that served science by taking up Locke's "underlaborer" task was approved; rhetoric that took something away from one man's rationality insofar as it made him subject to the interests of another was not. A modern rhetoric textbook summarizes that end of traditional rhetoric's journey in this way: "The members of the British Royal Society, founded in 1660, envisioned a world without rhetoric, a world where people would speak of things as they really were, without the colorings of style, in plain language as clear as glass, so many words for so many things."[11]

There is little in the history of traditional philosophy and rhetoric, in these admittedly sketchy presentations, that would give hope for their reconciliation or convergence. In the next section, however, I thematize a strand within both endeavors that offers a basis for the rebirth of rhetoric at the end of philosophy that Schrag discerns. That strand is interpretation, which is present in both rhetoric and philosophy—despite the fact that rhetoric traditionally understands itself as primarily engaged in persuasion, and philosophy, correlatively, traditionally understands its task as analysis that permits correct representation of things in words. Underneath both those self-portrayals, however, we can find an implicit reliance upon interpretation of persons, situations, and things. A certain amount of intellectual excavation is needed to identify that substructure; we can now turn to that task.

PART TWO: HERMENEUTIC

> Builders must at times return to construction sites they left behind, or go back even further.
>
> —Martin Heidegger, "A Dialogue on Language"[12]

> . . . philosophies of the past remain open to reinterpretations and reappropriations, thanks to a meaning potential left unexploited, even repressed. . . . if one cannot reawaken and liberate those resources . . . no innovation would be possible, and present thought would have only the choice between repetition and aimless wandering.
>
> —Paul Ricoeur, *Oneself as Another*[13]

When we take up the task of revisiting "construction sites"—here, the spaces of traditional philosophy and rhetoric—we must recognize the fact that talk of construction, in our contemporary intellectual context, carries a subtext of deconstruction. Thus the goal of excavating these spaces needs differentiation from that of deconstruction. As I understand the latter, deconstructive theory takes a wrecking ball (so to speak) to three traditional pillars of philosophy:

a. the separation of knowledge from power, which supports an epistemological conception of the *object* of communicative praxis,
b. the relation between the signifier and signified, which supports a semiotic conception of the communicative *process*,
c. and the assumption that human beings are selves who exercise unilateral agency in knowing their environment, which supports an individualistic conception of the communicative *subject* as the locus of power.[14]

Schrag has emphasized that the "deconstructivist strategy" through which these assumptions are refused is "the negating moment . . . through which the authority of the tradition is placed into question."[15] Those assumptions inform a conception of communication based in traditional philosophy and rhetoric—a conception that leaves the resources of hermeneutic (in Ricoeur's words) "unexploited, even repressed." Schrag finds both rhetoric and philosophy implicated in that repression: Whereas philosophy became "a formalized body of procedures which purportedly yield a representation of reality and a rational reconstruction of knowledge," attuned to a desire for transparent knowing of objects, rhetoric "congealed into a formalized body of procedures and principles" for knowing how to influence subjects.[16] He proposes, however, that correlative to deconstruction's "negating moment" is "an affirming moment . . . that provides a new beginning."[17] This "new beginning" could be a theorizing and practicing of philosophy and rhetoric as complementary modes of interpretation, rather than as opposed modes of extracting information from things and influencing persons. Excavation, in contrast to deconstruction, thematizes implicit facets of a phenomenon by articulating what else is present, along with its more evident constituents. Thematizing—arguing for the implicit presence of features which are thereby made explicit—is the first step toward proposing how that "what else" may account for the phenomenon as it presents itself, as well as serve as the basis for reconceiving it as it might be.

In what follows, I develop the beginnings of an affirmative moment by sketching Heidegger's ontological turn in hermeneutic and Ricoeur's explication of discourse as the process in which understanding happens. That will allow us to recognize hermeneutic's presence within traditional philosophy and rhetoric, and so, recognize that communicative praxis actually thrives in a hermeneutic space, rather than in a linguistic edifice resting on the assumptions regarding process, object, and subject that are evident in traditional philosophy and rhetoric, and are the target of contemporary deconstructive strategies.

One reason for the unnoticed (and perhaps repressed) presence of hermeneutic within traditional philosophy and rhetoric may be Plato's valorization of modes of communication which seem to do without strategies for interpretation. This preference is stated quite clearly in *Protagoras* (347–348) when he characterizes "talk about the poets" as "a commonplace entertainment to which a vulgar company have recourse . . . because they are not able to converse." He contrasts that talk to the conversation of "real gentlemen and men of education," who "are contented with one another's conversation, of which their own voices are the medium, and which they carry on by turns and in an ordinary manner." These conversation partners "do not require the help of another's voice, or of the poets whom you cannot interrogate about the meaning of what they are saying." Lack of a method which would enable them to "make proof of the truth in conversation," he continues, means that disputes about meaning "can never be decided." Nondecidability in regard to what we would call "author's intention" leaves us with a multiplicity of possible meanings, without any way of deciding among them; which is to say, without an evident and explicit method for moving from multiple interpretations to a singular meaning. That lack is overcome by Plato's method, as portrayed in the Socratic dialogues: dialectic is practiced in questioning-and-answering conversations that analyze the concepts at issue in terms of what is and is not involved in them, and eventually reach an agreed-upon meaning. Plato's dismissal of interpretation that does not lead to agreement on one meaning may well have inspired subsequent scholars to develop hermeneutic procedures and principles. Beginning with Aristotle in the *Rhetoric* and *On Interpretation*, and continuing until Heidegger's ontological turn and Hans-Georg Gadamer's antimethodical conception of understanding, hermeneutic focused on method—and in particular, on how to uncover a multiplicity of meanings within a written text and how to narrow down that multiplicity when we cannot interrogate the text's author(s).

Even within orality, a degree of distanciation occurs when (as in the *Protagoras*) reported speech or indirect discourse—e.g., "talk *about* the poets," rather than talk *with* a poet—is at issue. Eric Havelock holds that "it is only as language is written down that it becomes possible to think about it" and for it to become "separated visually from the person who uttered it."[18] Yet the separation intrinsic to indirect discourse encourages analyzing even oral/aural communication as an object, rather than as an activity or event. That objectivation encouraged traditional hermeneutic to become an epistemological endeavor, aligned with the objectivistic orientation in philosophy in the search for truth (or, truths) by means of analyzing ideas within texts and their contexts. In other words, insofar as the object of interpretation was indirect discourse or written texts, hermeneutic presupposed a certain distanciation from everyday aural/oral and tactile/kinesthetic activity, as it functions to influence the lives of human beings. Plato's unthematized hermeneutic relied on the device of Socrates' face-to-face conversations. Because that method was borrowed from the nonanalytic context of everyday talk, he was able to use it without attention to it. Beginning with Aristotle, however, hermeneutic is marked by a preoccupation with method that philosophical inquiry as well as rhetorical theory came to share.

There are three contemporary departures from that history of preoccupation with method that are particularly relevant to Schrag's proposal for resituating rhetoric and philosophy in a hermeneutic space. The first is Heidegger's resituation of hermeneutic from an epistemological to an ontological domain. In effect, he proposed that interpretation is not only something that we do when the meaning of words is unclear or debated. Rather, it is a basic structure of human being: in rather Aristotelian terms, our nature is as much to interpret as the acorn's nature is to become an oak. His analysis identifies and corrects traditional philosophy's preoccupation with relatively static objects (beings) at the expense of their ultimate context: temporally-developing Being. This context is the environment we engage in the course of working out our being-in-the-world, which is a situated being; a being-there (Dasein) rather than somewhere else, at some other time. Gadamer developed that thesis in relation to communicative activity, and so extended its implicit relevance to the dimension of interpretation within traditional rhetoric. The third departure is Ricoeur's proposal that we understand all of human action—not only the products of linguistic activity—by means analogous to those we use in textual hermeneutics. The importance of that analogy becomes clear in his discussion of discourse as a form of human action, which is basic for his development of an ontologically-oriented hermeneutic. Space constraints allow only a brief sketch of Heidegger's conception of understanding and Ricoeur's conception of discourse as the site for a conception of the communicative process, subject, and object which is quite different from that assumed in traditional philosophy and rhetoric. Yet even a brief sketch should enable us to recognize an intrinsic hermeneutical dimension of communication that was "unexploited, even repressed" in traditional philosophy and rhetoric.

In *Being and Time* (section 32), Heidegger analyses the knowledge we bring to inquiry as a "fore-structure" composed of three typically unnoticed conditions for interpreting any item in the environment as being a particular thing. In order to recognize something, we sift through a wealth of possibilities for involvement with that item—which is to say, for the meaning it could have for us. These possibilities are already available to us as members of a particular culture. On the basis of this inherited "fore-having" of possibilities, members of a culture develop individualized orientations that precede actual involvement with particular items in the environment. Thus, when we do engage anything, we do so with "fore-sight," by virtue of points of view that are activated by that involvement. In anticipation of turning to Heidegger's rather cryptic observation that message bearers both come from and go toward the message: Engaging anything is bringing to bear, in going toward a particular situation, the individualized "fore-sight" that comes from inherited "fore-having." Joining general possibilities for meaning ("fore-having") with individualized ways of engaging the environment ("fore-sight") is identifying something as this, rather than that—which is to say, interpreting it; understanding it as being in this category, rather than that; as related to other items in the environment in this way, rather than that way; as bearing this meaning, rather than that. Simultaneously, the environment comes toward engagement by lending itself to some, but not just any, modes of articulation. The articulation that emerges from each communicative event carries over into future engagements, in the form of a "fore-conception" which is a blend of cultural "fore-having" and individualized "fore-sight."

An interpretation, then, is "the working-out of *possibilities* projected in *understanding*"; it "is never a presuppositionless apprehending of something presented to us."[19] A good deal of this understanding happens without predicative activity, and especially, without needing to name the items we identify. But Heidegger notes that when we do name a thing, we do so on the basis of how we have already interpreted it. We do not simply "throw a 'signification' over some naked thing"; rather, the "thing in question already has an involvement which is disclosed in our understanding of the world."[20] The significance of a thing, then—the sense it has for those who discuss it, and the items in the environment that it indicates, or which it evokes as relevant to a particular discussion—is a result of the influence of the "fore-structure," as it makes that environment known. Rhetors are influenced by this process of interpretation, prior to any influence that they may extend to their audiences.

Michael Hyde has drawn our attention to Heidegger's ontological turn in hermeneutic as the basis for "a fundamental understanding of rhetoric" as "the making-known of Being in and through discourse."[21] Although defining what exceeds linguistic formulation is intrinsically impossible, we can understand "Being" as the abstracted conceptualization of the environment that encompasses all situations: Being is all that could be available for appropriation within human activity. "Discourse" is more amenable to definition. A brief outline of Schrag's and Ricoeur's characterizations may be helpful before we turn, in the last section of this chapter, to Heidegger's explication.

For Schrag, discourse is a constituent of "communicative praxis as an amalgam of discourse and action": "Discourse is here understood as a multifaceted event, comprised of speaking, writing, and language. Speaking has to do with the multiple forms of verbal communication, but also includes the deployment of gestural meaning and articulations through bodily motility."[22] That definition is taken up in Hyde's identification of the relation between discourse and Being: "Discourse brings the word to mind such that Being can be thought and eventually made-known to others through communicative practices."[23] These practices link the "fore-conceptions" available to a community in the semantic and syntactic resources of a language with individuals' situated actions of speaking and writing. We have an echo here of Husserl's concept of consciousness as always "consciousness of . . ."; as directed toward an intentional object, rather than enclosed within itself. Similarly, language as it is actualized in speaking and writing—that is, as discourse—ceases to be an enclosed system. Instead, it must be (as Schrag says) "*about* something, *by* someone, and *for* someone."[24]

Ricoeur also characterizes discourse as multifaceted; as a "dialectic of event and meaning" that affords us a measure of "distanciation" from activity that is situated in a particular space and time, by articulating that activity through meanings that we can access at any time and place.[25] The meanings evoked by words transcend the moment (of an event), yet they inform that event, even as the event informs its meaning. This difference in temporal character is the most basic difference between discourse and language: "To say that discourse is an event is to say, first, that discourse is realized temporally and in the present, whereas the system of language is virtual and outside of time."[26] Discourse, then, is a relation between an actual temporal activity and an atemporal system of possibilities—rather than a relation between a signifier (symbol) and a signified (thing) to which it refers.

The additional characteristics of discourse that Ricoeur identifies further emphasize its differences from language. In regard to the subject—the "who" of language—he notes that "language has no subject insofar as the question 'who speaks' does not apply" when we analyze language; however, "discourse refers back to its speaker by means of a complex set of indicators, such as personal pronouns."[27] This understanding of the differences between language and discourse enables us to realize that the dismissal of the subject in deconstructive theory follows from the nature of language, rather than discourse. Alternatively, beginning from discursive activity leads to understanding subjects as results of that activity, rather than as agents who cause it. Similarly, the objects of discourse are not things presumed as prior to discourse, but are foci of discursive activity that can be discerned and discussed by virtue of their articulation in discourse. The "signs of language refer only to other signs in the interior of the same system," Ricoeur notes, but "discourse is always about something."[28] Investigation of communicative praxis confirms that any "something" inevitably bears the influence of power sedimented in linguistic practices, which embody the "fore-conceptions" we bring to discourse. Ricoeur's last characterization emphasizes the divergent functions of these two resources: "While language is only a prior condition of communication for which it provides the codes, it is in discourse that all messages are exchanged."[29]

In sum, Ricoeur's analysis of discourse in terms of subjects (who are indicated in discourse), objects (that about which discourse speaks), and processes (temporal events that engage atemporal meanings) does not depend on the characterizations of those three components of discourse (and traditional philosophy) that I cited at the beginning of this section as the target of deconstructive critique. His discursive reinterpretations are based in how these components function within communicative praxis that's concerned with messages, rather than with preexistent things to be known or subjects to be influenced. His characterization of language as a *condition* for the exchange of messages in communicative praxis provides a clue for understanding Heidegger's conception of messages as both the starting point and the goal of message bearers. Before we turn to that concept, and to the understanding of "the essential being of language" that enables it, we need to consider the extent to which Schrag's and Ricoeur's concepts of language and discourse differ from general understanding of those resources within the histories of traditional philosophy and rhetoric that I've sketched.

When philosophy left rhetoric it rejected rhetoric's concern with the use of language to create messages for particular purposes. Traditional philosophy focused on conceptual and empirical investigations of the objects and subjects designated in and by language, and neglected the process of accomplishing that designating. When philosophy took up language again, it was as a conceptual object: Messages were analyzed as abstracted units of meaning, or as linguistic signs drawn from a self-referential system. In both approaches, the reality of messages as accomplishments that actualize the subjects who speak them, as well as the objects spoken of, was neglected; even, suppressed. Phenomenology's determination to describe "the things themselves," however, led to recognition that things in the lifeworld (the everyday cultural, social, political, and physical environment of human life) are accomplished in communicative praxis that constitutes, rather than reports on, those things as being this, rather than that; here, rather than there; now, rather than then. Thus, phenomenological analysis expanded from description of the appearances to multiple and dynamic interpretations of the possible conditions and goals implicated as appearances come to be present (or remain absent) in the lifeworld.[30] In other words, description of the lifeworld requires interpretation in terms of "fore-conceptions" embodied in a language. Thus, as Ricoeur says, there is a relation of "mutual belonging" between phenomenology and hermeneutics.[31]

Correlatively, although rhetoric retained a focus on the actuality of language in use, its concern was primarily directed toward strategies for influence in order to bring about particular goals. Until quite recently (even more recently than phenomenological philosophy's interpretive turn) rhetoric's concern was with influencing—shaping—actual practices, rather than with reflection that could discern how discourse shapes the very possibilities for those practices, as well as shaping the interests and very being of rhetors and their goals. However, contemporary investigation of the epistemic function of rhetoric and efficacy of discourse within scientific inquiry has instigated that reflection.[32] Those investigations support Hyde's conclusion: "The primordial function of rhetoric is to 'make-known' meaning both to oneself and to others. Meaning is derived by a human being in and through the interpretive understanding of reality. Rhetoric is the process of making-known that meaning."[33] This hermeneutic theme of "interpretive understanding" functions as a path along which rhetoric and philosophy expanded their traditional concerns with expressive strategies and theorizing knowledge. We can now consider how that path, as blazed by Heidegger, enables a resituating of philosophy and rhetoric in "a reclaimed hermeneutical space beyond epistemology and tropology."[34]

PART THREE: THE HOMECOMING

> The message-bearer must come from the message. But he must also have gone toward it.
> —Martin Heidegger, "A Dialogue on Language"[35]

> The self-preservation of what is alive takes place through its drawing into itself everything that is outside of it. Everything that is alive nourishes itself with what is alien to it. The fundamental fact of being alive is assimilation.
> —Hans-Georg Gadamer, *Truth and Method*[36]

From the perspective of a hermeneutically-informed phenomenology, the linguistic turn in contemporary philosophy was a partial recovery of communicative territory long-ago ceded to rhetoric. From this perspective, which understands language as the embodiment of fore-conceptions that can be accessed as possibilities for communicative praxis, a linguistically-focused philosophy appears as suffering from lack of actuality; as lacking the substance that could have enabled philosophy to resist the deconstructive winds that were able to bring down its house so easily, and leave it to wander about as a visitor in other disciplines' conversations. Resettling philosophy may well require reviving, and even resurrecting, it—given the starvation diet to which it was subjected during the long ascendancy of modes of philosophizing in abstraction from the everyday in order to engage in analysis of conceptual residue "purified" of its lifeworld context. Rather than simply resituating philosophy so that it may continue business as usual, although now in the house of language that had been maintained by rhetoric, I would argue that reconstructing the process, object, and subject that are implicated in communicative praxis is necessary.

Heidegger's oft-quoted identification of language as the house of Being suggests that a convergence of philosophy and rhetoric must occur on the ground of a different understanding of language than was favored by either philosophy or rhetoric when they first were domiciled together and during their centuries of separation. Heidegger's claim that "the essential being of language cannot be anything linguistic" suggests that the space for philosophy's homecoming is other than the compendium of lexical entries and syntactic structures commonly associated with "the essential being of language." The alternate conception that I want to propose starts from Heidegger's affirmative complement to his negative claim that "the essential being of language cannot be anything linguistic," namely: "The essential being of language is Saying as Showing."[37] "Showing what?" and "showing how?" are plausible follow-up questions, but his response is less than immediately enlightening:

> Saying is showing. In everything that speaks to us, in everything that touches us by being spoken or being spoken about, in everything that gives itself to us in speaking, or waits for us unspoken, but also in the speaking that we do ourselves, there prevails Showing which causes to appear what is present, and to fade from appearance what is absent. Saying is in no way the linguistic expression added to the phenomena after they have appeared—rather, all radiant appearance and all fading away is grounded in the showing Saying . . . Saying is the gathering that joins all appearance of the in itself manifold showing which everywhere lets all that is shown abide within itself.[38]

The enlightenment that these sentences do yield, for me, depends upon studying them against the background of an ontologically-oriented hermeneutic that incorporates the work of Heidegger on the fore-structure that informs interpretation, Ricoeur on the nature of discourse, and Husserl on situating analysis of essential structures in the life world. In what follows, however, I'll use that background rather than engage in any further explication of it. More specifically, I'll use it in relation to the need for reconceptualizing the process, object, and subject of inquiry of philosophical and rhetorical endeavors as the first step toward an affirmative response to the deconstruction of their modernist forms. The life world (which I take to be the actuality of human activities and their institutionalized sedimentation) is a processual phenomenon which only allows thematization in terms of subjects and objects when we take a distanciated analytic attitude toward it. I take that attitude here in order to examine three constraining habits that support modernist conceptions of the process, object, and subject rejected by deconstruction's "negating moment." In the course of setting out those habits, I also set out Heidegger's alternative way of understanding all three components. Following this alternative enables the "affirming moment" of Schrag's "new beginning"; a moment at which "the philosopher and rhetorician meet in this reclaimed hermeneutical space in the wake of their joint projects of deconstruction."[39]

The first constraining habit often leads to interpreting Heidegger's "Saying is Showing" claim literally, even though he explicates "showing" in nonocular terms: speaking, touching, waiting, and giving—far more than seeing—are the activities proper to the showing that is saying. All of those modes of embodied engagement with an environment are combined in presenting a particular interpretation of the life world. In order to avoid the habit of reducing those modes to a visual one, I suggest that we call this activity evoking, rather than showing: Saying is evoking, by means of the giving, waiting, touching, and speaking that constitute effective articulation, what is present as well as what is absent in the sayer's life world. The sayer is a rhetor, then, insofar as he or she effectively proposes an interpretation of the life world that, in its "disclosing and disguising," lets us affirm, and so identify with, a particular showing of what is actually and potentially present.[40]

The second constraining habit is understanding "showing" as designating; that is, as referring to some already existent thing in the world that awaits our gaze and articulation. A long and persistent history of understanding language as referential and communication as transmission is born from and supports this habit. Heidegger, among others, reorients us toward an alternative understanding of what signs are and do. "The Greeks of the Classical Age know and understand the sign in terms of showing—the sign is shaped to show," he says; but "Hellenistic times" replaced that showing with "a stipulation": the sign was henceforth taken to be "a manner of designation by which man's mind is reset and directed from one object to another object."[41] Deconstructing the referential theory of language that developed from that objectivating "stipulation" enables a very different conception of communicative praxis, for "if the showing character [of saying] is not based on signs . . . rather, all signs arise from a showing,"[42] the meaning of signs emerges in that activity, rather than being attached to preexistent objects.[43]

The third constraining habit is reification. "Everything spoken stems in a variety of ways from the unspoken," Heidegger reminds us; yet once it is spoken, "it begins to appear as if it were cut off from the speaking and the speakers."[44] Reflecting on this third habit together with the second leads us to an alternative conception of both the shown/said object and the subject who shows/says: rather than assume reifications of the "who" that speaks, as well as the "what" that's spoken of, we can reconceptualize both as emergent from discourse. Signs, then, evoke something of the multitude of (in Ricoeur's words) "potential worlds" that are the genuine object of interpretation; they evoke what is absent but could be present, as they articulate (say and show) a particular interpretation of the lifeworld. The "who" of speaking and hearing—that is, the subjects of discourse—are part of that invocation, for rather than the relation between speakers and speaking being one of cause and effect, "speakers are present in the very way of speaking."[45]

This reconception of the process, object, and subject of showing/saying should enable us to make some headway in understanding Heidegger's rather cryptic remark on messages that is the first epigraph for this section: "The message-bearer must come from the message. But he must also have gone toward it." This is a puzzling remark, insofar as we take the bearing of messages to be a matter of preexistent subjects transmitting meanings that are prior to discourse. The reconception of discourse's process, object, and subject that I've sketched here, however, reorients us toward an understanding of messages as *possibilities* for significance which are actualized in the process of communicative praxis. That activity also actualizes—constitutes—its participants. "The fundamental fact of being alive is assimilation," Gadamer reminds us in the second epigraph at the start of this section. We are, in effect, what we hear and what we show/say, just as much as we are the food we eat and the air we breathe. This is not to say that we are the determined results of the language we use. Rather, in going toward the discursive possibilities accessible in a community's language, we constitute ourselves through dynamic, and sometimes unexpected, identification with some of the multiplicity of possibilities we hear (first from others, and later from ourselves) in our life world experience.[46] Being alive is a matter of how we use those resources, more than of what they are; for in an important (and very difficult to articulate) sense, linguistic resources, unlike air and food, are not; they do not exist until they are made manifest in and by our showing/saying.

Thus the messages that bear us, and for which we are bearers, are not predetermined results of the language we use. In other words, significance is not imprisoned by extant linguistic practices. Rather, the productive function of language elucidated by Aristotle's concept of *poiesis* enables showing/saying to evoke *possibilities for being* otherwise, as well as to report on what *appears to be* the case.[47] Assimilation is the key process here: Discourse is alive insofar as it assimilates unforeseen and even unlikely associations emergent from interpretations of "the things themselves."[48] Auditors (including the rhetors who show/say) are thereby directed toward multiple possibilities for what is and could be the case, which is to say that the things about which we communicate are constituted, in communicative praxis, by contingent and dynamic assimilation and exclusion of possibilities. As philosophy and rhetoric engage in that praxis, they simultaneously constitute their hermeneutical "space beyond epistemology and tropology."

NOTES

1. Calvin O. Schrag, "Rhetoric Resituated at the End of Philosophy," *Quarterly Journal of Speech,* vol. 71 (1985): 164–174.

2. Ibid., 172.

3. Martin Heidegger, "A Dialogue on Language," in *On the Way to Language*, trans. Peter D. Hertz (New York: Harper and Row, 1962), 51.

4. Paul Ricoeur, *Oneself as Another*, trans. Kathleen Blamey (Chicago: University of Chicago Press, 1992).

5. Martin Heidegger, 199. See also “A Dialogue on Language,” 5.

6. Although hints of this lifeworld orientation may be found throughout Husserl’s work, the strongest formulation is in *The Crisis of European Sciences and Transcendental Phenomenology*, Part IIIA. Edmund Husserl, *The Crisis of European Sciences and Transcendental Phenomenology*, trans. David Carr (Evanston: Northwestern University Press, 1970).

7. For this notion of the convergence of philosophy and rhetoric, see Calvin O. Schrag and David James Miller, “Communication Studies and Philosophy: Convergence without Coincidence,” in *The Critical Turn: Rhetoric and Philosophy in Postmodern Discourse*, eds. Ian Angus and Lenore Langsdorf (Carbondale: Southern Illinois University Press, 1993).

8. Ernesto Grassi, “Why Rhetoric Is Philosophy,” *Philosophy and Rhetoric,* vol. 20 (1987): 68–78, 68.

9. Calvin O. Schrag, “Rhetoric Resituated at the End of Philosophy,” 167–168.

10. Granted, “all men” tacitly included only males of particular social status; still, the accepted discourse community was considerably wider than Plato’s.

11. Patricia Bizzell and Bruce Herzberg, *The Rhetorical Tradition* (Boston: Bedford Books, 1990), 642.

12. Heidegger, “A Dialogue on Language,” 22–23.

13. Paul Ricoeur, *Oneself as Another*, trans. Kathleen Blamey (Chicago: University of Chicago Press, 1992), 299.

14. My focus on these three supports of traditional inquiry is inspired by Dennis Mumby’s analysis of the influence of postmodern thought on communication theory in his “Modernism, Postmodernism, and Communication Studies: A Rereading of an Ongoing Debate,” *Communication Theory,* vol. 7 (1997): 1–28.

15. Schrag, “Rhetoric Resituated at the End of Philosophy,” 170.

16. Ibid., 170.

17. Ibid.

18. Eric Havelock, *The Muse Learns to Write* (New Haven: Yale University Press, 1986), 111–112.

19. Martin Heidegger, *Being and Time*, trans. John Macquarrie and Edward Robinson (New York: Harper and Row, 1962), 189 my emphasis, 191–192.

20. Ibid., 190–191.

21. Michael J. Hyde, “Rhetorically, Man Dwells: On the Making-Known Function of Discourse,” *Communication,* vol. 7 (1983): 201–220.

22. Calvin O. Schrag, *Communicative Praxis and the Space of Subjectivity* (Bloomington: Indiana University Press, 1986), 33–34.

23. Hyde, “Rhetorically, Man Dwells,” 206.

24. Schrag, *Communicative Praxis and the Space of Subjectivity*, viii; my emphasis.

25. Paul Ricoeur, *Hermeneutics and the Human Sciences*, ed. and trans. John B. Thompson (Cambridge: Cambridge University Press, 1981), 132.

26. Ibid., 133.

27. Ibid.

28. Ibid.

29. Ibid.

30. This expansion in the phenomenological enterprise involves movement from a static to a genetic phenomenology—from description of what appears, to analyzing the layers of sense that constitute those appearances—and then to a generative phenomenology that analyzes the historical evolution of what appears.

Paul Ricoeur emphases the intrinsic nature of this expansion: "Husserl continued to develop the properly temporal implications of perceptual experience. He was thus led, by his own analyses, toward the historicity of human experience . . . perceptual experience appeared more and more like an artificially isolated segment of a relation to the 'life-world', itself directly endowed with historical and cultural features." Ricoeur, *Hermeneutics and the Human Sciences*, 119.

The generative phenomenology that developed from that increased acknowledgment of historicity has been explicated by Anthony Steinbock: "In distinction from a genetic analysis that is restricted to the becoming of individual subjectivity, a synchronic field of contemporary individuals, and intersubjectivity as founded in an egology, generative phenomenology treats phenomena that are historical, geological, cultural, intersubjective, and normative from the very start." Anthony J. Steinbock, *Home and Beyond: Generative Phenomenology after Husserl* (Evanston: Northwestern University Press, 1995), 178.

31. Ricoeur, *Hermeneutics and the Human Sciences*, 101.

32. I am thinking here of Robert Scott's impetus for understanding rhetoric as epistemic, Harold Garfinkel's investigations of the ethnomethodology of work, work in the rhetoric of inquiry, and the work of Herbert Simons. For correlative work within philosophy, see David Hiley, et al. Robert L. Scott, "On Viewing Rhetoric as Epistemic," *Central States Speech Journal*, vol. 18: (1967): 9–16; Harold Garfinkel, *Studies in Ethnomethodology* (Englewood Cliffs, NJ: Prentice-Hall, 1967); John S. Nelson, et al., eds., *The Rhetoric of the Human Sciences* (Madison. University of Wisconsin Press, 1987); Herbert W. Simons, ed., *The Rhetorical Turn: Invention and Persuasion in the Conduct of Inquiry* (Chicago: University of Chicago Press, 1990); and David R. Hiley, James F. Bohman, and Richard Shusterman, eds., *The Interpretive Turn: Philosophy, Science, Culture* (Ithaca: Cornell University Press, 1991).

33. Michael J. Hyde and Craig R. Smith, "Hermeneutics and Rhetoric: A Seen But Unseen Relationship," *Quarterly Journal of Speech*, vol. 65 (1979): 347–363.

34. Schrag, "Rhetoric Resituated at the End of Philosophy," 170.

35. Heidegger, "A Dialogue on Language," 51.

36. Hans-Georg Gadamer, *Truth and Method* (New York: Crossroad), 223.

37. Heidegger, "The Way to Language," 123; cf. "The Nature of Language," 107.

38. Ibid., 126.

39. Schrag, "Rhetoric Resituated at the End of Philosophy," 170.

40. Heidegger, "The Way to Language," 115.

41. Ibid.

42. Ibid., 123.

43. John Stewart's reconceptualization of language as "articulate contact" provides a thorough critique of referential theories of language and transmission theories of communication. I would argue, however, that his equation of language and communicative activity takes inadequate account of institutionalized or (in phenomenological terms) sedimented prior and predominant usage. Thus it neglects the dimension of communicative activity ("language") that resists change as well as the potential for alternative understanding offered by language considered as a resource, rather than an activity. A theory that includes both language as source of possibilities and resistance, and communicative activity as locus of actual constitution of the lifeworld, responds to the needs of a variety of endeavors within philosophy and rhetoric (e.g., cultural studies, critical rhetoric, social movement rhetoric, critical theory, lifeworld phenomenology). John Stewart, *Language as Articulate Contact: Toward a Post-Semiotic Philosophy of Communication* (Albany: SUNY Press, 1995).

44. Heidegger, "The Way to Language," 120.

45. Ibid., 199; cf . "A Dialogue on Language," 5.

46. See my "Refusing Individuality: How Human Beings Are Made into Subjects," *Communication Theory,* vol. 7 (1997): 315–327.

47. For further discussion of *poiesis* in relation to Schrag's conception of communicative praxis, see my "In Defense of Poiesis: The Performance of Self in Communicative Praxis," in *The Task of Philosophy after Postmodernity*, eds. William McBride and Martin Matustik (forthcoming).

48. The phrase is Husserl's. It has often been misunderstood as a positivistic remnant similar to Durkheim's call for investigating "social facts as things." In both cases, I would argue, what's needed is an analysis of phenomena (what appears in a social and physical environment) that understands them as contingent and partial actualizations of multiple possibilities. Edmund Husserl, *Ideas Pertaining to a Pure Phenomenology and to a Phenomenological Philosophy, First Book*, trans. Fred Kersten. (The Hague: Martinus Nijhoff, 1983), 25.

10 Procreation in a Beautiful Medium

Eroticizing the Vectors of Communicative Praxis

RAMSEY ERIC RAMSEY

> Our faith comes in moments; our vice is habitual. Yet there is a depth in those brief moments which constrains us to ascribe more reality to them than to all other experiences. For this reason the argument which is always forthcoming to silence those who conceive extraordinary hopes of man, namely the appeal to experience, is for ever invalid and vain. We give up the past to the objector, and yet we hope. He must explain this hope. We grant that the world is mean, but how did we find out that it was mean? What is the ground of this uneasiness of ours; of this old discontent?
>
> —Ralph Waldo Emerson, "The Over-Soul"

> The guiding of thought and the deft coördination of deed is at once the path and honor of humanity.
>
> —W.E.B. Du Bois, *The Souls of Black Folk*

> Urge and urge and urge,/ Always the procreant urge of the world.
>
> —Walt Whitman, *Leaves of Grass*

EXPERIMENTING WITH LOVE

Calvin O. Schrag, who writes of love in his recent *The Self after Postmodernity*, argues that to get at what we can mean by this powerful concept we must understand that: "discourse about the ways of love requires experimentation with different vocabularies in efforts to articulate love's workings on the boundaries of transcendence and immanence."[1] It is to add to his already rich position of the fitting response that Schrag turns to love.[2] I suggest we must elucidate the discourse on love as we find it throughout the traditions of thought and we must experiment with these various vocabularies to guard against idolatry and blasphemy in our endeavors to undertake ethical communicative praxis. So as Schrag turns to vocabularies of Søren Kierkegaard and Emmanuel Levinas to undertake his own experiment in love, for our part we shall turn to vocabularies from Plato and the voices associated with this name in *Symposium*, from Henry David Thoreau, and from the prophet Micah to see what we might encounter concerning love and communicative ethics. I shall offer readings that willfully ignore certain challenges that come or are sure to come from Platonists, Thoreauvians, and theologians and I shall do so long enough, perhaps, to come nearer to Love and what we might say in these vocabularies concerning the ethics of the fitting response before a certain professionalism sets in.[3]

The fitting response demands, from we know not whence, an understanding of the erotic component both immanent and transcendent to it if we are to have any chance to be responsive to the other and otherness. This erotic understanding would show us that rather than talk of fitting responses we would begin better with talk of fitting responsiveness.[4]

IN-BETWEEN FROM THE BEGINNING

From Plato we have heard a many layered Love story. Just how many layers can, at least, be put this way: Plato has Apollodorus tell again a story (he is said to have a clearer version than an unnamed "someone" who heard the story from Phoenix, son of Philip) of what happened at Agathon's symposium (already now some years past) to a group of companions curious to hear the details. We say "tell again" because Apollodorus has already told the story to Glaucon "just the other day." But it is not really Apollodorus' story. (Or is it? Perhaps one task in all of this is to find out to whom discourses would be said to belong.) In any event, Apollodorus heard it from the same Aristodemus who was, unlike Apollodorus, present at the event and it was he who told it to Phoenix who in turn told it to the now suspect "someone." It is the case, however, that Apollodorus corroborated his story with another attendee, *viz.*, Socrates. There are more complications yet to add because the so-called centerpiece of the story being recounted is that story Socrates tells of his experience with the itinerant mystic Diotima, who herself begins with the account of a myth that deals, no less, with desire, consummation, and the birth of Eros. Oh, what a long walk to Eros, at least if we depart from Plato's

Symposium. At the risk of making this already impossible journey more impossible still, let us quote Apollodorus's caveat:

> Now, Aristodemus couldn't quite remember every detail of everyone's speeches, and *I* don't remember everything *he* told me either. But I'll give you a pretty accurate report of what he remembered of each speech, at least of the speeches which have stuck in my mind. 178a[5]

What might become stuck in our minds if we were to pursue this route not to mention if we were to take into our account the arrival of Alcibides in his drunken revelry praising he claims not love but Socrates?

How could we ever hope to find our way to love from such beginnings? How would we find our way to love if we sought to look for it? If we could be so bold as to say we could get close to love, then what is our likely fate if we wish to love or to be loving. One wonders if it can end anywhere but in idolatry or blasphemy with respect to that/whom/which is beloved.

So much as we know is said in *Symposium* about Eros and much more has been said about what is said there since. Amidst all that has been said it is the parents of Eros and the notion of procreation that shall concern us here (202e–207a). Diotima tells us that Eros is born of a union between Plenty and Poverty who consummate their desire under particular circumstances *viz*., the party celebrating the birth of Aphrodite. Yet there is more. We are told that Plenty is found passed out from an indulgence in nectar and that Poverty, who of course was not invited to the party but had come to beg, finds Plenty in Zeus' garden. Taking advantage of this opportunity she then lays with Plenty becoming pregnant with Eros.

With this as his lineage, Eros is neither god nor mortal but a mediator between gods and mortals; he is (along with here-unnamed other spirits) a middle ground making divine and human contact possible. Making, Diotima is said to tell us, "the universe an interconnected whole." This mediation enables the only means of communication between gods and mortals, as they cannot meet directly.

Although Eros allows this contact, his parentage has other consequences. He is always between having and being without— "neither destitute, but isn't ever well of either." This nondestitute lack makes Eros one who must get around and wander so as to search and hunt for what he needs. To pursue these ends, we are told, he is forever "thinking up captivating stratagems" and that he often goes about carrying out these plans with his skills in "magic, herbs, and words." So with words and magic and with herbs and cunning (who is, by the way, his grandmother) Eros makes a way in the space between the world of mortals and the world of the gods, so that we might make ours. If we are touched by Eros, if we are in some way related, then what might our inheritance be?

Against the backdrop of this account, communicative praxis would be like Eros: neither wholly materialist (mortal) nor wholly idealist (divine). It would be an in-between, a beautiful medium existing as it does as a space of procreation where we attempt to make ourselves and attempt to make our world. The beautiful medium of communicative praxis is that simultaneously impoverished and overflowing condition for the possibility of human relation. One of the paradoxes of the human condition so understood and exemplified by the consequences of communicative praxis is this: Abundance *and* lack surround us. This simultaneous too much and too little places demands on us and piques our desires, in a word it eroticizes us. When we are fittingly responsive we are eroticized and when erotic in this way we are, Diotima is said to tell us, on the verge of begetting *logoi*. That is to say, through communicative praxis we are on the verge of saying something to someone about something.

However, we bear responsibility for begetting *logoi*—for saying something to someone about something. Though we are responsible for these *logoi*, they are, nonetheless, not strictly ours. We must, it is true, answer for them and why they came *through* us, but still they are not ours even though our responsibility to and for them is absolute. Or more demanding still, they are more ours when they fail and less so ours if they would have their moment of success.

We take our standing in a divinely hued space, one Diotima is said to believe leads to procreation in a beautiful medium. Yet not every birth of discourse and action produces world-shattering effects. Indeed, it would be fittingly responsive, and we too often overlook this, to say "with pleasure" to the request "would you please pass the salt?" The simple request and the response are mundane and close to inconsequential to be sure, but they are no less embedded in both the life world and on the continuum of fitting responses possible for mortals. We too frequently lose sight of this everyday significance. This is exemplified when we are asked for cases and examples of fitting responses and we start too grandiose looking always for something world historical.[6] But world-historical responses come more from circumstances that are such than from persons who are such; certainly Marx taught us this lesson. Being-there in a world-historical circumstance is an accident of sorts and thus so is being great. No doubt not just anyone could be able to suffer such circumstances greatly, but a kind of Aristotelian magnificence is only a necessary, not a sufficient condition for greatness.

We are not alone in thinking this. Levinas, for instance, knows this well and shows us something similar to this when he argues that before philosophy there is ethics.[7] If this were not so Levinas argues, then the simple "after you" at an open doorway would be an impossible utterance for mortals. Such standing aside is a possibility of the greatest importance, because if we can yield here before the other at the doorway, then we can be said to have a chance to yield to even larger responses that fit social and political situations in which we find ourselves confronted by otherness.

Let us not, however, read this divinely hued space of eroticism too hastily as some version of either nostalgia or neopantheism. The areligious religiosity that informs these reflections would not be pantheistic because it still thinks G-d an unbridgeable distance. Nonetheless, it would without fail experience itself as panerotic—sauntering, struggling, and foraging the in-between—the space between and yet connective of gods and finite beings. Paneroticism is the condition for the possibility of a responsiveness that gives birth to responses for and with the other. Responsiveness (erotic) must be everywhere (pan).[8]

WANDERING AND WONDERING

I have come across this from Thoreau while wandering through his texts on my way to another destination therein, one recommended by a friend:

> I have met but one or two persons in the course of my life who understood the art of Walking, that is, of taking walks,—who had a genius, so to speak, for *sauntering*: which word is beautifully derived "from idle people who roved about the country, in the Middle Ages, and asked charity, under the pretense of going *à la Sainte Terre*," to the Holy Land, till the children exclaimed, "there goes a *Sainte-Terrer*," a Saunterer,—a Holy-Lander. They who never go to the Holy Land in their walks, as they pretend, are indeed mere idlers and vagabonds; but they who do go there are saunterers in the good sense, such as I mean. Some, however, would derive the word from *sans terre*, without land or home, home, but equally at home everywhere. For this is the secret of successful sauntering. He who sits still in a house all the time may be the greatest vagrant of them all; but the saunterer, in the good sense, is no more vagrant than the meandering river, which is all the while sedulously seeking the shortest course to the sea. But I prefer the first, which, indeed, is the most probable derivation. For every walk is a sort of crusade, preached by some

> Peter the Hermit in us, to go forth and re conquer this Holy Land from the Infidels.[9]

Although he prefers the first, Thoreau gives us no good reasons, indeed, no reasons at all to see these two derivations of *sauntering* as mutually exclusive. We shall take from each and argue it is best to see sauntering as a hybrid.

Thoreau ends by sending us on a sort of crusade, a sauntering with a purpose that seeks to regain the Holy Land from the Infidels. We must, of course, rethink these provocative terms with some care. To begin, *infidel* in the Aramaic means "those who are thankless." With this understanding we would see sauntering as a form of thankfulness and the thankful ones would walk toward the Holy Land trying to give thanks. Sauntering would be thankful for the erotic attachment to otherness in all its manifestations; it would be sauntering—in the good sense we mean—to try and say and try and give thanks for and to Eros. Walking becomes on this view a type of praying or mobile meditation. On the other hand, this sort of crusade to take back these lost Holy Lands would be a conquering—which is itself an overcoming—that does so with thanks and responsiveness. Such a return in not undertaken in the name of any star, of any cross, of any crescent. Pervaded by gratitude, conquering as overcoming would be a manner of coming back and of returning to places we may well have never been.

Thoreau says he knows of only one or two persons who know how to saunter in the good sense he means. Only one or two know how to *take* walks. If we ask: Whence or from what does one take so as to walk or seek in thankfulness, then our answer would have to have access to Thoreau's less preferred derivation of sauntering. We would have to say that one would take from Eros that is, from anywhere Eros is. This is akin to Thoreau's "equally at home everywhere" because the panerotic would allow for one to begin a sauntering, taking off in thankfulness from any homelessness (because home-there, nonetheless). From within an embedded freedom does one "take" so as to take a walk: "No wealth can buy the requisite freedom, and independence, which are the capital of this profession. It comes only by the grace of God."[10] Walking well, sauntering in excellence if we might make Greek this concept, is to avoid the banality of idling and vagabondry. These are the conditions to be avoided and we do so by staying close to the ever-present source of Eros—sauntering to stay ever-close to our homelessness. To be erotic is to be thankful; to love is to reconquer the Holy Land from those thankless ones (infidels). Thoreau's idleness is here seen as idolatry because in staying put one says one knows *already*, one knows with *certainty*, one knows where G-d *is*. Thoreau's vagabondry is seen here as blasphemy because in walking aimlessly one says G-d is *nowhere*, one says one knows that G-d *cannot be found*, one says that one knows *all* looking for G-d is in vain. As Aristotle knew before him, Thoreau knows it takes great courage to walk well.

Humility in walking or sauntering with Eros would come from understanding in the first derivation the notion of pretense which is linked to the space of our ever-abundance and our ever-lack. Although Thoreau tries to suggest that his walking (and that of those one or two unnamed persons he has met) is unpretentious, we would think otherwise of ourselves. Humility is knowing that all this seemingly must fail and we shall of necessity fall radically short of the call contained in the provocation because, in the end, all ends are haunted by pretense. As an unavoidable danger, a pretense that can always undermine our efforts must keep our sauntering humble. Walking is being thankful, being thankful is being grateful for the erotic attachment to the radical in-between of existence. All of this is a way toward a fitting responsiveness.

Could we not say Thoreau teaches us that certain bad habits de-eroticize us. Though they cannot obliterate the erotic, these bad habits remain an ever-present danger. Our habits inform and form our walking and the style of our gaits. If, as it must, walking has its active side, it so too has its moment of suffering, its ability to undergo and receive. These moments of suffering reception are also formed by habits. Saying that there are both divine and profane revelations, Thoreau comments on our ability to receive and to suffer them when he writes: "The same ear is fitted to receive both communications. Only the character of the hearer determines to which it shall be open, and to which closed."[11] He goes on to say that the mind can be "permanently profaned by the habit of attending to trivial things." These habits and the walking to which they lead make life for Thoreau either dyspeptic or eupeptic, though he knows as do we that the former is more readily available today. Nonetheless, he encourages us to imagine: "why should we not meet, not always as dyspeptics, to tell our bad dreams, but sometimes as eupeptics, to congratulate each other on the ever glorious morning? I do not make an exorbitant demand, surely."[12]

ALWAYS ALREADY ON NOTICE

To end, let us return to Micah and the notice. We have heard from the prophet that we have already been put on notice about loving and walking:

He has told you O man, what is good,
And what the Lord requires of you:
Only to do justice
And to love goodness,
And to walk humbly with your God;
Then your name will achieve wisdom. (6:8)

How difficult it is to walk humbly with the near-god Eros who ever-connects us in such provocative ways to Otherness. But we have hope even in this difficult task because each provocation is a calling forth, a voicing that says to us that we must care about and do justice and care for and love goodness all the while we struggle to maintain humility. To care we must be responsive to the situation and let come through us in the doing predicated on communicative praxis what can be said to be fitting. There will be no conquering in the good sense we mean without justice and humility.

If we are to take back holy lands from infidels and surely the prophets call for this as much as Thoreau, then we must first give up our selves the addiction to which is thankless. Consequently, sauntering understands our selves are not first there and then are asked how they shall respond. Rather, they are not altogether there as selves *until* called, until the provocation calls them forth into the selves they are able to become there. Selves are not first a voicing who say: "here I am—I know how I shall respond already," as if subjectivity could in any full sense precede the calling or provocation. Selves become through an attending to a voicing that comes initially from otherness. As a sauntering self, one trying to overcome the addiction to self, I say: provocation, erotic calling forth, responsiveness, therefore I shall be called forth to become this for awhile. The possibility of filling ourselves out in something approaching fullness (but never achieving it) would be in direct proportion to the degree of fitting responsiveness we embody. Our habits hear and receive these calls through which we receive the provocations of the ever-erotic situations that call us forth. This is a measure of our responsiveness.

So walking humbly with this near-god-like Eros would be a sauntering, a homelessness that is equally at home in every situation because within each situation it would be erotically attached and responsive enough to care about justice and goodness. It would saunter looking for the way that opens toward the Holy Land in each situation (the everywhere and nowhere home). Walking would be responsive to what both stands blocking the way of the opening toward home and that toward which it would carefully attend so as not to profane anything in what would otherwise be its arrogant desire to get to the opening at all costs.

This twofold concern is constitutive of the ought of sauntering. Fitting responsiveness would have to know how both to take matters into its hard working hands and how to practice letting go and waiting if it were to meet the requirement to do justice and love goodness.

Wandering, sauntering, conquering—all in the good sense we mean—attempts the coördination called for in the epigraph from Du Bois with a fitting responsiveness whose most fecund philosophical articulation we owe to Schrag. It seeks its erotic fit with and within otherness. Love explains the hope to which Emerson refers above and with which we began and without which we would not be able to continue.

A SOCRATIC ECHO

Anyway, these are some things I have heard about love's many workings. I, for one, would desire to be persuaded by some of them.

NOTES

1. Calvin O. Schrag *Self after Postmodernity* (New Haven: Yale University Press, 1997), 145.

2. Calvin O. Schrag *Communicative Praxis and the Space of Subjectivity* (Bloomington: Indiana University Press, 1986). I have tried to add corporeal resonance to the fitting response as a part of *The Long Path to Nearness: A Contribution to a Corporeal Philosophy of Communication and the Groundwork for an Ethics of Relief*, (Amherst, NY: Humanity Books, 1998) and a political vector in "A Contribution to Communicative Ethics: Bad Faith and Its Relation to Schrag's Fitting Response," *Phenomenological Inquiry*, vol. 20 (October 1996): 118–127.

3. For an insightful argument as to why we must not only avoid professionalism but why our writing styles themselves need to be reconsidered see Patricia Huntington, *Ecstatic Subjects, Utopia, and Recognition* (Albany: SUNY Press, 1998). She works out their a position via Heidegger and Irigaray that argues if we wish to make postmetaphysical moves, then we need to create and put into practice a variety of a postmetaphysical poetics. More to the point, see her wonderful example of how this looks in practice in her beautiful "Stealing the Fire of Creativity," *Feminist Interpretations of Martin Heidegger*, Nancy Holland and Patricia Huntington, eds. (University Park, PA: Penn State University Press, 2001), 351–376.

4. See David James Miller, "Immodest Interventions," *Phenomenological Inquiry*, vol. 2 (October 1987).

5. Plato, *Symposium* I use here the translation of Robin Waterfield (Oxford: Oxford University Press, 1994).

6. Permit me this aside: Cannot Schrag say, like Kant with respect to moral behavior, that there has never been in the history of human finitude a fitting response. No less for admitting this, is the power of the concept. All so-called cases or examples are of a fitting responsiveness even if each fails the test for which no mortal has the key to judge it *a* fitting response. No less powerful for not having been or for being closed within itself as a fitting response because becoming responsive or now we say erotic is, if we could still talk this way, an end-in-itself that is always somehow also outside of itself. Outside of itself means that it is always touching those conditions of otherness that will both undo it and cause it to have endless reverberations. Always would it become simultaneously more and less than it "is" in the ways it could be taken to be.

7. See Emmanuel Levinas, *Levinas Reader*, trans. and ed. Sean Hand (Oxford: Blackwell Press, 1989), cf., 107.

8. See, Ramsey Eric Ramsey "Communication and Eschatology: The Ethics of Relief, the Work of Waiting, and areligious Religiosity," *Communication Theory*, vol. 7, no. 4 (November 1997): 343–361.

9. Henry David Thoreau, "Walking," *Civil Disobedience and Other Essays*, ed. Philip Smith (New York: Dover, 1993), 49–74, 49. I owe my finding this essay to my work with Stephen Pluháček who asked me to read Thoreau's "Life Without Principle." I crossed paths with "Walking" on my way there.

10. Ibid., 50.

11. Thoreau "Life Without Principle," in *Civil Disobedience and Other Essays*, 75–90, 86.

12. Ibid., 90.

Selected Publications by Calvin O. Schrag

BOOKS AND MONOGRAPHS

Existence and Freedom: Towards on Ontology of Human Finitude. Evanston: Northwestern University Press, 1961.

Experience and Being: Prolegomena to a Future Ontology. Evanston: Northwestern University Press, 1969.

Radical Reflection and the Origin of the Human Sciences. West Lafayette: Purdue University Press, 1980.

Communicative Praxis and the Space of Subjectivity. West Lafayette: Purdue University Press, 2003. (Originally published: Bloomington: Indiana University Press, 1986.)

Communicative Rhetoric and the Claims of Reason. Evanston: Northwestern University School of Speech, 1989.

The Resources of Rationality: A Response to the Postmodern Challenge. Bloomington: Indiana University Press, 1992.

Philosophical Papers: Betwixt and Between. Albany: State University of New York Press, 1994.

The Self after Postmodernity. New Haven: Yale University Press, 1997.

God as Otherwise Than Being: Toward a Semantics of the Gift. Evanston: Northwestern University Press, 2002.

EDITED BOOKS

Patterns of the Life-World, ed. with James Edie and Francis Parker. Evanston: Northwestern University Press, 1970.

Foundations of Morality, Human Rights and the Human Sciences, ed. with A.-T. Tymieniecka. Albany: State University of New York Press, 1983.

Phenomenology in a Pluralistic Context (Selected Studies in Phenomenology and Existential Philosophy), ed. with William L. McBride. Albany: State University of New York, 1983.

Phenomenology in America: Origins and Developments, ed. with Eugene F. Kaelin. Dordrecht: Kluwer Academic Publishers, 1989.

Women Philosophers: A Bio-Critical Source Book, ed. with Ethel M. Kersey. Westport: Greenwood Press, 1989.

JOURNAL ARTICLES AND BOOK CHAPTERS

"Phenomenology, Ontology and History in the Philosophy of Heidegger." *Revue Internationale de Philosophie* 44 (2): 1–16 (1958).

"Existence and History." *Review of Metaphysics* 13 (1): 28–44 (1959).

"Kierkegaard's Teleological Suspension of the Ethical." *Ethics* 70 (2): 66–68 (1959).

"Whitehead and Heidegger: Process Philosophy and Existential Philosophy." *Dialectica* 13 (1): 42–56 (1959).

"Kierkegaard's Existential Reflections on Time." The *Personalist* 42: 149–164 (1961).

"Faith, Existence and Culture." *Journal of Religious Thought* 18 (2): 83–91 (1961).

"John Wild on Contemporary Philosophy." *Journal of Philosophy and Phenomenological Research* 22 (3): 409–411 (1962).

"Ontology and the Possibility of Religious Knowledge." *Journal of Religion* 42 (2) (1962).

"The Lived Body as a Phenomenological Datum." *The Modern Schoolman* 39 (3): 203–218 (1962).

"Towards a Phenomenology of Guilt." *Journal of Existential Psychiatry* 3 (12): 333–342 (1963).

"The Meaning of History." *Review of Metaphysics* 17 (4): 703–717 (1963).

"The Structure of Moral Experience: A Phenomenological and Existential Analysis." *Ethics* 73 (4): 225–265 (1963).

"Existentialism and Democracy." *Pacific Philosophy Forum* 2 (4): 95–100 (1964).

"Heidegger and Cassirer on Kant." *Kant-studien* 58 (1): 87–100 (1967).

"Re-thinking Metaphysics." In *Heidegger and the Quest for Truth*, ed. M.S. Frings. Chicago: Quadrangle Books, 1968.

"Substance, Subject and *Existenz*." *Proceedings of the American Catholic Philosophical Association* 42: 175–182 (1968).

"Struktur der Erfahrung in der Philosophie von James und Whitehead." *Zeitschrift fur Philosophische Forschung* 23 (4): 479–494 (1969).

"The Phenomenon of Embodied Speech." *The Philosophy Forum* 7 (4): 3–27 (1969).
"Heidegger on Repetition and Historical Understanding." *Philosophy East and West* 20 (3): 287–295 (1970).
"Philosophical Anthropology in Contemporary Thought." *Philosophy East and West* 20 (1): 83–89 (1970).
"The Life-World and Its Historical Horizon." In *Patterns of the Life World*, ed. with James Edie and Francis Parker. Evanston: Northwestern University Press, 1970.
"The Historical as a Feature of Experience." *University of Dayton Review* 8 (1): 7–16 (1971).
"The Transvaluation of Aesthetics and the Work of Art." *Southwestern Journal of Philosophy* 4 (3): 109–124 (1973).
"Praxis and Structure: Conflicting Models in the Science of Man." *Journal of the British Society for Phenomenology* 6 (1): 23–31 (1975).
"The Crisis of Human Sciences." *Man and World* 8 (2): 131–135 (1975).
"The Topology of Hope." *Humanitas* 13 (3): 269–281 (1977).
"A Phenomenological Perspective on Communication." *Resources in Education*, the ERIC index, Nov. 1979 (microfiche).
"The Concrete Dialectic of Self-with-Society." In *Experience Forms: Their Cultural and Individual Place and Function*, ed. George G. Haydu. The Hague: Mouton, 1979.
"The Fabric of Fact: Beyond Epistemology." *Eros* 7 (2): 83–97 (1980).
"A Response to 'A Response to *Radical Reflection*.'" *Reflections: Essays in Phenomenology* (Winter): 40–45 (1981).
"The Texture of Communicative Praxis as New Context for Subjectivity." In *Phenomenology and the Understanding of Human Destiny*, ed. Stephen Skousgaard. Washington, D.C.: University Press of America, 1981.
"Being in Pain." In *The Humanity of the Ill: Phenomenological Perspectives*, ed. Victor Kestenbaum. Knoxville: University of Tennessee Press, 1982.
"Philosophical Anthropology as an Analytic of Mortality." In *Transparencies: Philosophical Essays in Honor of Jose Ferrater Mora*, ed. P. N. Cohn. Atlantic Highlands: Humanities Press, 1982.
"The Idea of the University and the Communication of Knowledge in a Technological Age." In *Communication Philosophy and the Technological Age*, ed. Michael J. Hyde. Tuscaloosa: University of Alabama Press, 1982.
"A Response to My Critics: Professors O'Neill and Mays." *Journal of the British Society for Phenomenology* 14 (1): 40–49 (1983).

"The Challenge of Philosophical Anthropology." In *The Phenomenology of Man and of the Human Condition*, ed. A. T. Tymieniecka. Dordrecht: Reidel, 1983.

"The Question of the Unity of the Human Sciences Revisited." In *The Phenomenology of Man and of the Human Condition*, ed. A.-T. Tymieniecka. Dordrecht: Reidel, 1983.

"Decentered Subjectivity and the New Humanism." *Alaska Quarterly Review* 2 (3–4): 115–129 (1984).

"Rhetoric Resituated at the End of Philosophy." *Quarterly Journal of Speech* 71 (2): 164–174 (1985).

"Subjectivity and Praxis and the End of Philosophy." In *Hermeneutics and Deconstruction*, ed. Don Ihde and Hugh Silverman. Albany: State University of New York Press, 1985.

"On the Hermeneutics of Gadamer and Habermas." Co-authored with Chong-Mun Kim. *Korean Journal of Philosophy* 12–13: 135–148 (1986).

"Husserl's Legacy in the Postmodern World." *Phenomenological Inquiry* 12: 125–133 (1988).

"Liberal Learning in the Postmodern World." *The Key Reporter* 54 (1): 1–4 (1988).

"Authorial Reflections." In *American Phenomenology: Origins and Developments*, ed. Eugene Kaelin and Calvin Schrag. Dordrecht: Kluwer Academic Publishers, 1989.

"Rationality between Modernity and Postmodernity." In *Life-World and Politics: Essays in Honor of Fred Dallmayr*, ed. Stephen K. White. Notre Dame: University of Notre Dame Press, 1989.

"Explanation and Understanding in the Science of Human Behavior." In *Reconsidering Psychology*, ed. James E. Faulconer and Richard H. Williams. Pittsburgh: Duquesne University Press, 1990.

"Communication in the Context of Cultural Diversity." *Phenomenological Inquiry* 16: 111–117 (1990).

"Interpretation, Narrative, and Rationality." *Research in Phenomenology* 21: 98–115 (1991).

"Husserl's Legacy in the Postmodern World." In *Husserl's Legacy in Phenomenological Philosophies*, ed. by A.-T. Tymieniecka. Dordrecht: Kluwer Academic Publishers, 1991.

"Reconstructing Reason in the Aftermath of Deconstruction." *Critical Review* 5 (2): 247–260 (1991).

"The Phenomenological Sociology of George Psathas: Appraisal and Critique." *Phenomenology and the Human Sciences* 16 (3): 1–10 (1991).

"Communication Studies and Philosophy: Convergence without Coincidence." Co-authored with David J. Miller. In *The Critical Turn: Rhetoric and Philosophy in Postmodern Discourse*, ed. Ian Angus and Lenore Langsdorf. Carbondale: Southern Illinois University Press, 1992.

"Traces of Meaning and Reference: Phenomenological and Hermeneutical Explorations." In *Current Advances in Semantic Theory*, ed. Maxim Stamenov. Philadelphia: John Benjamins, 1992.

"Phenomenology and the Consequences of Post-modernity." In *Reason, Life, Culture*, ed. A.-T. Tymieniecka. Dordrecht: Kluwer Academic Publishers, 1993.

"Reason and Life: The Transversal Logos." In *Reason, Life, Culture: Phenomenology in the Adriatic Countries*, ed. by A.-T. Tymieniecka. Dordrecht: Kluwer Academic Publishers, 1993.

"Transversal Rationality." In *The Question of Hermeneutics*, ed. T.J. Stapelton. Dordrecht: Kluwer Academic Publishers, 1994.

"Method and Phenomenological Research: Humility and Commitment in Interpretation." Co-authored with Ramsey Eric Ramsey. *Human Studies* 17: 131–137 (1994).

"The Kierkegaard-Effect in the Shaping of the Contours of Modernity." In *Kierkegaard in Post/Modernity*, ed. Martin J. Matu?tík and Merold Westphal. Bloomington: Indiana University Press (1995).

"Ultimacy and the Alterity of the Sublime." In *Being Human and the Ultimate*, ed. Nenos Georgopolous and Michael Heim. Amsterdam: Rodopi, 1995.

"Reminiscences on Paul Tillich: The Man and His Works." *North American Paul Tillich Society Newsletter* 21 (1): 3–8 (1995).

"The Story of the Human Subject in the Aftermath of Postmodern Critique." *Revue roumaine de philosopie* 1–2 (1996).

"Philosophy at the End of the Twentieth Century with a Note on Lucien Blaga." *Romanian Review* 51 (327): (1996).

"At the Crossroads of Hermeneutics, Rhetoric, and Ethics." *Man and Ideas: The Journal of the Yeungam Center for research in Eastern and Western Philosophy* 10 (1997).

"Hermeneutical Circles, Rhetorical Triangles and Transversal Diagonals." In *Rhetoric and Hermeneutics in our Time*, ed. by Micahel Hyde and Walter Jost. New Haven, Conn.: Yale University Press, 1997.

"The Recovery of the Phenomenological Subject: In Conversation with Derrida, Ricoeur, and Levinas." *Journal of the British Society for Phenomenology* 28 (1997).

"La recuperation du sujet phenomenologique." In *Analecta Husserliana* vol. L. Dordrecht: Kluwer Academic Publishers (1997).

"From Experience to Judgement in the Aftermath of the Postmodern Critique." In *Analecta Husserliana*, ed. by A.-T. Tymieniecka. Dordrecht: Kluwer Acamdemic Publishers, 1998.

"My Dialogue with Twentieth Century Continental Philosophy." In *Portraits of American Continental Philosophers*, ed. by James Watson. Bloomington: Indiana University Press, 1999.

"Response to Contributors." In *Calvin O. Schrag and the Task of Philosophy after Postmodernity*, ed. by Martin Beck Matuštík and William L. McBride. Evanston: Northwestern University Press, 2002.

Contributors

Stanley Deetz is professor of communication at the University of Colorado at Boulder. He specializes in the study of organizational communication from a critical/cultural/philosophic perspective. His research primarily focuses on relations of power in work sites and the way these relations are produced and reproduced in everyday interaction. Normatively his work attempts to produce communicative practices that lead to more open discussions and representative decision making. He is co-author of *Leading Organizations through Transitions* (Sage, 2000) and *Doing Critical Management Research* (Sage, 2000), author of *Transforming Communication, Transforming Business* (Hampton, 1995) and *Democracy in an Age of Corporate Colonization: Developments in Communication and the Politics of Everyday Life* (SUNY, 1992), and editor or author of eight other books. He has published over 100 essays in scholarly journals and books regarding stakeholder representation, decision making, culture, and communication in corporate organizations and has lectured widely in the United States and Europe. He offers an on-line course on communication and cultural change for the executive masters at Seton Hall University. Current projects investigate disciplinary and unobtrusive control processes in knowledge-intensive work.

Cynthia Gaffney, assistant to the editors, is an instructor in the Department of Communication Studies at Arizona State University West. She teaches courses that take a philosophical approach to communication and rhetoric.

Amy Grim is a doctoral candidate in communication at the University of Colorado at Boulder, where she studies vernacular public discourse and organizational communication from a rhetorical perspective. She is currently working on her dissertation project that investigates public discourse about euthanasia.

Michael J. Hyde is the University Distinguished Professor of Communication Ethics, Department of Communication, Wake Forest University, and a Fellow of The W. K. Kellogg Foundation. He is the author of the award-winning book, *The Call of Conscience: Heidegger and Levinas, Rhetoric and the Euthanasia Debate* (University of South Carolina Press, 2001).

Lenore Langsdorf is a professor at Southern Illinois University, Carbondale. Her research and teaching is focused on the philosophy of communication, using resources from both the Euroamerican (Husserl, Gadamer, and Ricoeur) and American pragmatic (Dewey, Mead) traditions. Her current work develops a phenomenology of communicative action; recent publications that develop aspects of that project are "The Real Conditions for the Possibility of Communicative Action," in *Perspectives on Habermas*, ed. Lewis Edwin Hahn (Open Court, 2000), "In Defense of Poiesis: The Performance of Self in Communicative Praxis," in *The Task of Philosophy After Postmodernism*, eds. William McBride and Martin Beck Matustik (Northwestern University Press, 2002), "The Doubleness of Subjectivity: Regenerating the Phenomenology of Intentionality," in *Ricoeur as Another: The Ethics of Subjectivity*, eds. Richard A. Cohen and James L. Marsh (SUNY Press, 2002), and "Reconstructing the Fourth Dimension: A Deweyean Critique of Habermas's Conception of Communicative Action," in *Habermas and Pragmatism*, ed. Mitchell Aboulafia (Routledge, 2002).

Alexander Lyon is assistant professor of communication at the University of Arkansas at Little Rock. His research and teaching interests center around the critical investigation of organizational communication.

Raymie McKerrow is associate provost for graduate studies and professor at the School of Interpersonal Communication, Ohio University. His research has focused on the intersection of postmodernism, rhetoric, and culture. He teaches graduate seminars in feminist rhetoric, rhetoric and culture, and Foucault and social change.

David James Miller is the communication liaison for the Louisiana Business Leadership Network. For the last six years he has been involved in disability work and has done so full-time for the last two years. He spent ten years prior to this teaching philosophy and communication at the undergraduate and graduate levels. His academic publications include: "Communication Studies and Philosophy," coauthored with Calvin O. Schrag, in *The Critical Turn: Rhetoric and Philosophy in Contemporary*

Discourse (Southern Illinois, 1993); "The Philosophy of Communication" in the *Encyclopedia of Phenomenology* (Kluwer, 1997); "Wittgenstein: Time for a New Philosophical Practice" in *Continental Philosophical Review* (1998). He has coauthored pieces on women and work with Patty Sotirin, including "Secretarial Positioning: Gender Ambivalence and Harassment" in *Gender and Conflict* (1994). He has also published translations of Jean Baudrillard's work, including "Modernity" in the *Canadian Journal of Political and Social Theory* (1987).

Michael J. Millington is the director of the Louisiana Business Leadership Network where he facilitates employer initiatives to hire workers with disabilities. He taught in the field of rehabilitation counseling for nine years, has produced twenty-four juried publications and book chapters. He has been involved in disability work for seventeen years as a service provider, administrator, teacher, and researcher. The experience of disability in the context of employment has been the central theme of his work. His journal publications include "A Preliminary Investigation of the Role of Differential Complexity and Response Style in Measuring Attitudes toward People with Disabilities" (1996); "Planning Strategy in Disability Management" (1998); "Validity and the Employment Expectation Questionnaire—Beta Version: Do Attitudes Mediate Outcomes?" (2000). His book chapters include "The Constructs and Practices of Job Placement" (1998), and "The Business Perspective on Employers, Disability, and Vocational Rehabilitation" (forthcoming).

Dennis K. Mumby is professor of communication studies at the University of North Carolina at Chapel Hill. An organizational communication scholar, his research focuses on the relationships among power, discourse, and identity in the workplace. He has published in journals such as *Communication Monographs*, *Management Communication Quarterly*, *Discourse and Society*, and *Academy of Management Review*.

Majia Holmer Nadesan is associate professor of communication studies at Arizona State University West. Her research addresses the practices and discourses that contribute to the contribution of subjectivity in everyday life. In particular, she focuses on the hegemonic role economic discourses play in delimiting possibilities for interpreting self and others and for constraining the existential opportunities for each.

Stephen Pluháček is visiting scholar in the department of humanities at Michigan Technological University. He is the translator of Luce Irigaray's *Between East and West* (Columbia) and with Heidi Bostic, translator of

Irigaray's *The Way of Love* (Continuum). With Bostic and Irigaray he is currently at work on a book titled *Questions for Continuum.*

Ramsey Eric Ramsey is associate professor at Arizona State University West and faculty director of the Barrett Honors College. He is author of *The Long Path to Nearness* (Humanities, 1998) as well of several articles appearing in such journals as *Rethinking Marxism*, *Philosophy and Rhetoric*, and *Communication Theory*. He has lectured and delivered papers internationally in the Czech Republic, Spain, Romania, Costa Rica, Mexico, and Cuba. He is editor of the Philosophy/Communication book Series from Purdue University Press.

Index

Praise for

THE CONFIDENCE EQUATION

"A grounded, heartfelt guide to real confidence—practical, inspiring, and refreshingly human."

—**Jessica Baum, LMHC,** author of *Anxiously Attached* and *SAFE*

"A must-read for anyone who's ever faced adversity or doubt."

—**Ian Seidenfeld,** 2020 Paralympic gold medalist

"With humor, heart, and scientific insight, Rosenfeld offers introverts a powerful framework for cultivating authentic confidence. This book is a gift for anyone who's ready to overcome self-doubt their own way."

—**A. Janet Tomiyama,** professor of psychology, UCLA

"A simple, science-backed recipe for feeling comfortable in your own skin. Rosenfeld knows the science better than anyone, and he's lived the struggle firsthand. If you want confidence, stop guessing at it—and start using the confidence equation."

—**Kurt Gray,** endowed chair and professor of psychology,
The Ohio State University

"Dan Rosenfeld has a gift for turning personal experience into broader wisdom. In *The Confidence Equation,* he excavates the most actionable insights from his own story with remarkable introspection—often vulnerable and always illuminating—and connects them seamlessly to what we might discover in our own lives."

—**Anthony Burrow,** professor of psychology, Cornell University